D0713064

HAROLD BLOOM

Harold Bloom

THE RHETORIC OF ROMANTIC VISION

David Fite

The University of Massachusetts Press

Amherst, 1985

Copyright © 1985 by The University of Massachusetts Press
All rights reserved
Printed in the United States of America
Designed by Barbara Werden
Typeset in Linoterm Zapf Book by The University of Massachusetts Press
Printed and bound by Cushing-Malloy, Inc.

Library of Congress Cataloging in Publication Data

Fite, David, 1953—
   Harold Bloom: the rhetoric of Romantic vision.

   Bibliography: p.
   Includes index.
   1. Bloom, Harold.   2. English poetry—History and criticism.
3. American poetry—History and criticism.   4. Criticism—United States.
5. Romanticism.   I. Title.
PR29.B57F5   1985   821'.009'145   85—5864
ISBN 0—87023—484—6 (alk. paper)

For my parents
Orville *and* Mary Grace Fite

CONTENTS

PREFACE

This book is offered as neither a celebration nor an indictment of the critical project of Harold Bloom. Rather, it attempts to explain how that project developed, and to locate Bloom's extreme version of revisionary Romanticism within relevant contexts in modern literary theory. Bloom is a notoriously difficult critic, one whose relentless appropriation of esoteric paradigms and increasing air of gothic self-referentiality have combined to intimidate or dismay many an interested reader. If finally much of this difficulty exists on the "surface" alone, as I think it does, then it is quite possible that an exegesis designed to clarify the unfolding logic of Bloom's enduring values will succeed in opening his work to an even wider audience and a greater range of debate than it now enjoys.

Before presenting a book of this sort one does well to anticipate objections. In Bloom's case the objections may take two forms. Detractors would argue that Bloom is not, in fact, an important critic or theorist at all, but rather a minor figure whose perversities failed to win a sizable audience even during the boom years of the seventies, and whose work as a whole already appears to be fated for enshrinement—along with disco music, pet rocks, sensitivity training, and Jimmy Carter—in the museum of gorgeous fads and irrelevancies engendered by that unhappy era. Those who regard Bloom in this fashion probably will not be reading this book. But it seems necessary to respond to them, anyway, with a few brief remarks on the nature of the contemporary literary House of Fame.

In one sense, the detractors are right. Bloom's most recent books, *Agon* and *The Breaking of the Vessels*,[1] do not appear to have occasioned anything near the rousing critical response afforded his major works of the seventies, from *Yeats* early in the decade to *Deconstruction and Criticism* (a collaboration with the other Yale critics) at the end. Bloom's revisionary challenge was fresh then, and, like many of the best revisions, it produced a healthy shudder and a shock in the literary establishment. The most recent work, on the other hand, tends largely to consolidate previous Bloomian positions on issues in reading, Romanticism, and literary history; the story of "influence" is extended and fleshed out (in essays on Gnosticism) and nuances are explored (in essays on Freud), but the basic insights remain the same and the polemical exigencies impelling them have only been re-presented, not revised. If Bloom in his recent writings sometimes has become, alas, boring, there could be no greater defeat for a man who has strived so relentlessly, with undeniable prophetic intent, to *unsettle* us, to force us to confront anew the violent transgressions he sees at the heart of reading and poetic history.

Yet this defeat, should we choose to grant it, might be said to figure as the inevitable obverse side of Bloom's very real victory. Ironically enough, Bloom, the fiercest canonizer of our time, has himself been canonized over the course of the past decade; in the process his willful and mighty critical voice has been tamed, tidied up, made altogether safer and saner than he no doubt would like. The project called Bloom, or the "anxiety of influence," has become, in short, yet another perspective, one important theoretical voice among many others to be dutifully studied and judiciously assessed in graduate schools, conferences, and all the rest of the institutional forums that help professional academics to define themselves today. If his books no longer shock or surprise, it is perhaps a tribute to the "strength"—a central Bloomian virtue— that his voice has shown in legitimizing itself, and thereby legitimizing the questions concerning literary influence and the nature of reading and Romanticism which have been Bloom's major areas of preoccupation.

I am aware, then, that my book, in seeking to "explain" Bloom, opens itself to another objection, perhaps more formidable than the first: that in "explaining" him it continues the process of regularizing or domesticating his work in unproductive ways. Such could be maintained, obviously enough, of any critical work—who among us is not still haunted by the heresy of paraphrase?—but the charge has been made especially salient lately as one "introduction" or "survey" after another has been published to clarify the difficulties in writers such as Derrida, Lacan, and Barthes—all of them practitioners of intensely self-reflexive modes of discourse that are meant to exist not as stable bodies of doctrine but as subversive and dis-

ruptive emblems of the power of language itself, the power of language's exploding, unfettered, even erotic, signifiers. While Bloom
remains strategically logocentric in ways that these theorists certainly do not, he is also a writer who deliberately blurs all distinctions between criticism and poetry, a writer who, as Wallace Martin
has observed in his thoughtful introduction to the canonizing
volume, *The Yale Critics*, may best be understood by studying not
his doctrines themselves but the " 'experience of their psychological meanings.' "[2] I would amend Martin only in this fashion (and
perhaps Martin would see it as more an exfoliation than a correction): Bloom's work is particularly interesting because the doctrines
within it are meant or mapped—incessantly and almost obsessively
schematized by Bloom himself—to have an interesting use, which
is nothing less than the rescue of the poetic imagination for our
time. The "experience" of Bloom's meanings is thus most profitably
approached through an examination of the underlying principles
and logic controlling a determinedly "useful" body of doctrine. In
the manner of Kenneth Burke, one reads Bloom not so much for
what he says as for what he hopes to accomplish in saying it, both
for himself and for his fitful fellowship of readers of poetry in a
"belated" time. That Bloom's hopes for poetry and Romanticism are
important is an assumption that this study makes; that they are
important in ways other than those that Bloom intends is an argumentative possibility toward which the exegetical machinery of the
first four chapters advances.

This book is perhaps clearly enough written to serve some
readers as a less painful substitute for the "experience" of Bloom
himself. My rue over this is moderated somewhat by the countering
hope that other readers will find here enticement to turn, or return,
to the many books of the still blooming critical project of my subject, there to confront one of the most challenging and audacious
theoretical voices of the past several decades. We live now, obviously, in a new chaos of dizzying literary theories, and we are burdened
with the freedom to make of these theories what we can. One irony
of this situation is that, in an academic profession imperiled by
forces both internal and external, a true growth industry has arisen
in recent years featuring criticism written about criticism. Some
would see the phenomenon as emblematic of the decadence into
which the profession has lapsed; mired within a dark but easeful
bog of spurious "self-evident truths," they cry out for a return to the
"poem itself," to the "world of literature," as if these things (poems,
worlds) existed innocent of the necessary mediation that criticism

both examines and enacts. Others, at an opposite extreme, see in this recent metacritical state of affairs a bracing manifestation of the triumph of intertextuality, as language (not voice) threads its serenely nihilistic way through the endless volumes of the Library of Babel. I prefer a middle, if not a golden, meaning; at a time of fascinating and, yes, enervating richness in theory, to write a critical book about a critic, it seems to me, is to try to help us talk to each other a little more clearly about what it is we are about.

This book began as a dissertation at the University of Southern California. I would like to thank Jackson Cope and Vincent Farenga for reading various sections of the manuscript. Peter Manning offered generous and extraordinarily painstaking counsel on the book as a whole. Marjorie Perloff directed the dissertation with great sensitivity and a rigor born of selfless concern, and it is to her that I am most indebted. I am also deeply grateful to William Cain and Daniel O'Hara for their very helpful comments on a subsequent draft of the manuscript, and to Bruce Wilcox, the director of the University of Massachusetts Press, who has offered not only shrewd advice but friendly and energetic support.

I would like to thank others who, in various ways they may not realize, helped me to write this book: Lovene Wood, Gordon Dossett, Greg Van Houten, Dennis Vellucci, Elizabeth Giffen, Andy Ballauer, Henry Binder, Charles Phipps, S. J., Joseph Sendry, and my former teachers Gerald Hunt, William Pratt, and W. Ross Winterowd. While I was working on this project I lived in Sin Palace, at the foot of the green hills of Los Gatos. I'd like to thank my friend Louis Hernandez, who presided over the palace with wit and passion. Finally, I owe more than I need ever hope to say to Karen McNally, in whose exuberance there could be no brighter beauty.

ACKNOWLEDGMENTS

Acknowledgment is made for permission to reprint selections from material under copyright.

To Alfred A. Knopf, Inc.: from *The Collected Poems of Wallace Stevens*, © 1923, 1931, 1935, 1936, 1937, 1942, 1943, 1944, 1945, 1946, 1947, 1948, 1949, 1950, 1951, 1952, 1954 by Wallace Stevens; from *Opus Posthumous*, edited by Samuel French Morse, © 1957 by Elsie Stevens and Holly Stevens. Reprinted with permission of Alfred A. Knopf, Inc.

To Macmillan Publishing Company: from *The Collected Poems of William Butler Yeats*, "The Second Coming," © 1924 by Macmillan Publishing Company, renewed 1952 by Bertha Georgie Yeats; "At Algeciras—A Meditation Upon Death," "Byzantium," and "A Dialogue of Self and Soul," © 1933 by Macmillan Publishing Company, renewed 1961 by Bertha Georgie Yeats; "The Tower," © 1928 by Macmillan Publishing Company, renewed 1956 by Georgie Yeats; "The Gyre," © 1940 by Georgie Yeats, renewed 1968 by Bertha Georgie Yeats, Michael Butler Yeats, and Anne Yeats; from *A Vision* by W. B. Yeats, © 1937 by W. B. Yeats, renewed 1965 by Bertha Georgie Yeats and Anne Yeats; from *Essays and Introductions* by W. B. Yeats, © Mrs. William Butler Yeats, 1961. All reprinted with permission of Macmillan Publishing Company, Michael B. Yeats, and Macmillan London, Ltd.

To Viking Penguin, Inc.: from John Ashbery, *As We Know*, © 1979 by John Ashbery; from John Ashbery, *Self-Portrait in a Convex Mirror*, © 1972, 1973, 1974, 1975 by John Ashbery; from John Ashbery, *Houseboat Days*, © 1975, 1976, 1977 by John Ashbery. Reprinted with permission of the publisher, Viking Penguin, Inc.

HAROLD BLOOM

INTRODUCTION

Early in 1959 a young scholar from Yale named Harold Bloom published his first book, a brief, polemical study of Shelley's major poems entitled *Shelley's Mythmaking*. Blessed with the imprimatur of the prestigious Yale University Press, and armed with a thesis derived from the Jewish theologian Martin Buber which condemned almost every major previous critic of Shelley for the "sin" of reading the poetry as philosophy rather than poetic "mythmaking" (SM, 118),[1] Bloom's book guaranteed itself considerably more attention than fledgling scholarly efforts typically receive. Much of the attention was unfavorable. The anonymous reviewer for the *Times Literary Supplement* of 21 August 1959, in a review entitled "Elephants and Shelley," is representative of the scandalized:

> From a *point de départ* of nth degree remoteness, namely a distinction made by the theologian Buber between I-Thou and I-It relationships, [Bloom] proceeds, through the ritually prescribed cloud of witnesses, to offer, as his general interpretation of Shelley, a "mythopoeia" that involves the omission of "Adonais," and such other essential poems as do not fit it, and leaves both the reader and the truncated cadaver of the poetry at a point *n* degrees remote from any easily ascertainable *point d'arrivée*. (P. 482)

Closer to home, another scholar who had already made his mark in Romantic studies, Earl Wasserman, joined the chorus of detractors with his critique of *Shelley's Mythmaking* in the *Yale Review*, but offered at the same time a perspective that saw into the life of things to come. Despite the fact that Bloom has "repeatedly misread the poems," despite all the distortions he has forced upon Shelley by imposing "irrelevant or only partially relevant *a priori* assumptions," Bloom's critical approach, Wasserman concluded in 1959, would prove to be more important and more influential than a safer, saner perspective, because Bloom's vision of Shelley's work grants "the modern reader a sense of kinship with that poetry."[2] If "every age takes from literature what it most wants," then Bloom, Wasserman observes, "by creatively reinterpreting—that is, isolating, exaggerating, and playing a novel light upon—the quasi-religious mythmaking in Shelley's poems," has made those poems "potentially significant to the twentieth-century mind."

In the years since Wasserman wrote his review, Harold Bloom has become perhaps the most important commentator on Romantic and twentieth-century poetry in the English language. He has assumed a status as quite likely the most praised and most reviled critic of our time, and unarguably the most prolific. Bloom has now written, from *Shelley's Mythmaking* in 1959 through *Agon* and *The Breaking of the Vessels* in 1982 (and including one work of fiction, *The Flight to Lucifer: A Gnostic Fantasy*), fourteen full-length books, totaling over 4,000 pages, and has edited numerous others. Through both his own reviews and those of scholars guided by the light of the Bloomian lamp, his celebrated and notorious theory of the "anxiety of influence" now looms as a formidable presence in academic and intellectual journals ranging from *Diacritics* to the *New Republic* to the *Times Literary Supplement*. As De Vane Professor of Humanities at Yale, he has come to be regarded as a central representative of the most prestigious academy in American letters, an academy that has featured other distinguished— and controversial—critics of Romantic and modern literature such as Geoffrey Hartman, J. Hillis Miller, Paul de Man, and Jacques Derrida. Bloom's books are avidly read and often fervidly reviewed. Commentators as luminous as Kenneth Burke, Edward Said, Helen Vendler, and Bloom's colleagues de Man and Miller have hailed his work as a brilliant and important contribution to the intellectual history of our time. Burke calls his thinking "exceptionally subtle and complex";[3] Said says Bloom's is "antithetical criticism at its fiercest and most brilliant," and sees his readings to be "almost unparalleled in skill and thematic nuance." Miller affirms that Bloom "is perhaps the most dazzlingly creative and provocative of critics writing in English today." Vendler finds in his work "a repository of vivid engagement with poems" and a "real excellence in . . . formulation of larger questions." De Man hazards the guess that Bloom, "in his understanding of Romanticism" and the nature of reading, "has been ahead of everybody else all along."

Still other scholars have declared themselves suspicious of
Bloom, with some even going so far as to denounce his writings as
solipsistic charlatanry of the highest order. Frank Kermode, while
acknowledging that Bloom "is a very remarkable critic" with "a
great, almost selfish passion for poetry," complains that his dense
and elliptical style puts "horrible and ugly obstacles in the way of
civilized non-coterie readers." Charles Altieri calls Bloom "brilliant" but sees in his work "an incredible sloppiness and arrogance
towards logic and discursive reasoning which makes me wonder
how literary criticism maintains even the minimum level of respect-
ability it has among intellectual disciplines." Christopher Ricks,
Howard Nemerov, and David Hirsch see almost no redeeming features in the Bloomian project. Ricks calls his theory of the anxiety of
influence a "lurid melodrama" and detects in it "the revenge of an
itchy critical intelligence against the larger, more manifold, and
more enduring creative intelligence of poets." Howard Nemerov
draws from Bloom's work the "melancholy" lesson that "the effort
to render English unintelligible is proceeding vigorously at the
highest levels of learning." Hirsch labels Bloom a "minor critic" with
a "narrow obsession" whose theories are "repugnant to common
sense." Even his detractors, however, are forced to concede what
one of them, Robert Towers, calls the "remarkable fact" of Bloom's
influence, an influence wielded not only by the "strength" of his
ideas, but also by his Yale associations, his amazing productivity,
and his frequent appearances as poetry critic and cultural pundit in
a host of journals. Romantic scholars of all schools and critical
persuasions cite him in footnotes; poets long desperately for in-
clusion in the Bloomian canon of crucial contemporaries; critics as
eminent as Joseph Riddel and M. H. Abrams write articles on his
theories. Recently, even the feminist literary historians Sandra M.
Gilbert and Susan Gubar have employed Bloom's predominantly
patriarchal theories as part of an impressive study of the woman
writer in the nineteenth century, *The Madwoman in the Attic*.

Throughout his twenty-five-year odyssey to the position of near-
oracular preeminence that his adversaries suggest he is all too
happy to accept, Bloom's fundamental subject has never changed.
From *Shelley's Mythmaking* to *Wallace Stevens: The Poems of Our
Climate* to his latest review in the *New Republic*, he has eloquently,
relentlessly, and combatively explored one terrain and one terrain
alone: the possibilities and the perils implicit in what the prologue
to *The Visionary Company* calls the "faithless faith" of the great
Romantic poets (p. 1), that faith in the redemptive "autonomy" of

the poet's imagination, which for Bloom represents the heart of all "strong" and central poetic vision from Milton through A. R. Ammons and John Ashbery. That Bloom as a critic has now achieved such a "strength" and centrality of his own, however embattled, confirms the acuteness of Wasserman's remarks apropos of *Shelley's Mythmaking*, and suggests that we would do well to examine the relationship between Bloomian critical vision and the spirit of our age. The story of Romantic poetry and its continuing "influence" that Bloom has offered over the last two decades, at times with almost intimidating prophetic intensity, clearly has been, for some readers, the vision that our age demands, just as for others it has come to serve as an exemplary culmination of all the worst tendencies of contemporary criticism. In this volume I will study the nature of Bloom's conception of the Romantic imagination as he develops it in his early books on the English Romantics, and then extends it through his theory of the anxiety of influence to cover all poetry written in England and America since Milton. The salience of the Bloomian critical canon for our time, the ways in which the fully developed "map of misreading" either give or fail to give our age what it needs, will be closely examined, and the appropriateness of Bloom's Romantic precepts as guides to the evaluation of contemporary poetry, in particular, will be carefully assessed. Bloom has strived, in his many works since *The Anxiety of Influence* itself, to elucidate the powerful "assumptions" about the nature of poetry, Romantic quest, and the reading experience that have always controlled his criticism. In so doing, he has elaborated a profound and unsettling rhetoric of Romanticism based on the imaginative relations between poetic fathers and poetic ephebes, or sons, which unpersuaded scholars contend is both inaccurate and reductive when taken as a picture either of Romanticism itself or of the modern and contemporary poetry to which the rhetoric is also meant to apply. This volume will examine the assumptions governing Bloom's enterprise, and the methods, judgments, and values that his criticism displays in working out those assumptions.

Bloom began as a brilliant, wayward son to his critical fathers Northrop Frye, Frederick Pottle, and M. H. Abrams—the last two Bloom's teachers and the dedicatees, respectively, of *Shelley's Mythmaking* and *The Visionary Company*. These two earliest books, along with their companion volume of 1963, *Blake's Apocalypse: A Study in Poetic Argument*, presented a portrait of the six great English Romantics—Blake, Wordsworth, Coleridge, Byron, Shelley, and Keats—that was notable for its strong affinities to the work of

Frye on myth and romance, Abrams on the Romantic imagination and the structure of the Romantic lyric, and Pottle on the "case of Shelley."[4] Chapter 1 of this study will consider Harold Bloom's early theory of the Romantic imagination, a theory very well represented by the titles of his first three books. From the very start, Bloom is drawn to Romantic poetry by the "moral heroism" of its "agnostic faith in the mythopoeic mode," by the heroism, that is, of its refusal "to be anything but poetry, anything but mythmaking" (SM, p. 118). The greatest Romantic poets, the six of the "visionary company," are allied, for all their many differences, by their "common theme of imagination," and by their passionate Stevensian knowledge "that the theory of poetry is the theory of life" (VC, p. 3). A sensitive reading of such poetry, Bloom contends here at the beginning of his career, will discard conventional source hunting and mining of extraliterary esoterica for the more serious task of mapping the "poetic arguments" in the poet's works, arguments, of course, that have to do solely with the various aspects of the creative imagination.

With the publication of the Blake study, Bloom had already established himself as one of the most important critics of English Romantic literature. The abiding presence of William Butler Yeats and Wallace Stevens even in this early triad of books indicated, however, that Bloom's own vision would not be content to rest on the "visionary company" alone. From 1963 to 1970, he published extensively in journals and various collections on a wide range of topics. Many of these occasional pieces were gathered in *The Ringers in the Tower*, a 1971 compilation whose essays on Browning, Ruskin, Pater, Stevens, Emerson, Whitman, and A. R. Ammons dramatically revealed the capaciousness and ambition of Bloom's developing critical project. Even more dramatic, though, was the publication the previous year of his massive, controversial, and inescapably brilliant study of the Irish poet William Butler Yeats. Entitled simply *Yeats*, this book broke Bloom's seven-year absence from major publication with a resounding blast at the authority of established critical tradition. "Yeats was a poet very much in the line of vision," begins the preface to this new study, and the lines of literary tradition are already being redrawn; "his ancestors in English poetic tradition were primarily Blake and Shelley, and his achievement will at last be judged against theirs" (p. v).

For most of this century, of course, no poet had been more lionized by the critical establishment than Yeats. With Eliot and Joyce, he stood at the center of the Modernist canon promulgated by the New Critics and their epigones. As such, he was widely regarded as the greatest lyric poet of his time, perhaps even, the eminent critic R. P. Blackmur was moved once to observe, the greatest lyricist since the seventeenth century.[5] The tale of Yeats's career was fashioned to meet the needs of an age that conceived itself to be in revolt against Romanticism, an age presided over by the severely "classical" Eliotic theory of an imagination liberated from suspect personality into the craftsman's adequacy of precise and sinewy diction, meter, and form. The Modernist masters did not deny that Yeats had begun as a Romantic, but they saw the rest of his career precisely as a triumph over such inauspicious poetic beginnings. As John Hollander has put it, "the consensus of the modernist movement praised Yeats as the heroic slayer of his own early Romanticism";[6] for the New Critics, Yeats attained greatness only when he hardened his diction, toughened his mythology and his use of personae, and sharpened his wit to produce the outstanding body of work from *In the Seven Woods* in 1904 to the *Last Poems* in 1939.

Bloom's central response in *Yeats* to this Modernist reading was to counter its assumptions about poetry, the imagination, and the reading experience, and thereby to change the verdict on the poet by altering the very grounds of admission into the literary canon. Bloom does not deny that Yeats's poetry underwent a great transformation following *The Wind among the Reeds* in 1899; he simply affirms that by and large, despite the frequent excellence of the rhetoric of the middle and later Yeats, it changed for the worse. The heavily praised Yeats poems central to the Modernist canon, poems such as "Leda and the Swan," "The Second Coming," "Among School Children," and "The Circus Animals' Desertion," are seen by Bloom to disguise with the vigor of their rhetoric the essential emptiness, incoherence, and occasional viciousness of their imaginative arguments. Yeats, for Bloom, all too often fails as a poet over the last forty years of his life because he forsakes the visionary power of the pure Romantic imagination that he had displayed in his youth, because he capitulates as a poet to reductive and morally bankrupt ways of seeing the world that have nothing to do with the strength of real poetic vision. Yeats as Gnostic, Yeats as hunter of "spooks" and Dublin theosophists (*Yeats*, p. 240), Yeats as worshipper of the " 'composite god' " of historical process (p. 470): Bloom laments all these components of the Yeatsian vision as fundamentally antipoetic, as a going against the grain of Yeats's proper Shelleyan and Blakean Romanticism. All the personae of the public Yeats—the self-styled Anglo-Irish bard, the neo-Augustan satirist of the foibles of political man, the lover of aristocracy and violent hero-

ism—are repugnant to Bloom as well. Yeats's main problems as
a poet, Bloom claims against most previous critical authority, are,
first, that he desires too frequently to be something other than
a poet—a philosopher, say, or a theosophist, or a statesman—and,
second, that he wants such disastrous things because, finally, he
does not believe strongly enough in the creative power of the Romantic imagination. Chapter 2 of this study will examine the logic
and the methods of Bloom's submission of an established Modernist master to the tribunal of his "visionary company," and will assess
the indictment of the latecomer on the grounds of a lapsed faith in
the visionary imagination that necessarily follows.

Of course, for many critics and poets in the past decade, the
central importance of Bloom's *Yeats* has not resided in its revisionist reading of Yeats himself as a fallen and diminished Romantic, but
in the radically different conception of literary history and the nature of poetic meaning upon which Bloom's treatment of Yeats
depends. In his preface to *Yeats*, Bloom announced that the book
was but "a prolegomenon to a larger study of poetic influence"
(p. vii). When the first part of that study was delivered in a remarkable tetralogy of volumes appearing in the four-year span from 1973
through 1976, the fierceness of its polemics and the prodigious
energy of its execution of an uncompromising thesis quickly established Bloom as the one inescapable critic of nineteenth- and
twentieth-century poetry writing today. *The Anxiety of Influence* in
1973 presented the argument that all "strong" poetry since Milton
has been written under a grim and increasingly oppressive psychology of belatedness which forces poetic sons to wrestle with the
mighty dead of blocking precursors "so as to clear imaginative
space for themselves" (p. 5). *A Map of Misreading* in 1975 elaborated
a complete theory of reading out of the earlier volume's sketchy list
of the six "revisionary ratios" that necessarily obtain in the Romantic crisis lyric and across the career of the poet as the latecomer
confronts his "melancholy at his lack of priority," and makes his
poems out of "the illusion of freedom, out of a sense of priority being
possible" (AI, p. 96). *Kabbalah and Criticism* in the same year added
to the roster of sources for Bloom's system, which already included
thinkers as varied as Freud, Vico, Nietzsche, Kenneth Burke, William
Blake, and the scholars Walter Jackson Bate and Angus Fletcher, by
revealing a crucial model for Bloom's map of revisionary evasions to
be the kabbalistic rhetoric of the medieval *Zohar* and its reinterpre-
tation by the sixteenth-century commentators Moses Cordovero
and Isaac Luria. *Poetry and Repression* in 1976 rounded out the

tetralogy with full-scale applications of the by now quite elaborate Bloomian theory to texts by Blake, Wordsworth, Shelley, Keats, Tennyson, Browning, Yeats, Emerson, Whitman, and Stevens. The appearance, also in 1976, of another collection of miscellaneous pieces, *Figures of Capable Imagination*, and in 1977 of the magisterial study, *Wallace Stevens: The Poems of Our Climate*, served to consolidate Bloom's massive revisionist reading of Romantic and modern poetry. His two most recent volumes, *Agon* and *The Breaking of the Vessels*, with their painstaking discussions of the Gnostics, Plato, and pre-Socratic rhetoric, show that Bloom is no longer content with considering the nature of the revisionary imagination in the modern era alone, but is now determined to locate the origins of revisionism in the very origins of Western literary culture.

The general outline of Bloom's theory of the anxiety of influence is now common critical currency. Ever since Milton justified the ways of Satan for imaginative man, all poets in the Western tradition have had to battle with a sublimity, an imaginative achievement not their own, an achievement that, precisely by coming before them, threatens their own claims to imaginative priority and *thereby* establishes the conditions for meaning in their poems. Poets cannot escape the imperatives of influence; those who attempt to "idealize" about the bloody parricide of poetic relations will succeed only in creating weak poetry, weak criticism.[7] "Figures of capable imagination," Bloom says, borrowing a phrase from Stevens, "appropriate for themselves" (AI, p. 5) by strongly, even savagely, misreading the poems of central precursors, and thus winning through to an achievement of their own—an achievement that *only* exists, however, by virtue of its desperate battle with what came before. Bloom's theory, despite its oedipal model, thus has "nothing in common with anything now miscalled 'Freudian literary criticism' " (PR, p. 25), since to say that a poem is an "achieved anxiety" (AI, p. 96) is *not* to say, as orthodox Freudians do, that the poem somehow represents a sublimation, or an overcoming, of that anxiety. A poem is itself a *process* of repression, Bloom contends, not a product of a completed sublimation, and the stronger the poem—the stronger, that is, its misinterpretation of a precursor— the more "poetry, revisionism, and repression verge upon a melancholy identity," which it is the duty of the critic to map (PR, p. 27).

This mapping of the anxieties of influence also has little to do with the conventional scholarly operation known as source study. "By 'poetic influence' I do not mean the transmission of ideas and images from earlier to later poets," Bloom cautions (AI, p. 71); in fact, "what I mean by the study of poetic influence turns source-study inside out." Since "the meaning of a strong poem *is* another strong poem," and since this meaning works on a much deeper level than the mere mimicking of literary style or borrowing of received ideas, then the "antithetical" critic's responsibility is to assess the ways in which the precursor poem "is being misinterpreted, revised, corrected, evaded, twisted askew"—in short, misread—by the latecomer (FC, p. 9). The map of revisions presented by Bloom in his many books of the seventies attempts to chart the characteristic evasions of the Romantic crisis lyric by isolating six "revisionary ratios," and dividing these into their imagistic and rhetorical, as well as psychic, components. *Clinamen, tessera, kenosis, daemonization, askesis, apophrades*: the names for these ratios are deliberately flamboyant, as is the "precariously assimilative" and sometimes bewildering paradigmatic method behind them.[8] Bloom in his recent enterprise often seems determined to resist easy absorption—if only because, according to the Bloomian theory of misreading, too quick an understanding is likely to sacrifice strength for the chimera of a weak, idealizing, and finally impossible interpretive accuracy. "There are no interpretations but only misinterpretations," Bloom announces in the most urgent and polemical piece he has ever written, "A Manifesto for Antithetical Criticism," in *The Anxiety of Influence*, "and so all criticism is prose poetry" (p. 95); it is, in fact, the "discourse of the deep tautology—of the solipsist who knows that what he means is right, and yet that what he says is wrong" (p. 96).

The final four chapters of this study will examine Harold Bloom's theory of the anxiety of influence, probing its rhetoric and the logic of its "deep" tautologies, assessing the nature of its appeal to what Bloom continually calls our "belated" age, and, finally, determining the appropriateness of its vision of literary history and critical canon making. The development of the theory of the anxiety of influence in Bloom's writings correlates directly with the enlarging of his critical scope in the late sixties and early seventies to include the work of poets, especially Americans, who have labored after the great age of English Romanticism. The theory is presented, then, as not only a map, but quite consciously a story—a story of Romanticism as a "vast visionary tragedy" (AI, p. 10) whose heroic but self-defeating conception of the autonomous imagination, as it is embodied in the poems of the "visionary company," has determined the progressive diminishings of poetic creation ever since.

Bloom does not shrink from the dark implications of his story; he is, as Geoffrey Hartman has observed, "totally a kaka-angelist, a bearer of bad news."[9] If reading, for Bloom, is "a belated and all-but-impossible act" (MM, p. 3), then the misreading that is strong poetry and strong criticism grows increasingly desperate, ever more precarious, as the shadows of literary history lengthen. "Romantic tradition differs vitally from earlier forms of tradition," Bloom says, in that it is "*consciously late*," and "canon-formation," which "for us, has become a part of Romantic tradition," must be performed in just such a spirit of acutely self-conscious belatedness (p. 35). Thus, we have Bloom characteristically observing, in a 1975 year-end review of poetry for the *New Republic*, that "America is the Evening Land, or the last phase of Mediterranean culture," and going on to evaluate the year's offerings in terms of the melancholy deduction that "this late in tradition all reading (and writing) is heavily shadowed by the past."[10] The winners in this process of canon making, defined as those who have struggled most nobly with the inevitability of their own imaginative defeat before an overly rich and now oppressive tradition, are Yeats, Hardy, Hart Crane, and, above all, Stevens, among the moderns, and Ashbery, Ammons, Robert Penn Warren, James Merrill, Elizabeth Bishop, Geoffrey Hill, and Seamus Heaney, among more recent poets. The losers are virtually all those poets associated with the Modernist canon of our New Critical heritage, especially Eliot, Pound, Auden, and Robert Lowell, but also William Carlos Williams, Louis Zukofsky, Charles Olson, and, in our present time, poets as different as John Berryman, Robert Creeley, and Allen Ginsberg.

What kind of authority does Bloom's theory of the anxiety of influence possess? Is his canon of modern and contemporary poets based upon fruitful assumptions about the nature of reading and of poetic meaning, or is it, as detractors complain, an unproductive exercise in barren and myopic Romantic nostalgia? Why is Bloom such an important figure within our intellectual climate—at times as important, it seems, to his opponents as to those who find in his theories the suasions of true critical prophecy? Chapter 3 will address the initial question by establishing the contours of the theory of influence itself, not only in relation to Bloom's chosen precursors but also, and even more important, in relation to his own earlier readings of the visionary company. Much of Bloom's work in his latest phase represents a deep and subtle rereading of his own earlier visionary Romanticism, with the key to the rereading being his switch from the master trope of "vision" to that of "influence" as a way of explaining the imaginative life of poetic works. While Bloom's cunning borrowings from thinkers such as Nietzsche, Freud, Luria, and the second-century Gnostic, Valentinus, are important and will be duly considered, his appropriation *of himself*, especially of his earlier "vision" of Blake, is just as crucial to his enterprise and will receive much of my attention. Chapters 4 and 5 follow the third chapter's mapping of the theory of influence with a detailed consideration of the project of canon making that develops out of that theory, and with a lengthy description of the tale of American poetic history delivered by Bloom in his recent work. Bloom's treatment of Emerson, Whitman, and Stevens is the subject of chapter 4, which continues in the expository mode of the previous chapters as it delineates the methods by which Bloom assimilates American poetry into his paradigms for the "anxiety of influence." In chapter 5, I abandon exposition for an analysis of the *costs* of Bloom's campaign to save Romanticism in modern poetry. Probing the nature and the quality of the choices that Bloom as a canonizer makes when he moves beyond the realm of the visionary company, I first examine his reading of the two contemporary poets whom he has most frequently and most forcefully lauded, A. R. Ammons and John Ashbery, and then offer a reading to counter his overly narrow portrait of the two as heroically spent visionaries in the "central" Emersonian line of American poetry.

Because the issues raised by Bloom's canonizing project for Romanticism and modern poetry have to do finally with the *uses* of poetry and the place of imagination within culture, my sixth chapter will provide an in-depth examination of Bloom's theories of influence and reading in the context of other conceptions of poetry, rhetoric, and Romanticism that have achieved preeminence in the critical climate of the past several decades. Both Bloom's method for "misreading" and his Romantic canon for the modern find their polar opposite in the rigorous Poundian poetics of Hugh Kenner; his theories of rhetoric, language, and the nature of poetic meaning feature a revealingly intimate quarrel with the self-reflexive linguistic nihilism of his deconstructionist Yale colleague Paul de Man; his Romanticism in its final phase stands as a fully explicit repudiation of the more moderate and more optimistic Wordsworthian Romanticism of his former teacher M. H. Abrams. Chapter 6 of this study will assess the appeal of Bloom's determinedly "belated" Romantic cosmogony by treating his theories as part of a collective dialogue on the *responsibilities* of poetry and of criticism in our time. Kenner, de Man, and Abrams serve as exemplary figures in this discussion not only because they are themselves widely regarded as important theorists on the contemporary scene, but because their work bears so deeply on the issues raised by Bloom's enterprise as a whole.

What *is* the proper life of poetry? of language? of the imagination within culture? What *are* the responsibilities of the critic to the poem being read? to literary history? to a modern culture that, as many of our finest critics agree, seems to have lost any sense of the continuing relevance of literature and the humanities? If Harold Bloom's work is an important contribution to the intellectual climate of our time, as his many followers proclaim, it is important not because it adds yet another "theory of Romanticism" to an already crowded and impressive roster, nor because it furnishes an abundance of fascinating, polemical readings of poetical works in the Romantic tradition. Rather, Bloom's self-styled critical prophecy on the fate of Romantic vision, influence, and reading finally attains the embattled "centrality" it so strongly desires because it endeavors to answer, with its own highly imaginative "map of misreading" and its dramatic narrative of the bloody battles of influence, those larger questions about poetry, imagination, and culture that continue to trouble us in what Bloom would describe as our time of most urgent need.

O N E

The Visionary Company
in Its Own Time

The theory of the visionary Romantic imagination presented in
Harold Bloom's three earliest books seems in retrospect—an even
more privileged prophetic perspective than that enjoyed by Earl
Wasserman in 1959—to belong fully, almost inevitably, to the new
age of Romantic myth that had already been inaugurated in literary
criticism by Northrop Frye in his landmark studies, *Fearful Symmetry* and *Anatomy of Criticism*.[1] The first Frye book, a study of the
mythic universe of William Blake, appeared in 1947 and revolution-
ized a Blakean critical industry that had seldom before veered from
its original nineteenth-century inclination to view the poet as either
an inspired mystic or a raving madman or, more often, some odd
combination of both. *Anatomy of Criticism*, published ten years
later, drew heavily on Blake's "iconography" of the creative imagination (FS, p. 421) to elaborate an encyclopedia of modes, symbols,
myths, and genres envisioned by Frye as presiding over a distinct,
and distinctly definable, literary universe. In the years immediately
following the publication of *Anatomy of Criticism*, Harold Bloom
was himself busy formulating a theory of poetry that could double
as a theory *toward* a revivified critical life, and he found in the
Blakean categories of his critical father profound instruction in the
"mythography" and "mythopoeia" of the life-giving Romantic
vision.[2] Appropriating from Frye important models for describing
romance in English literary tradition, and sharing with him a passionate commitment to the "work of imagination" as "a decisive act
of spiritual freedom," a "vision of the recreation of man" (AC, p. 94),
in the first stage of his career as a critic, Bloom presented an
anatomy of his own—an encyclopedic chart of the mythmaking
creations of the visionary company. This chapter will examine
Bloom's early map of Romanticism, and will attempt to elucidate its
crucial relation to a formidable critical precursor.

It is an illuminating exercise to list some of the main points
Northrop Frye makes in *Fearful Symmetry* against established readings of William Blake. Frye argues strenuously that Blake is neither
a mystic nor a madman, neither a Christian nor an esoteric philosopher. He contends that Blake *is* a great poet, but that his greatest
poems are not the traditionally admired "Songs of Innocence" and
"Songs of Experience" and other shorter lyrics. Rather, Blake's central achievement resides in the long prophecies of his later years,
prophecies that must be read, Frye emphasizes, as complex visionary constructions, and furthermore, as visionary constructions
bearing startling affinities to the line of English poetry deriving from
Spenser and Milton, and to the tradition of Hebraic prophecy most
strongly associated with the utterances of Ezekiel.[3] What is instructive here, of course, is that all these very points could easily be
abstracted from *Shelley's Mythmaking, The Visionary Company,* and
Blake's Apocalypse as the central contentions of the early Bloom
about Blake. Bloom frequently acknowledges his debt to Frye in his
first three books, and specifies, in the preface to the revised edition
of *The Visionary Company,* that the debt pertains not only to the
interpretation of Blake, but to the criticism of Romantic poetry as
a whole.[4] In fact, the two critics share several crucial beliefs about
Romanticism, beliefs developed out of encounters with Blake, but,
in Bloom's case, also formulated through the happy medium of
Frye's already established reading of the poet. Both critics, seeing
the world through a Blakean lens, glorify the power of the mythmaking visionary imagination; both insist, against established critical
authority, that visionary poetry requires a reading in terms of *itself,*
in terms of the types of visionary moments that it tries to present.
And both critics go on, then, analogizing in Blakean fashion from
these types, to construct an anatomy of the imagination out of the
similitudes of imaginative quest.

Where Frye and Bloom do differ, however, even at this early
stage—a divergence whose extraordinary repercussions for
Bloom's later theory of the anxiety of influence I will explore in
chapter 3—is in their views of larger literary tradition, and in their
consequent motivation, as critics, for anatomizing that tradition.
Frye employs Blake's "iconography" of the imagination to chart the
archetypes, myths, and symbols of the literary universe, but does so
in the service of a conception of literary tradition as an "ideal order"
that he has derived from what he calls the "very fundamental criticism" of T. S. Eliot (AC, p. 18). The role of the critic for Frye is to describe and to classify that tradition as rigorously and capaciously as

possible, eschewing direct concern with value judgments of any kind (p. 20). Bloom, on the other hand, is inclined from the very start of his career to view literary tradition not as an "ideal order" but as a *competition*—a competition that the critic necessarily confronts, and about which he *must* make evaluations and decisions. Bloom's decision, of course, in *Shelley's Mythmaking*, *The Visionary Company*, and *Blake's Apocalypse*, is to valorize the visionary imagination almost exclusively, and thus to erect—or resurrect—a much more circumscribed canon than that charted by Frye in *Anatomy of Criticism*. The apparent objectivity of Frye's method, as he maps not only romance, but comedy, tragedy, and satire, not only myths, but symbols, modes, and genres, does not for long obscure the fact that romance nonetheless remains for him first among equals in its status as a mediation between the divine and the human in the tales men tell. Bloom, in contrast, presents himself quite consciously as a Romantic critic writing about a body of Romantic poetry whose values and central concerns he not only defines but shares; the precarious but redemptive power of the autonomous visionary imagination is his sole subject—and his own passionate value judgment against his chief competition, the anti-Romantic doctrines of the New Critical regimen that had dominated the American academy for three decades.

There are four central characteristics of the visionary imagination as it is defined by Bloom, under the strong influence not only of Frye but of M. H. Abrams as well, in his early triad of books on the English Romantics. First, the visionary imagination represents a complex triumph over all that is merely "given," especially over that natural world whose charms are a potential trap for the creative person. Second, the visionary impulse, in struggling to achieve expression, characteristically enacts a quest, a journey whose travelings can be mapped as a distinctive kind of Romantic crisis lyric. Third, the moments of pure vision or pure mythmaking in a Romantic poem—the moments approximating Blake's "Pulsation of the Artery"[5]—are evanescent, because the visionary imagination, after a brief transparent flash, necessarily lapses from sublimity back into the constrictions of mere language. Fourth, this sublimity, since it exists by virtue of its passage beyond all context to an absolute purity of vision, in some sense has no referent and is always focused on the problematics of pure visionary desire—the desire, in Wordsworth's terms, for "something evermore about to be."[6]

Several remarks that Bloom makes in his 1971 preface to the revised edition of *The Visionary Company* furnish a useful framework for discussing his view of the place of nature in Romantic poetry. First, Bloom observes that the book's "central contention" is the radical one that "the Romantics were not poets of nature." Second, he claims against a number of "negative critics," including C. S. Lewis and René Wellek, that his study does "not translate" the mind-nature dialectic of Romantic poetry solely "into Blakean categories," but rather seeks out "the crucial analogues and rivalries that connect these poets ..." (p. vii).[7] That many commentators besides Lewis and Wellek have found the second claim to be rather unconvincing suggests key questions about the early Bloom enterprise: What precisely is the *source* of his vision of the mind and nature in Romantic poetry, and what is the critical context in which we can best appreciate that vision?

M. H. Abrams, with whom Bloom studied at Cornell University, gave us, in his classic 1953 volume, *The Mirror and the Lamp*, our central, and perhaps by now rather shopworn, metaphors for the contribution of Romantic aesthetics on the issue of mind and nature. The first figure, the classical one, provides an emblem of the mind as a "reflector of external objects," an accurate recorder of the givens of the sensory world.[8] The second, marking "the prevailing romantic conception of the poetic mind," sees the imagination in creation as a "radiant projector" that imbues the life of the given world with a profound life of its own. Bloom, in his three early volumes, meets his teacher on the question of Romantic mind, and then extends the light of the lamp even further. "What does ally" the Romantics, he says in the first chapter of *The Visionary Company*, echoing both Abrams and Frye, is "one of the great traditions of English poetry, the prophetic and Protestant line of Spenser and Milton, which reaches its radical limits in the generation after Wordsworth" (pp. 7 − 8). The "characteristic concern" of this line, he says, is "with the double transformation of the individual and of nature," a transformation that involves the "apocalyptic ambition" to "humanize nature, and to naturalize the imagination" (p. 8). While for Abrams, whose central Romantic protagonist is always Wordsworth, the lamp of the Romantic mind remains a "projector," the poet's eyes and ears, to paraphrase "Tintern Abbey," only *half*-creating what they also perceive as independent objects, for early Bloom, who loves Wordsworth but canonizes the apocalyptic humanist Blake, the lamp is a much more radical power, a power moving *away* from a mere naturalizing of imaginative life *toward* the transformation of both man and nature into the lineaments of a solely visionary imagination.

Several passages from Blake that especially preoccupy Bloom might be taken as the guiding light for his reading of the other Romantics on the question of the relation between mind and nature. The first, from Blake's *Milton*, one of the longer prophecies so important to both Bloom and Frye and crucial to the later development of Bloom's theory of the anxiety of influence, tells us that "The Imagination is not a State: it is the Human Existence itself" (2.32.33). That is, the "Real Man," for Blake, *is* the "Imagination" (CP, p. 783); the visions of the intensely creative imagination, the visions—to use the Buberian language of *Shelley's Mythmaking*—of the "I-Thou" relation, create completely for us that world of unmediated communion or purely subjective relational events that gives us true life. The sweep of such a visionary power is best seen in another key Blakean passage, this from the conclusion to *Jerusalem*, Blake's longest and most difficult prophecy. Here the four Zoas, the four great powers or faculties in every man whose disunity has brought about the fallen world of experience, "take their places," Bloom says, "in a wonderfully active Eden" (VC, p. 122):

> And they conversed together in Visionary forms dramatic which
>   bright
> Redounded from their Tongues in thunderous majesty, in
>   Visions
> In new Expanses, creating exemplars of Memory and of Intellect
> Creating Space, Creating Time according to the wonders Divine
> Of Human Imagination. . . .   (4.98.28–32)

This could be the text for Bloom's own reading of Romanticism. "Visionary forms," for Bloom as well as Blake, are not merely projections onto the already given of the phenomenal world; at their best, as Blake's attempt to build a myth of Man regenerate through the "Human Form Divine" of the active imagination shows, they totally create for us the only life that really matters, the life-in-life of vision. Bloom uses Blake precisely to reverse the conventional notion that, above all, the Romantics longed for a union or a oneness with a natural world and a cosmos that could somehow save them. Against this reading, he cites the complex Blakean conception of nature—a conception that he is at pains to show does not, after all, merely present simple, static oppositions. Blake's rejection of the natural world, Bloom says, is "dialectical or provisional" (BA, p. 336) insofar as the "unorganized innocence" of the state of Beulah depicts to a "limited but genuine extent" a nature that is "paradisal." Bloom goes on immediately to claim, however, that this "soft" view of na-

ture, found mainly in the overesteemed early Blake, is later transcended in the much greater and more authentic long prophecies,
poems whose emphasis is on "the extent to which nature is fallen,"
the extent to which "the attractions of Beulah" begin "to be eclipsed
by its dangers" (p. 298). The danger of too great a faith in the Beulah
world of nature proceeds tautologically from the primary and defining value of the creative imagination; too large a final faith in nature,
for Bloom, means, simply enough, too weak a faith in vivifying
autonomous vision.

Upon this Blakean distinction Bloom builds the entire evaluative
framework of his early canon of Romantic poetry. In some sense, he
tells us, *all* the "great Romantics . . . distrusted the Beulah of earthly
repose, the natural garden of a world" that they "longed for," and
yet that was so dangerous for them. In some sense, all the major
Romantics passed beyond Beulah "to a myth that promised a humanism that could transcend nature's illusions" (vc, p. 407). And in
still another more precise sense, then, the story of Romantic poetry
for Bloom must be a story of successes and failures in grappling
with the imperatives of the visionary impulse, successes and failures to be charted in comparative fashion on the basis of relative
attainment to Blakean ideals. In this scheme, Shelley is returned to
a position of preeminence as an apocalyptic humanist on the same
level of aspiration, if not attainment, as Blake himself, while the
established Romantics of critical tradition—Wordsworth, Coleridge, Byron, and Keats—are, in varying degrees, devalued. Bloom,
in fact, has almost nothing to say about Byron, apparently including
him in *The Visionary Company* (devoting to him only forty-four
pages of a total of 465) mainly as a gesture of hollow and rather unconvincing obeisance to that very tradition of reading Romanticism
that most of the rest of the volume seeks to overthrow. Byron's career is encapsulated in a few trenchant lines. Lacking "faith in his
own imaginings" (p. 281), he "never left the world, nor could he ever
abandon any of the existing conceptions of it." As the "most social"
of the Romantics and therefore the "least Romantic," he is an unwilling partisan of the visionary sensibility and, finally, a failure
(p. 3). Coleridge, the one Romantic not only tolerated but positively
esteemed by the New Critics, receives even less attention than
Byron—thirty-nine pages of *The Visionary Company*, none of them
on the *Biographia Literaria*, none of them on Coleridge's voluminous writings in theology and philosophy, which, for Bloom, have
"only a life in death" (p. 237). Whereas Blake discovered in the
theory of poetry an authentic theory of life, the "philosopher-

theologian" in the "official" Coleridge (p. 21) "found what seemed a rock to build upon," but what turned out to be, for the poet, "only a fear of blind matter, and the torments of the formless, a poet's true Hell" (p. 235). "Coleridge could not be a fanatic, even of the Imagination" (p. 228), Bloom tells us, and this is what, after the visionary triumphs of "The Rime of the Ancient Mariner" and "Kubla Khan," destroyed him as a poet.

The crucial antipode to Blake in Bloom's discussion of nature's ambivalent place in imaginative activity is, of course, Wordsworth. For Bloom, the critic's most salient task in reading Wordsworth is to explain the forty-year senescence of the poet after his one great decade of achievement. Just as Coleridge's "The Rime of the Ancient Mariner" is read in *The Visionary Company* as a foreshadowing of "the eventual fate of its creator, when the activity of the whole soul will yield to torpor" (p. 212), so, too, all the monuments of Wordsworth's visionary power at its apex—"Tintern Abbey," *The Prelude*, the great ode—are examined for clues as to the imminent and precipitous decline in imaginative strength of their creator. These clues center, as we might expect, in what Bloom sees as the precarious Wordsworthian myth of a benevolent nature, a myth explicated time and again in *The Visionary Company* in terms of the contrasting Blakean vision of the apocalyptic "Real Man" of the imagination. First, though, Wordsworth is given his due. He is, Bloom says, "the first poet ever to present our human condition in its naturalistic truth, vulnerable and dignified, and irreducible, not to be explained away in any terms, theological or analytical, but to be accepted as what it is." Wordsworth's belief in the "goodness of the natural heart" (p. 140), his "naturalistic celebration of the possibilities inherent in our condition, here and now" (p. 128), found embodiment in "a heroic mode of naturalism" (p. 198) whose "human glory" was bequeathed to poets as luminous as Keats, and, in our century, Wallace Stevens (p. 128).

And yet, for all Wordsworth's grandeur, the Wordsworthian myth of a benevolent nature is suspect—a perilous flirtation with the cunning charms of Beulah. Blake himself condemned Wordsworth's doctrine of the exquisite congruence of "external World" and "individual Mind" (PW, p. 590) with the terse dismissal: "You shall not bring me down to believe such fitting & fitted" (CP, p. 667). His condemnation—and perhaps Northrop Frye's interpretation of it in *Fearful Symmetry*[9]—are implicit in much of Bloom's commentary on Wordsworth in *The Visionary Company*. If for Blake the imagination either "totally destroys Nature and puts a thoroughly

Human form in its place, or else Nature destroys the Imagination," then for Wordsworth, "as for Stevens, the earth is enough," and poetry is rightfully offered as a sort of "commentary" on the relation between our imaginative lives and the sensuous givens of the neutral world (VC, pp. 127 – 28). The danger in this myth of a benevolent nature meeting a lamplike imagination is that it does not allow the poet ever to consider that "more sinister manifestation of Nature-as-temptress" represented by figures such as Keats's Belle Dame, Blake's Vala, and the duplicitous "Shape all light" of Shelley's late fragment, "The Triumph of Life" (p. 144). The result, says Bloom, is that when at last Wordsworth does darken his vision of nature in the final poems of his great decade, "Peele Castle" and "Ode to Duty," he cannot "bear to indict Nature" for having deceived him, and so "turns . . . upon himself," dismissing the "very bliss of solitude he once held essential for vision," and, in effect, abandoning that "autonomy of his own imagination" which was both his glory and "his freedom" (pp. 187 – 88).

This reading of Wordsworth shows quite strikingly the extremity of Bloom's stand on issues crucial to Romanticism. His claim that he has not translated the other poets of the visionary company into his own iconoclastic Blakean categories is difficult to endorse in the light of comments such as the following on Wordsworth's career, made by way of explicating Blake's "The Book of Thel" and "The Crystal Cabinet":

> "Tintern Abbey," the "Intimations" ode, and "Peele Castle" trace the stages by which the bard of Beulah, desperately trying to maintain a vision of a married land against the lengthening shadow of organic mortality, gradually gives way to orthodoxy and timidity and at last falls into the Ulro of the "Ecclesiastical Sonnets," and beyond that, the final abyss of the sonnets favoring capital punishment. This cycle from the poet of "possible sublimity" and "something evermore about to be" to the Urizen who could write of "Fit retribution, by the moral code," *is* the natural cycle that Beulah alone as a vision must at the last come to. (VC, p. 31)

And if there is justice in feeling that the imaginative life of Wordsworth perhaps is distorted when rigidly charted according to a "visionary" geometry derived from Blake, so too, obviously, can a strong case be made that Bloom's readings misrepresent the other great Romantics as well, and for the same reason. "La Belle Dame sans Merci," for example, yields easily to a reading precisely opposite Bloom's own, if one chooses to see the temptress in that poem as a figure not of seductive nature but of the Romantic imagination itself. Certainly Keats, with his frequent broodings over what in the "Ode to a Nightingale" he calls the "deceiving elf" of imaginative "fancy," gives us ample reason to read the poem in that fashion.[10] That Bloom chooses *not* to see Keats ever as an ironist of the imagination, that he chooses instead to read Keats solely according to the principles of Blakean "vision," is, of course, just the sort of highly polemical act that alienated many of his reviewers at the time—and that has helped him since to gain the uncommon fame as a critic that he enjoys today.

The other three characteristics of the visionary imagination presented by Bloom in his early work—its quest patterns, its brief moments of epiphanic and sublime transparency, and its final non-referentiality—are all related, and all derive from the initial postulate that, at best, the visionary imagination triumphs over and transforms the recalcitrant objectness of the natural world. Bloom's emphasis on the quest motif in romance owes much to Frye's seminal schema in *Anatomy of Criticism*, which posits all four myth forms, romance, comedy, tragedy, and irony or satire, as "episodes in a total quest-myth" (p. 215). Quest romance is distinguished by its complete tripartite form, featuring an *agon* or conflict, a *pathos* or death struggle, and an *anagnorisis* or discovery, the last of which involves, says Frye, the "recognition of the hero, who has clearly proved himself to be a hero even if he does not survive the conflict" (p. 187). The romance, as the "nearest of all literary forms to the wish-fulfillment dream" (p. 186), thus accomplishes a crucial mediation, Frye goes on to say, insofar as its hero, although mortal, nonetheless seeks and displays attributes associated with divinity.

Bloom in his early work, and in his important transitional essay of 1968, "The Internalization of Quest Romance," both assimilates and profoundly transforms Frye's anatomy of agonistic Romantic quest.[11] Whereas for Frye "the meaning of a poem, its structure of imagery, is a static pattern" (AC, p. 158), and its archetypes, in Geoffrey Hartman's apt phrase, "neo-Kantian forms that serve to objectify our experience of art,"[12] for Bloom, from the very start, the meaning of a poem resides in the dynamic, *temporal* relation between the poet's desires and his poem's quest toward their fulfillment. Frye's consciously spatial model of the quest myth depends on his belief that the critic comes *after* the reading experience, and can then objectively describe the static, atemporal pattern of the literary work. In Bloom's hands, the theory of quest is transformed into an agon, *fully* engaging the critic-as-reader, of the Romantic warrior in a death struggle first with nature, then with the even more formidable foe of a blocking agent within the self that would seek to thwart the poet's quest for visionary powers. "Internalized" in this fashion, the quest motif in Romanticism is embodied in what Bloom calls "psychologized versions of the ancient patterns" of search and attendant "alienation" (VC, p. 399), patterns whose end is to confer upon the quester the Romantic equivalent of divinity: intense imaginative activity.

In *The Visionary Company*, Bloom tends to emphasize the alienation made inevitable by the inability of nature to furnish an adequate and responsive context for the immensity of the quester's desires. The key texts for this discussion are Shelley's "Alastor" and Keats's *Endymion*—both poems powerful versions of Wordsworth's *The Excursion*, and both featuring the same preoccupation with the exigencies of the isolate, and wandering, visionary self. Readers who might object that such a reading is fruitful for "Alastor" but a grave distortion of the rich, and perhaps partly Platonic, tensions of *Endymion*,[13] are advised that there is a discrepancy in the poem between Keats's overt emphasis and the real, if hidden, drama behind it. The real quest of Endymion, Bloom says, ends with the youth's emergence from the Cave of Quietude, called "a den of Ulro, a deathly isolation" (p. 376), and his acceptance, which is unlike the response of Shelley's relentless hero in "Alastor," of the need to remain in the ordinary world. *Endymion* is thus wrested into the confines of Blakean geometry, pitting the visionary imagination against the charming but dangerous phenomenal world of our ordinary lives, but to so wrest it Bloom is forced to dismiss the remaining section of the poem, that featuring the vanishing of Endymion with the Indian maid newly transformed into a moon goddess, as "a mechanical end," a "desperate" and "premature union" of "the real with the ideal" (p. 378). It was, of course, just this sort of critical operation that led reviewers of the time such as the anonymous *TLS* scribe mentioned in my introduction to accuse Bloom of thesis-mongering—a charge that has only intensified with the years.

While *The Visionary Company* highlights the first stage of quest romance, the disjunction between nature and the infinite Blakean desires of the imaginative man, "The Internalization of Quest Romance" takes as its subject the larger and for Bloom even more important second stage, the drama of the imagination confronting that in the poet's own self that threatens visionary flight. We would anticipate the story of Bloom's development by lingering for too long here on this crucial essay—its themes will be discussed at some length in chapter 2 as a necessary prelude to the culminating theory of the anxiety of influence—but it is instructive to note that the enlarged scope of Bloom's later conception of quest romance is really but the logical consequence of his commitment from the start to an exaltation of pure vision over nature. In "the Real Man, the Imagination, stage," Bloom observes in characteristically Blakean language, "nature is the immediate though not the ultimate antagonist." The final foe "to be overcome," he says, the "recalcitrance in the self," is, in fact, "what Blake calls the Spectre of Urthona" and Shelley, "the unwilling dross that checks the spirit's flight" (RT, p. 22). With the quest fully internalized through the terminological offices of a dread spectre of one of Blake's four Zoas, Bloom is able to make explicit, in this key transitional essay, what had been often only implicit in *The Visionary Company*: not just "Alastor," not just "Endymion," but *all* Romantic poetry is a questing "made in the name of a humanizing hope that approaches apocalyptic intensity" (RT, p. 15). All Romantic poetry, then, is a crisis poetry featuring as hero the poet himself and his "creative process" locked in a deathly struggle for power with "imaginative inhibitions" of "every kind," especially those arising from within (p. 19).

In *The Visionary Company*, Bloom had accepted Frye's Blakean definition of an "apocalypse" as "the imaginative conception of the whole of nature as the content of an infinite and eternal living body which, if not human, is closer to being human than to being inanimate" (AC, p. 119). Now in an essay written seven years later, he confronts more fully the implications of that definition, and, for the first time in his published work, explicitly criticizes Frye for an inadequate treatment of the romance form. Frye "still speaks of the Romantics," Bloom observes, as "seeking a final unity between man and his nature," but this, in fact, is precisely *not* what they are seeking, at least not in the "purest version of the quest form" (RT, pp. 20–21) as it is now seen by Bloom to be delivered in the "greatest" and "most drastic" Romantic quests, Blake's *Jerusalem* and Shelley's *Prometheus Unbound*, respectively (p. 19). Against an anatomy by Frye that clings too closely, for all its own Blakean impulses, to the rhythms of nature and natural recurrence as a basis for charting the literary universe, Bloom now posits, in the last phase before his turn to influences and anxieties in *Yeats*, an imaginative iconography featuring the problematics of "desire wholly taken up into the imagination" (p. 24), and imagination attempting then to fulfill a desire that can never be fully realized by the act of writing the poem.

This conception of the Romantic imagination as an infinite and inexpressible desire in the process of trying to utter itself is crucial to an accurate understanding of Bloom in *all* his phases, including the very earliest in *Shelley's Mythmaking*, for it not only underlies his notion of Romantic "mythopoeia" and the cherished Romantic sublime, but also, in turn, dictates the *kind* of reading he gives Romantic and modern poetry—a reading that, again from the very start, challenges the main assumptions of the Modernist approach to literary texts. In *Shelley's Mythmaking, The Visionary Company,* and *Blake's Apocalypse,* Bloom tends to distinguish between two types of sublime Romantic achievement, the first a lesser epiphanic moment still tied to the world of nature, and the second a greater apocalyptic rapture that, if only for one brief, purely visionary moment, seems to leave all the entrapments of natural context behind. Bloom's definition of "epiphany" as the point "where a cyclical order of nature and a higher eternal order come together" (VC, p. 14) is taken directly from Frye's *Anatomy of Criticism,* where it appears to have been gleaned from Blake.[14] *The Visionary Company* makes the Blakean connection explicit; the point of epiphany in Blake is "the upper limit of Beulah," from which we "look down benevolently to the natural world, free of its cyclic variation, and up to the eternal world," but from which, as well, "we are still more involved in nature than the apocalyptic world need be" (p. 14). Wordsworth, not surprisingly, furnishes the central examples of the creative beauty, as well as the potential dangers, of this vantage point. Bloom cites, in particular, the great passage from book 6 of *The Prelude,* in which Wordsworth describes his reaction to his guide's assertion that they "had crossed the Alps":

> Imagination—here the Power so called
> Through sad incompetence of human speech,
> That awful power rose from the mind's abyss
> Like an unfathered vapour that enwraps,
> At once, some lonely traveller. I was lost;
> Halted without an effort to break through;
> But to my conscious soul I now can say—
> 'I recognise thy glory:' in such strength
> Of usurpation, when the light of sense
> Goes out, but with a flash that has revealed
> The invisible world, doth greatness make abode,

There harbours; whether we be young or old,
Our destiny, our being's heart and home,
Is with infinitude, and only there;
With hope it is, hope that can never die,
Effort, and expectation, and desire,
And something evermore about to be.   (6.592 — 608)

Even here, Bloom notes, in a passage verging on the purely visionary, Wordsworth's emphasis is naturalistic, his senses are "transcended by a natural teaching" (VC, p. 153). Yet, it is the transcendence itself, or, rather, the imagination's marshaling of strength to achieve it, that is "the vital element" in the passage, and, as we have already seen, it is the failure of Wordsworth to retain such strength that dooms him, after his few brief years of greatness, to the "Ulro" of an orthodox death-in-life as a poet. The explanation for this failure now comes clearly into focus as being entirely Blakean. If a poet, having attained a point of epiphany, does not then pass beyond the gate of upper Beulah to the fully apocalyptic world, then "he is doomed to the vision of eternal recurrence and Beulah becomes the static state of Ulro" (p. 30).

The greatest moments of sublimity in Romantic poetry come, Bloom claims, from the sudden "raptures of prophecy" in Blake and Shelley (VC, p. 146), and it is to the crucial sharings, and the equally important divergences, of these two Romantic prophets that we must turn if we are completely to capture Bloom's own "visionary" contribution to the Romantic tradition. By now we have elucidated the tremendous importance of Blake to Bloom; we have seen how extensively and how resourcefully Bloom uses the iconography of imagination provided by both Blake and Frye on Blake to make a map of his own for Romanticism. Yet, Bloom's first book, after all, is about Shelley, and there is ample evidence throughout his writings to suggest that Shelley, not Blake or Stevens or Emerson, remains the poet closest to his own heart's desires. Why is Shelley so important to him? Do Shelley's visionary flights, like Blake's, condition in any way the terms of Bloom's reading of the other poets of the visionary company? The introduction to *Shelley's Mythmaking* establishes a telling framework within which to answer these questions—and to assess the nature of that sublime central to Bloom's reading of the Romantics. His main contention in *Shelley's Mythmaking* is that Shelley is neither a Christian nor a Platonist, but rather a wise and passionate poet of the "mythopoeic" mode, a mode defined by Bloom as featuring unmediated relations within the realm of the poet's consciousness, from which the poet may then "dare to make his own abstractions, rather than adhere" to the formulations of already established myths (p. 8). Shelley, Bloom says, stands with Blake as the greatest mythopoeic poet of Romanticism but also crucially diverges from the earlier, more confident Romantic prophet insofar as Blake was "a system maker, a mythographer who catalogues his meanings" (p. 10), while the more cynical Shelley gives us a myth that remains "quite simply . . . myth: the process of its making, and the inevitability of its defeat" (p. 8). Thus, a key passage from Blake would be something like the following, from book 2 of *Milton*:

> Judge then of thy Own Self: thy Eternal Lineaments explore
> What is Eternal & what Changeable? & what Annihilable!

> The Imagination is not a State: it is the Human Existence itself
> Affection or Love becomes a State, when divided from
>   Imagination
> The Memory is a State always, & the Reason is a State
> Created to be Annihilated & a new Ratio Created
> Whatever can be Created can be Annihilated Forms cannot
> The Oak is cut down by the Ax, the Lamb falls by the Knife
> But their Forms Eternal exist, For-ever. Amen
>   Halle[l]ujah   (2.32.30 – 38)

This speech of the seven angels to Milton summarizing Blake's doctrine of states is, for Bloom, a moment of sublimity, but the sublimity is a function of the greatness of Blake's "argument," of the "moving passion" with which Blake believes "in the truth of the awakened imagination, and the holiness of the affections of the altogether human as opposed to merely natural heart" (BA, p. 364). In other words, Bloom sees the grandeur of this passage residing in what the passage *says*, in the mythographic cataloging of the imagination that it provides—and Bloom then uses that as a key to his own charting of that visionary impulse that he, too, believes is "Human Existence itself." Contrast this to a sublime moment in Shelley, the conclusion of "Epipsychidion," where the poet realizes, with passionate woe, the impossibility of attaining an earthly paradisiacal union with Emilia:

> We shall become the same, we shall be one
> Spirit within two frames, oh! wherefore two?
> One passion in twin-hearts, which grows and grew,
> 'Till like two meteors of expanding flame,

Those spheres instinct with it become the same,
Touch, mingle, are transfigured; ever still
Burning, yet ever inconsumable:
In one another's substance finding food,
Like flames too pure and light and unimbued
To nourish their bright lives with baser prey,
Which point to Heaven and cannot pass away:
One hope within two wills, one will beneath
Two overshadowing minds, one life, one death,
One Heaven, one Hell, one immortality,
And one annihilation. Woe is me!
The winged words on which my soul would pierce
Into the height of love's rare Universe,
Are chains of lead around its flight of fire.—
I pant, I sink, I tremble, I expire![15]

Bloom reads mythopoeia such as this from Shelley, even in *Shelley's Mythmaking*, through the frame of Blake's mythographic account of the imagination. Against "the pastoral vision of Beulah-land" in the preceding 200 lines of the poem, Shelley is now seen to dramatize the defeat of the poem's myth, a defeat inherent in the myth's "paradoxical double commitment to an awareness of human limitations and to the transcendent value of an infinite desire" (p. 218). While this passage, like Blake's, is read for what it says, for its imaginative argument, the sublimity of the lines here, that which moves us in them, inheres in their passionate acknowledgment of the *obverse* side of the Blakean universe. This passage, Bloom contends, achieves grandeur by recognizing the *inability* of either earthly relationships or linguistic expression to meet the immensity of the imagination's desires. "Epipsychidion," by dramatizing the inadequacy of language and Beulah love, thus extends the argument of "Alastor" on the trap of nature, and completes, for Bloom, the passage of the sublime beyond *all* context to a region where desire confronts only the infinitude, rapturous, ineffable, and finally tautologous, of its own longings. Shelley, as the prototypical Romantic prophet of myth that is its own subject and its own inevitable defeat, temperamentally is much closer to Bloom than Blake ever could be, precisely insofar as Shelley's "moral heroism," his "agnostic faith in the mythopoeic mode" (SM, p. 118), speaks more intimately and with greater urgency to Bloom's sense of the temper of our own time, a time seen by Bloom even in his early work to be belated, "atomized," and faithless (RT, p. 18). If the very success of Blake's myth—"possibly the most formidable and organized ever created by a single man" (SM, p. 117)—guarantees its use by Bloom as a mythographic map for the questings of imaginative men, then the defeat of Shelley's ensures that the modern mapmaker will search always, and only, for the sublime of that drama of doomed desire that ascends, like "a larger intelligibility" for our tormented time (VC, p. 464),[16] out of the words, so inadequate and impoverished, on the page. And thus we arrive at the peculiarities of Bloom's *method* for reading Romanticism—and at the stridencies of his rhetoric against all other readers who would deny the salience of pure Romantic vision.

Since literary tradition for Bloom is a competition and not an ideal order, his first three books are best viewed as an extended polemic against the tradition immediately preceding him, the tradition that, through most of the twentieth century, had slighted all the Romantics but Coleridge, and that had been especially contemptuous in its dismissal of the prophet of humanized apocalypse, Shelley. Bloom's battles with the spectre of Irving Babbitt's "New Humanism," with the New Criticism of Tate, Ransom, Brooks, and Warren, and finally and perhaps most fiercely, with what he calls the "neo-Christian matrix of modern Anglo-Catholic letters" represented by T. S. Eliot, W. H. Auden, and C. S. Lewis (RT, p. 207),[17] are based upon fundamental differences in values, assumptions, and beliefs about virtually every form of cultural activity known to engage humans. Essentially, Bloom rejects *any* orthodox cosmogony, especially Christian, that would see man as a limited creature, and that would, under the rubric of conceptions as varied as original sin, classicism, decorum, and societal duty, invoke that limitation as right and necessary. For Bloom, again under the strong light of his own radical Blakean lamp, orthodox cosmogonies are but myths grown old and rigid, systems that can only enslave. Against all such stale myths, against what he sees as their limited and limiting view of man, Bloom preaches the apocalyptic humanism of Blake and Shelley, and presents a reading method to go with it, a method derived directly from the central poems of Romanticism as Bloom conceives it and intended completely to counter the established reading regimen of his critical adversaries. Where the New Critics, seeing literary tradition as an ideal order, habitually took care to cultivate the effect of a certain distance from the works they examined, a distance meant to serve as a correlative to the "objectivity"—the wit, irony, and paradox—of the work itself, Bloom, basing his reading method on a powerful but narrow definition of

Romanticism as a primarily visionary mode, fully engages the imaginative life of the works he admires, and thus replaces New Critical "objectivity" with his own distinctly passionate advocacy of, and prophecy about, the Romantic cause.

Bloom's readings in *Shelley's Mythmaking, The Visionary Company*, and *Blake's Apocalypse* are best described as "visionary paraphrases." His characteristic method, one owing much to Blake and Frye, is to quote a passage from a poem, summarize its "imaginative argument," and then elucidate the analogues and parallels obtaining between that argument and the arguments of other poems by poets of the visionary company, especially Blake and Shelley. One bewildered reviewer of the original edition of *The Visionary Company*, Robert O. Preyer, described the process in particularly witty fashion:

> There is little in the way of critical evaluation: "from this point the poem soars into greatness," we read. Other poems are called "brilliant," "profound," "superb," or "beautiful," and the reader's attention is directed instead toward a tissue of correspondencies, analogies, analogues, and similarities which the author constantly observes as he reflects on the entire corpus of works which belong within the autonomous world of the Visionary Mode. One gets the impression that *all* these works are simultaneously present to the author's consciousness at any given moment—and that he is incapable of forgetting. The result is astonishing, but not infrequently astonishment and admiration are followed by claustrophobia, the sense of being imprisoned in a suffocating House of Art which in turn dissolves into the appearance of a House of Mirrors.
>
> In his fits of total recall Mr. Bloom appears to throw down on the page hot slabs of melded relationships rather than paragraphs.[18]

A cryptic observation that Preyer goes on to make—"it is as though the author cannot endure the presence of an occasional poem"—takes us even closer to the heart of Bloom's visionary method of reading. Bloom, as he will later clarify through his intense valorization of Emerson, is in love with the idea of "a poetry never yet written"[19]—a poetry, furthermore, that *never could be* written, since to write a poem is, in the Buberian language of *Shelley's Mythmaking*, already to transform the unmediated "Thou" of the poet's conception into an object, into the "It" of the object world of unredeemed experience (p. 89). Thus, a poem for Bloom is

32

not, *cannot* be, what it is for the New Critics: an artifact, words on
a page. Such a conception has in it the chill of death-in-life for him.
Rather, Bloom says, a poem must be seen as the promise of a "fulfillment" that "is never the poem itself but the poem beyond that is
made possible by the apocalypse of imagination" (RT, p. 19). Shelley's "A Defence of Poetry," called by Bloom "the most profound
discourse on poetry in the language" (BA, p. 334), traces the etiology
of the inevitable fall into language of this promise that remains
always evermore about to be: "but when composition begins,
inspiration is already on the decline, and the most glorious poetry
that has ever been communicated to the world is probably a feeble
shadow of the original conception of the Poet" (SPP, p. 504).

Bloom, interested solely in the transcendent desire that exists
beyond, or before, its inevitable limitation into language, reads the
poems of the visionary company not for the words on the page but
for the visionary gleam those words may embody, and for the battle
with limitation that the presence of the poem-as-object implies. All
poems then become commentaries on the process of their own
mythmaking, an activity that Bloom sees as nowhere more profound than in Shelley, and best typified there by the battle for meaning in the much belabored "Ode to the West Wind." The charges
against Shelley by modern critics such as T. S. Eliot, F. R. Leavis, and
Allen Tate are commonplaces in our critical lore, and are well
summed by Bloom's teacher, Frederick Pottle, in his 1952 essay,
"The Case of Shelley." Of all the Romantics, Shelley most incurred
the contempt of an age in revolt against Romanticism. Called variously sentimental, self-dramatizing, self-pitying, immature, febrile,
and, most damning of all, a poor and a careless craftsman, Shelley
was transformed by the New Critics from one of the most praised
and popular poets of the nineteenth century into the man on the
dump of a Romantic tradition gone rancid with age.[20]

Bloom's resuscitation of Shelley's reputation is based on his contention that the New Critics, led astray by unproductive and pernicious assumptions about the role of poetry in society and about the
place of imagination in poetry, grievously misread the man who was
the most complex and the most "urbane" of all the Romantic
prophets. If some of Shelley's followers have done him a disservice
in attempting to reduce his deeply individualistic mythopoeia to
the doctrines of a Plato or a Godwin, an even graver disservice has
been wrought by those like Leavis and Tate who have failed, because
of their assumption that poetry can never, and ought never, to affirm
the possibility of an "I-Thou" relation, even to read Shelley's lines

with a minimal critical competence (SM, p. 74). "Of all the Romantics," Bloom contends, Shelley "needs the closest reading" (VC, p. 282), but as we might expect, what Bloom means by a close reading has little to do, in *Shelley's Mythmaking* and *The Visionary Company*, with that painstaking New Critical attention to the manifold ambiguities and paradoxes of the poem as a crafted object on a page that was de rigueur in the academy of the time. Rather, since Bloom's readings reflect his opposite sense that the object on the page somehow exists as a commentary, thwarted and cryptic, on the problematics of its own impetus as a visionary creation, what we get is a determined devaluation of the image as a staple of poetic discourse, and a corollary reaffirmation of the importance of poetic propositions. "Once we dispense with the odd modern critical dogma that what poetry is *about* is irrelevant to its aesthetic value," then we can also see that "image, far from being the primary pigment of all poetry, is irrelevant to much of the highest poetry, whether in the Romantic tradition or not" (VC, p. 172).

Thus, "Ode to the West Wind," the victim of what to Bloom is one of the most unconscionable hatchet jobs in the history of modern literary criticism, does not represent the woeful miscarriage of craft and literary intelligence that F. R. Leavis, dissecting the roiled imagistic strands of the poem, claimed it did.[21] The poem, Bloom says, features a moving dialectical drama of the stance of the mythmaking poet toward a west wind that is itself imbued with the breath of the spirit of apocalypse, and as such is never merely an object or an "It" to the poet *within* his poem. The poem's poignancy and its grandeur derive from the crucial opposition between stanzas 4 and 5, where the poet at first despairingly seeks, as a Thou, to be treated as an It, and then, in the famous final lines, surmounts visionary despair to affirm once again "the humanizing possibility of mythmaking" and "the value of the relationship which can create poems" (SM, p. 86). Shelley is a poet difficult for readers with inclinations as reductive as Leavis's to understand because such readers are not able to see that Shelley's ironies are those of prophecy, his often vague and seemingly convoluted images those of vision. Shelley's ironies, Bloom says, do not traffic in merely verbal or "metaphysical" wit, but present the far more profound visionary's "awareness of the terrible gap between aspiration and fulfillment" (RT, pp. 114–15). Shelley's images, similarly, are not intended to be imagistic in the early Modernist manner, but, rather, are visionary— and uncompromisingly visionary in their maker's effort to subvert them in the very act of presenting them.[22] Shelley makes visualiza-

tion difficult for us, Bloom notes (VC, p. 319), but he does so deliberately, not carelessly, in order "to arrive at a more radical kind of
verbal figure" in which the world might be wholly, if also skeptically,
"taken up into the mind" (RT, p. 109). That he "never altogether
achieved" such a language is not, Bloom argues with great passion,
an indictment of him, but simply an acknowledgment of the blocking power of what "Adonais" calls the world of "unwilling dross"
(43.384), the world against which Shelley battled as heroically as any
poet who ever lived, to a poet's inevitable defeat. For a poetic agon
much less heroic—but for a Bloomian critical argument considerably more refined—we may now turn, in chapter 2, to Bloom's
Romantic re-vision of that Modernist master Yeats.

T W O

Yeats and the
Spectre of Modernism

Yeats is, in many ways, the pivotal book in Harold Bloom's career as
a critic. The publication of *Shelley's Mythmaking, The Visionary
Company,* and *Blake's Apocalypse* in the five-year span from 1959
through 1963 had established Bloom as one of the truly indispensable critics on the great age of English Romanticism. Although his
uncompromising thesis that the Romantics were poets not of
nature but of "vision," and his concomitant elevation of Blake and
Shelley to positions of preeminence within the Romantic canon,
proved unsettling to more orthodox Romantic scholars, even those
who remained unconvinced were usually quick to acknowledge
that the brilliant young Romanticist conducted his argument with
great passion, rigor, and tremendous erudition. Robert Preyer,
whom we have already seen to be as troubled by Bloom as any critic,
delivered an evaluation of *The Visionary Company* in 1961 which
might be taken to be characteristic of the response of many readers
to the Bloom enterprise over the years. "It is extremely difficult,"
Preyer says at the start of his review, "to provide a substantive account of this perceptive, irritating, repetitive, and even profound
'Reading of English Romantic Poetry.' "[1]

Perceptive, irritating, repetitive, difficult, and even profound:
such was the strange mixture of exasperation and respect that
greeted Bloom's visionary Romanticism in the early phase of his
career—and that greets him still. At the center of that ambivalent
response was a concern with the almost obsessive narrowness of
Bloom's focus. There were misgivings about a man who violated the
rules of critical decorum by consciously presenting himself as a
Romantic writing about a body of Romantic poetry whose central
assumptions, values, and beliefs he shared, a man who, in turn, read

the central poems of the central Romantics with a forbiddingly firm
and well-cultivated scorn toward any attempt to transform those
poems into something he decreed they were not—any attempt, that
is, to see in them anything other than the purity of mythmaking
poetic vision. One sympathetic critic, James E. Benziger, observed of
The Visionary Company that "the chief weakness of this remarkable
study is a certain onesidedness; it has not the variety of the materials it considers."[2] With the publication of *Blake's Apocalypse* in
1963 to complete the triad of books on the visionary company, this
one-sidedness had come to loom as the major threat to Bloom's
critical enterprise. The question proposed by Preyer in his review of
The Visionary Company seemed to stand for all misgivings about
Bloom's methods, his values, and his vision. What escape could
there be, Preyer asked, from the imposing, astonishing, and finally
claustrophobic House of Visionary Art that Bloom was laboring so
energetically to construct?

The answer was seven years in the coming, and when it was
delivered in 1970 with the publication of Bloom's longest and perhaps most challenging book, *Yeats*, it proved to be not so much an
answer as a deliberate refusal even to countenance the question.
Yeats, a massive, synoptic reading of a great twentieth-century poet
in terms of his origins as a visionary Romantic, is the pivotal transitional volume in Harold Bloom's career because it demonstrates so
forcefully, indeed eloquently, the character of Bloom's developing
offense against established literary tradition—and the quality of his
defense against the questions that such a tradition would present
him. Bloom's *Yeats*, by reading all of a central modern poet's work as
a complex, sometimes perverse, generally inferior, response to the
writings of his great poetic precursors, Blake and Shelley, served to
broaden the expanse of the House of Visionary Art while at the same
time securing even more firmly all the portals of that dwelling
against any opening onto traditions different from the visionary. In
so doing, the book both extended the Blakean argument of Bloom's
early work on the primacy and the sublimity of the visionary imagination, and presaged the central thesis of the later volumes that
such a sublimity can only be earned through the grievous expense
of a dark and treacherous competition for visionary space between
poetic latecomers and their descendants-in-imagination. Part of
this expense, Bloom says in *Yeats* and in his many other volumes of
the seventies, inheres in the simple melancholy we experience following *our* recognition as readers that the source of our cherished
sublime in literature is such baleful and inhumane ground. Bloom's

own style in the phase inaugurated by *The Anxiety of Influence* in 1973, a style thick with what unpersuaded critics have labeled melodramatic posturing, is intended to embody the anguish that Bloom says we should all feel, an anguish to accompany the crumbling of our illusions about the "ideal order" we had naively thought literature to be. The main subject of this chapter will not be that anguish (the agonistic quality of Bloom's own rhetoric of *pathos* will be discussed in chapter 6); it will be the other major expense of competition featured in the new Bloomian theory, an expense proceeding logically from the premise that where there is a battle, necessarily there is a loser. Bloom's impassioned and polemical rereading of Yeats is most important for its two related and controversial contentions that Modernist poetry as represented by Yeats, no matter how strongly it *tries* to be anti-Romantic, remains Romantic nonetheless, and that, as such, what it delivers necessarily is an inferior Romanticism, a Romanticism diminished by the inexorable force of its own visionary belatedness.

In examining the intricate network of values and beliefs with which Bloom, via Yeats, meets the spectre of Modernism, we might find it helpful to use once again the schema advanced in the previous chapter for Bloom's theory of visionary Romanticism. "Yeats's immediate tradition," Bloom announces in his introduction to *Yeats*, "could be described as the internalization of quest romance, and Yeats's most characteristic kind of poem could be called the dramatic lyric of internalized quest" (pp. 4 – 5). Yeats's poems, that is, assume the dialectic of nature and the imagination in Romantic poetry, and then, at their best, pass beyond that confrontation to the deeper dialectic of poetic desires questing for visionary fulfillment amid a universe of death. The key text for placing Yeats within the Romantic tradition thus becomes Shelley's "Alastor," the "single poem that most affected [Yeats's] life and art" (p. 8), and the first great poem by a man who, of all the Romantics, has shown the most power to provide "developing imaginations with a paradigm for the torments of their own processes of incarnating the poetical character in themselves" (p. 17). Shelley's lyric portrayal of a young man doomed to wander the earth in a relentless and finally destructive search for "the spiritual form of his total desire" (p. 90) is seen by Bloom to figure heavily and fruitfully in Yeats's early poetry, especially in "The Wanderings of Oisin," which becomes one of Bloom's main reclamation projects when he rescues it from a history of critical neglect. More important than any specific influence, though, is the furnishing by "Alastor" to Yeats of an entire rich world for Yeats's poetic imagination to build itself upon. As Bloom describes it, the world bequeathed Yeats by Shelley is one in which the initial antagonist is nature, and the quest is for a mysterious and elusive epipsyche or beautiful woman who will wondrously complete the life of the quester. The inevitable ruin in such a world, Bloom says, is the ruin of imagination veering into a sublimity too fierce in its solipsism, and then enduring a destructive self-conscious separation "both from others and itself" (p. 90). Translated into Yeatsian terms, "Alastor" incarnates in him the germ of his crucial conceptions of the "antithetical," defined by Bloom as meaning "anti-natural" (p. 21), the Maud Gonne figure, or "representation of the *Mask* as Image," which the poet must desire and also must never have,[3] and the *daimonic* man, the poet of phase 17 of *A Vision* for whom Yeats's desired "Unity of Being" is most possible, yet who must also suffer, if his quest be false, the pangs of an "enforced self-realization" (AV, p. 140), which is the equivalent of what Bloom calls the "agony of self-consciousness" afflicting Shelley's haunted and doomed young quester (*Yeats*, p. 91).

Already, one of the dangers of Bloom's mapping operation is apparent: the danger, as Preyer warned, of becoming lost within the bewildering corridors of analogues and parallels that abound in the Bloomian House of Visionary Art. And yet the essential point is simple enough: Yeats appropriates from, and in some way, however perverse, always shares with Shelley a "conviction that the most poetic images are necessarily those of unfulfilled and unfulfillable desire" (*Yeats*, p. 350). He finds, too, in Shelley, who died so young and whose last real poem ("The Triumph of Life") was an unfinished testament to visionary despair, a moving emblem of his own deepest concern, the "rage" against growing old which preoccupied him in his own final phase as a poet.[4] Yeats's poetry at its most compelling, Bloom says, is built upon a Shelleyan quest for imaginative immortality, and an equally Shelleyan despair over the fate of that quest in a world seemingly designed to thwart it. Now the main argument of *Yeats* enters. While Yeats at his best is a strong Shelleyan prophet, and thus a quester who believes completely in the profound Blakean prescription from "The Marriage of Heaven and Hell" that "Where man is not nature is barren" (Blake, CP, p. 38), he is also a poet who is often not willing or able to confront the imperatives of that total commitment to the visionary imagination so forcibly mandated in the works of his key Romantic precursors. Instead, Bloom says, Yeats distorts that mandate by cunningly, eloquently, and sometimes viciously misreading the works of Shelley and Blake,

and by then using that misreading to generate and justify the
Gnosticism and perverse theosophical systematizing of his own
poetry, including the formulations of the "considerable if flawed
major poem," *A Vision* (*Yeats*, p. 211). In attempting to explain how
Yeats makes his precursors over in the lesser image of himself, and,
just as important, why he feels compelled to do so, Bloom delivers
his indictment of modern and Modernist poetry, and adumbrates
his famous theory of the anxiety of influence.

Yeats, as much as he loves Shelley and recognizes what Bloom
will call Shelley's (and Blake's) "infinite desire to break through
natural barriers and so uncover an altogether human universe"
(p. 60), also accuses his ancestral prophet of two grave sins against
the imagination. First, in the early essay of 1900, "The Philosophy of
Shelley's Poetry," he charges that, although Shelley does at times
intuit an enticing and authentic spiritual world, he then lacks the
authority and the theosophical roots fully to realize that world in
his poems and ends up producing poetry that at times suffers from
"an air of rootless fantasy."[5] Second, Yeats, in his discussion of
phase 17 in *A Vision*, criticizes Shelley for lacking the "Vision of Evil"
that would have made him one of the very greatest of poets, a vision
that Yeats seems to equate with the ability to conceive of the world
as a "continual conflict" (AV, p. 144). As we might expect, Bloom sees
both charges to be drastic and pernicious misreadings of Shelley's
world, misreadings that in turn, he says, aid Yeats in buttressing the
foundation of his own departures from what is most vital to visionary Romanticism. Here is the concluding stanza from Shelley's "The
Sensitive-Plant," to which Yeats's first accusation pertains:

> For love, and beauty, and delight
> There is no death nor change: their might
> Exceeds our organs—which endure
> No light—being themselves obscure.   (SPP, p. 219)

Observing that Shelley in these lines "seems in his speculations
to have lit on that memory of Nature the visionaries claim for the
foundation of their knowledge,"[6] Yeats goes on to condemn his
predecessor for not fully confronting the imperatives of such oc-
cultic faith, a condemnation that to Bloom is more revealing for the
light in which it shows Yeats's desperate need for a faith, any faith,
than for any insight it may offer into the passionate "visionary
skepticism" of Shelley (*Yeats*, p. 188). What Yeats conjures from this
passage, Bloom sardonically observes, is "a palpable spirit-world,
a universe of squeaking phantasms that can be invoked by a Soho

medium or a self-induced trance." Bloom, repudiating as always any imputation of Platonic or spiritualist orthodoxy in the poetry of Shelley, contends that these lines quite clearly confirm the central lesson of Shelley's work: "our senses are inadequate to the full humanity of our desire" (p. 61). Bloom's Shelley, against Yeats's, is the skeptical young man of the "Notes on *Queen Mab*" who remembers always the injunction: "All that we have a right to infer from our ignorance of the cause of any event is that we do not know it...."[7] Yeats, Bloom says, "despite his own temperamental skepticism, adopted always the contrary attitude, inferring from his ignorance a range of occult causes" (*Yeats*, p. 188).

Yeats's second charge against Shelley, that he lacked a "Vision of Evil," is to Bloom even more ridiculous than the first, and just as revealing about the unfortunate turn that Yeats's own systematizing took. Shelley, in fact, was "afflicted," Bloom claims, "by an all-but-excessive consciousness of the prevalence of evil" in the world, while Yeats's own work must be seen often to endorse "most things that are to be abhorred, including violence and prejudice...." Why the misreading, then? Because, Bloom says, Yeats is attempting to build the self-serving myth of the poetic latecomer, the myth that the earlier poet was somehow an "incipient" version of his descendant, but a version doomed to failure because lacking an essential component of the latter's vision (pp. 61–62).

Bloom's contention that it is in *every* case the latecomer who lacks range and depth of vision is most fully focused in his treatment of the complex relationship between Yeats and that other great exemplar of pure Romantic wisdom, Blake. The categories of chapter 1 are again pertinent: if Shelley furnishes Yeats with a model for meeting the poet's impossible immensities of desire, then Blake, the one completely successful "mythographer" of visionary imagination in the history of poetry, a man with "conceptual powers unique among the poets" (*Yeats*, p. 226), provides his descendant an iconography for charting poetic quest. Much of *Yeats* is devoted to supporting Bloom's argument that the central failing of Yeats's poetry is the malignant and distinctly un-Blakean manner in which he uses the map bequeathed him by his precursor. Many Yeats critics, of course, had already explored the ground of Blake's influence on Yeats, an influence especially notable in the system of *A Vision*, in the gyres which are its equivalent of the Blakean vortex, in the twenty-eight phases of the Great Wheel of incarnation which Yeats derived from his study of Blake's twenty-seven phases or churches of history. Bloom diverges from most earlier critics, and

especially from their most eloquent representative, Thomas
Whitaker,[8] in arguing that the influence of Blake on Yeats consists
not of a healthy and benign transmittal of ideas and images from
earlier to later poet, but, rather, of "creative misinterpretation" of
Blake by his lesser descendant, misinterpretation so great that
"sustained parallel studies of Blake and Yeats are never likely to
prove fruitful" (p. 309). *Milton* is the relevant text for Bloom here, as
it so often was in chapter 1, and as it will continue to be in chapter 3.
Bloom is especially preoccupied by a scene from book 2 of the brief
epic, where the seven angels are about the business of instructing
Milton in the Blakean doctrine of "States":

> Distinguish therefore States from Individuals in those States.
> States Change: but Individual Identities never change nor cease:
> You cannot go to Eternal Death in that which can never Die.
> Satan & Adam are States Created into Twenty-seven Churches
> And thou O Milton art a State about to be Created
> Called Eternal Annihilation that none but the Living shall
> Dare to enter: & they shall enter triumphant over Death
> And Hell & the Grave! States that are not, but ah! Seem to
>   be.   (2.32.22 − 29)

The very next strophe delivers the famous formula that the
imagination is not a "State" but "Human Existence itself." Yeats,
says Bloom, errs profoundly in taking from Blake's cosmogony the
doctrine of states, but then formulating a theory of imagination and
of poetry out of *that* doctrine, without seeing that in Blake the
imagination does not reside in any of the states themselves but
supersedes them all. In theory, Yeats thereby condemns the poet
always to exist within the Blakean world of Beulah, a world that
Bloom, following Blake, says is marked by mere receptivity, passive-
ness, and the tyranny of cyclical recurrence.[9] Yeats himself asserted
in the "Packet for Ezra Pound" at the beginning of *A Vision* that,
beyond a few suggestions on the "historical logic" of the twenty-
eight "incarnations," there "was nothing" in Blake's "unfinished
confused Prophetic Books" that could "help" him in formulating
the system presented in the book (AV, p. 12). Against this, Bloom
argues that Yeats, in the deepest recesses of his poetical character,
did not *want* to be helped by the real Blake, the great visionary myth-
maker of a confident Romanticism, but instead chose to misread the
prophetic books, transforming them into a second-rate hash of
theosophical gobbledygook and Gnosticism having little to do with
Blake but much to do with the failure in vision of Blake's belated

poetic son. The key transformation involves the relation of the twenty-seven states or churches and the important figure, also in *Milton*, of the "Covering Cherub," or "Shadow of Milton," a figure that, as we will see in chapter 3, has come to represent for Bloom the very heart of the darkness of poetic influence. Shortly after the doctrine of states is announced, the "Twenty-seven Heavens &. their Churches" are named by Blake, and then placed:

> All these are seen in Miltons Shadow who is the Covering Cherub
> The Spectre of Albion in which the Spectre of Luvah inhabits
> In the Newtonian Voids between the Substances of Creation
> (2.37.44 − 46)

In the edition of Blake that he edited with the pre-Raphaelite painter and poet Edwin J. Ellis, Yeats interprets this passage to mean that "the Cherub is divided into . . . twenty-seven passive states through which man travels" and through which "Blake found . . . the whole story of man's life. . . ." In this edition he also defines the covering cherub, in a manner anticipating his own central conception of *A Vision*, as the "mask of created form in which the uncreated spirit makes itself visible."[10] Against both these Yeatsian interpretations, Bloom first cites the malevolent reality of the cherub in Blake, and in Blake's source for the figure, Ezekiel:

> Thou *art* the annointed cherub that covereth; and I have set thee *so*: thou wast upon the holy mountain of God; thou hast walked up and down in the midst of the stones of fire.
> Thou *wast* perfect in thy ways from the day that thou wast created, till iniquity was found in thee.
> By the multitude of thy merchandise they have filled the midst of thee with violence, and thou hast sinned: therefore I will cast thee as profane out of the mountain of God: and I will destroy thee, O covering cherub, from the midst of the stones of fire.[11]

The cherub is not in any way for Blake an aid to imaginative fulfillment; quite the contrary, the figure represents what Bloom, even as early as *Blake's Apocalypse*, had called the "barrier between creative desire and artistic completion" (p. 359), and what he now explicitly labels "the negative or stifling aspect of poetic influence" (*Yeats*, p. 6). Furthermore, Bloom observes, making his most telling point, the cherub in Blake is never explicitly associated with history, and the fact that from a multitude of possibilities Yeats chooses this one particular figure, so malevolent and oppressive, to help him find his way into his own doctrine of historical incarnation, is as startling an instance of the "true imaginative inwardness" of poetic influence and misinterpretation as any poet has ever given us. Yeats's description of the twenty-seven churches as "passive," and as representing the "whole story of man's life," is as spectacularly inadequate on Blake, Bloom contends, as it is judicious in accounting for the phases of the moon in Yeats's own work. "To Blake these Churches are not necessarily passive," Bloom says, "and in them he certainly did not find the whole story of our life" (p. 78). Rather, it is through the "Eternal Annihilation" of the twenty-eighth state, of the "State about to be Created" featuring Milton himself, that what Bloom calls the "awakened humanity in a man" arises to embrace the imagination which "cannot pass away" (BA, p. 349)—the imagination, that is, as "Human Existence itself." Yeats, Bloom observes, misreads Blake so as not to see this all-important passage beyond the cycles of a fallen history, and thus, at the very center of his thought, presents, through the twenty-eight spokes of the Great Wheel, a world in which true imagination and authentic and fully human love can never live.

What, then, does Yeats have to offer us in *A Vision* and in the poetry engendered by that book? If he misreads and mis-takes Shelley and Blake so grievously, what is such misprision in service of? What precisely *is* Yeats's vision, and what is wrong with it? In defining his position, Bloom is quite aware of his adversary relation to a whole body of critical opinion, ranging from the New Critical strictures of Allen Tate to the acolyte's eloquence of Thomas Whitaker to the preeminent Yeatsian domain of Richard Ellmann (to whom *Yeats* is dedicated). For all their many differences, what these critics have in common is a greater willingness than Bloom evinces to accept Yeats as not only a great poet but also as a wise thinker. *A Vision*, of course, has always been at the center of the great debate on Yeats. The master's contention that the volume had been dictated to his wife by spirits was one of those scandals of the Modernist era that, like Pound's descent into dictator worship or the discreet anti-Semitism of Eliot, seemed best dealt with tactfully, if indeed confronted at all. Yet there were several attractive ways for mainstream critics to handle the problem of *A Vision* and the relation of its theory of history and imagination to Yeats's poetry. Many chose to invoke the spirit of a Spenglerian age, aligning *A Vision* in loose confederation with other massive undertakings of the time such as the cultural anthropology of Frazer and Weston and the Viconian mythmaking of *Ulysses* and *Finnegans Wake*. Myth in this view became Modernist insofar as it was used in the Eliotic manner of "The Waste Land," the manner prescribed in Eliot's famous essay on *Ulysses*, which recommends mythic parallelism as a legitimate tool of the modern artist in the face of a complex, fragmenting, and inchoate time.[12] Another persuasive option, this one for those still dubious about *A Vision* and yet unwilling to damn Yeats's poetry on that account, was to argue that the vast majority of Yeats's work could profitably be read without recourse to the systematized ideas and body of symbols inherent in it. *A Vision* could then be relegated to ancillary status as helpful background—a suggestion for "supplementary reading" in the rich but sometimes admittedly rather odd symbolic universe of the greatest modern poet.[13]

Bloom will not endorse either of these two approaches to the conundrum of Yeats's philosophy. The second, he says, is a transparent attempt to evade the obvious: the philosophy and symbols of *A Vision* are integral to Yeats's poetry, and often destructive of it. While the categories and cycles of *A Vision* may not be "adequate to Yeats's own imagination," they are nonetheless almost always operative within it, and contribute prominently to the vicious and reductive poetic arguments marring many of his supposedly greatest poems, including "The Second Coming," "Leda and the Swan," "The Gyres," and the Byzantium poems. The other bid to bypass the troublesome question of Yeats's systematizing is, in Bloom's eyes, much more imposing and thus much more malign. The Modernist conception of myth as a tool to be employed by the writer, a sort of conceptually powerful trick of the trade for ordering the raw welter of his materials, is inimical to Bloom, who, as we have shown, sees poetry at its best to be *identical* with the act of mythmaking itself. Yeats's own position on *A Vision*, that the book primarily serves to furnish metaphors for his poetry, is labeled by Bloom a misrepresentation of the real center of the volume, which is, inescapably, its esoteric philosophy. *A Vision*, Bloom sums, "is nothing if it is not wisdom literature," and yet the terrible failing of the book is that "it is sometimes very unwise" (*Yeats*, p. 210).

Bloom's exegesis of the Yeatsian philosophy in *A Vision* is the best and most brilliant part of his study. Occupying over eighty pages in the heart of the book, Bloom's reading of *A Vision* as the "culminating work" (p. 210) in Yeats's quest for the meaning of history and the poetic imagination becomes the basis of his notoriously polemical evaluations of all the poetry from *The Wild Swans at Coole* onward—all the poetry, that is, of the late middle and later Yeats which had been canonized by modern criticism as the foremost sustained poetic achievement of our century. If the early Shelleyan Yeats of "The Wanderings of Oisin" and "The Shadowy Waters" is a much more formidable poet than most modern critics had acknowledged, and if the middle Yeats of *In the Seven Woods*, *The Green Helmet*, and *Responsibilities*, with his absurd "anti-Romantic revisionist" tendencies (p. 162), is much less distinguished than had hitherto been supposed, then the Yeats of *The Wild Swans at Coole* through the *Last Poems* is, for Bloom, the most complex and the most puzzling Yeats of all, since the poems of these later years alternate between an imaginatively appropriate fidelity to the great line of Romantic vision and a completely repugnant departure from that line into the dehumanizing and reductive world of Gnostic theosophy presented by *A Vision*.

The germ of all the errors of *A Vision* is exhibited for Bloom in a comment Yeats makes apropos of Blake in his 1893 edition of Blake's writings: "The chief difference between the metaphors of poetry and the symbols of mysticism is that the latter are woven together into a complete system."[14] The notion implicit here that, as Bloom acidly puts it, "poetic metaphors are the blocks for building theosophical mansions, and poetry is a gnosis that has yet to go the whole way" (*Yeats*, p. 70), is fully realized in the grand edifice of *A Vision*, a "theosophical mansion" whose chart of the twenty-eight phases of the Great Wheel is meant, in Yeats's words, to help him hold "in a single thought reality and justice" (AV, p. 25). Working from his interpretation of Blake's covering cherub, Yeats in *A Vision* constructs a geometry of the creative imagination realizing itself through cycles shared by biography and history, cycles that are strictly determined by the dialectical logic of the interplay between the Yeatsian faculties of Will, Mask, Creative Mind, and Body of Fate. Bloom, reading *A Vision* in terms of "its most direct ancestors," Blake's epics, and "another forerunner," Shelley's *Prometheus Unbound* (*Yeats*, p. 212), maintains that the book must be assailed at the very start for the "curious assumptions" behind its main dialectic of the "antithetical" and the "primary." Yeats's "antithetical" is defined by Bloom as "the thrust toward individuality" in man (p. 217), a thrust that we have already seen Bloom label " 'anti-natural' (not 'unnatural')" (p. 21). "Primary," on the other hand, is identified by Yeats with the "complete passivity, complete plasticity" of phase 1 (AV, p. 183), and is summarized by Bloom as a "counter-movement toward" a highly suspect "unity" (*Yeats*, p. 217). This conception of a subjective and creative antithetical pole in dialectical opposition to a primary pole of inert objective knowing is clearly derived, Bloom says, from Shelley's "rather fearful Either-Or" pitting the "lonely ecstasy of the artist" as Alastor figure against the objective wisdom of a society that can so often stultify and repress (p. 224). And yet, as usual in Bloom's critical universe, the taking is seen only to famish the receiver; Yeats's "subjective" is entirely too much an affair of spooks and the supernatural, while his "objective" is not really a formidable enough foe for its opponent, revealing Yeats's propensity for closing off most of the agonistic possibilities of a true Romantic rhetoric. If the epics of Blake and Shelley present quests that attain maturity and imaginative grandeur precisely by realizing that the greatest visionary struggles are those that occur *within*, then Yeats's crude caricature of a dialectic, stalled as it is at the level of a monolithic but empty "antithetical," can only confront the imperatives of the first or "promethean" stage of imaginative battle, and, after that, must return to the confines of quest as mere "cyclic renewal," with the corollary "renewed necessity for heroic defeat," which is a dominant *topos* of the Yeatsian poetic universe (p. 230).

Bloom, of course, has no quarrel with "heroic defeat" as such— his own theory of poetry exploits the *pathos* implicit in such a notion—but he does argue that the specifically Yeatsian conception of heroism is empty, violent, vicious, and antipoetic, and he suggests that the heroic ideal of Yeats is so reductive precisely because, at least according to *A Vision*, all quests, imaginative or otherwise, can only exist within the cyclical and thoroughly deterministic world of that "fallen" history that Yeats catastrophically embraces via his misreading of Blake's doctrine of the covering cherub. Bloom's condemnation of Yeats's Gnosticism—and his Blakean basis for doing so—are nowhere better revealed than in the following long and crucial passage from Bloom's exegesis of the Great Wheel:

> Blake and Shelley both posited a Fall of Man where the more naturalistic Wordsworth and Keats did not, but their versions of the Fall are neither orthodox Christian nor Gnostic, though Yeats confounded Blake with Blavatsky and would not see the difference. For Blake and the Gnostics, as opposed to orthodoxy, the Creation and the Fall are one event. It is in meeting a fallen world, in learning how to live in history, that Blake and the Gnostics, and so Blake and Yeats part (as do Shelley and Yeats also). To Yeats, the fallen world or shadow of history contains the *daimon* of the *antithetical* or subjective man, of the poet who seeks to

redeem time. So the other self, that can lead one toward Unity of Being, is both natural and temporal, and must be met by an embrace of the shadow. Yeats does not seek to exorcise the shadow by clarifying it, or by compelling it to a full manifestation of itself. This is deliberately Yeats's choice; it is the crucial moral choice that the Gnostic makes for himself. Not to see that Blake makes quite another choice from the start is not to see Blake, and makes a mockery of the life and work of a prophet who was as great a moral figure as Ezekiel or Jeremiah. To Blake the shadow or serpent was a selfhood, but not the "other" or creative self; it was the stifler or Covering Cherub, the separating or inhibiting force of nature and history, sanctified by an inadequate version of reason, and by an unjust organization of society. (Pp. 217 – 18)

It is the anti-Blakean attempt of Yeats to find the "daimon" of his antithetical self within the shadows of a fallen and thus imprisoning history that, in Bloom's eyes, engenders most of the other flaws of Yeats's Gnosticism, especially his celebration of a natural Jungian religion, and his consequent yearning toward a collective folk wisdom of the unconscious or *anima mundi*, a wisdom to be attained, of course, through the unhappy medium of the Gnostic adept. Such an *anima mundi*, representing nothing but "a saving construct of the therapeutic idealist, of the subjectivist driven in on his own desperation," delivers a "natural religiosity" which is the exact opposite of the glorious "final form of Protestant inwardness" marking the Romantic imagination of Blake and Shelley (p. 221). At the end of Yeats's quest, "one finds neither a more human man nor God the Father, but rather an individual fantasy that precedes or hopes to precede a fantasy of the uncultured, a new natural religion" (p. 222). The prophecy and the affirmation that so many Modernist critics have seen Yeats provide in poems such as "The Gyres" and "Lapis Lazuli" become "inhumane nonsense" (p. 438), the "tragic joy" of "The Gyres" merely a paean to what Bloom, citing Buber, calls the "composite god" of a vicious and dehumanizing historical process (p. 470). Such a process, Bloom says, denies us our freedom and our dignity, the freedom that in Blake and Shelley resides "in the imagination which struggled with the will" (p. 275), the dignity that inheres in the passion and the profundity of that very struggle.

Yeats's one attempt to build for the imagination a City of Eternal Art through Byzantium, associated with phase 15 of *A Vision*, the "phase of complete beauty" (AV, p. 135) where contemplation and desire are one, fares no better in Bloom's schema.[15] It too delivers a reductive and antihuman view of the imaginative possibilities of man, because its strained "supernatural subjectivity" vaults too quickly beyond not only all the merely natural but, Bloom contends, all the specifically *human* as well. Unlike both Blake and Shelley, who, in Bloom's view, present complex dialectical accounts of the relation between vision and nature and are thus skeptical of any easy and empty transcendence, Yeats, misreading his precursors to simplify them, delivers in Byzantium's "artifice of eternity" an all too palpably self-serving supernatural salvation that succeeds only in devaluing "all human existence" before and beneath it (p. 242). Yeats's Byzantium, Bloom concludes, "is no country for men, young *or* old, and the monuments it contains testify to aspects of the soul's magnificence that do not support humanistic claims of any kind whatsoever" (p. 347).

It is especially as a vision of last things that Yeats's Byzantium seems cold and limited to Bloom, "a casting-away rather than a refining of the human" (p. 392). As usual, Yeats suffers in comparison to Blake, whose Last Judgment in the apocalyptic "Night the Ninth" of *The Four Zoas* yields the liberating picture of "the infinite & Eternal of the Human form" (l.374) only after "all Tyranny" is "cut off from the face of Earth" (l.80). Yeats's Byzantium does not deliver "a state of imaginative liberty at all" (p. 347), Bloom contends. While the moments of pure visionary aspiration toward a referentless sublime in Blake and Shelley can be characterized by their status as representative expressions of the desire toward imaginative freedom living in the hearts of *all* people, Yeats's visionary journey to Byzantium finally stands for nothing beyond itself, nothing beyond the intensely personal, highly circumscribed, and typically aristocratic conception of transcendence offered by a poet who, in his worst incarnations, was often too eager to be gathered out of time into the disdaining dome of eternity.

Where, then, in Bloom's view, resides the greatness of Yeats's poetry in its later phases? If *A Vision* represents a culmination of Yeats's thought and a framework for much of his later work, how, then, can Bloom agree with his critical adversaries that the later Yeats is indeed the greatest Yeats, that *The Tower* and *The Winding Stair*, in particular, are his two most distinguished volumes of lyrics? These questions take us to the heart of Bloom's method for reading Yeats, a method completely consonant with the tactics of visionary appropriation that I outlined in chapter 1, tactics now used seven years later in Bloom's own career and a hundred years later in the history of literary "mythmaking" to secure for the canon of Romantic art one of its most formidable prodigal sons. The Yeats of *The Wild Swans at Coole* through the *Last Poems* remains a great Romantic and a great humanist, Bloom contends, only when he finds the courage to doubt or to refute the system that he himself had set up in *A Vision* and that so often enslaved him, and advances instead, with bold confidence in the visionary imagination, into those regions of internalized quest and pastoral romance that had always been the mark of authentic High Romantic art. Thus, "Nineteen Hundred and Nineteen" is praised for its argument "forsaking [Yeats's] emerging system, and returning to the great Romantics, particularly to the teaching of Blake and Shelley as to how the poet's imagination needs to meet a time of political disillusionment" (p. 358). "A Dialogue of Self and Soul" is admired for the concluding affirmations of the "Self," which "fights free" of "everything in Yeats that has mythologized at its expense" (p. 375) to the grandeur of the lines, "We are blest by everything, / Everything we look upon is blest" (CP, p. 232). "At Algeciras—A Meditation upon Death" is rescued from relative obscurity by the stirring proclamation of its last stanza against the shadow of death—"for once" in Yeats, Bloom says, a reply that "is confidently in the power of the imagination" (p. 384):

> Greater glory in the sun,
> An evening chill upon the air,
> Bid imagination run
> Much on the Great Questioner;
> What He can question, what if questioned I
> Can with a fitting confidence reply. (CP, p. 241)

And if Yeats remains great in a lyric such as this, which, with its "visionary affirmation" casting off the challenges of Blake's "Idiot Questioner," can be called Yeats's "most genuinely Blakean poem" (p. 382), then he also retains visionary immortality insofar as he continues to work in the other, the Shelleyan, part of the Romantic visionary tradition. While the exuberant mythographer Blake confers upon Yeats whatever confidence he still owns in the imagination, the mythopoeic quester Shelley continues to move Yeats profoundly within the tradition of "Romantic pastoralism . . . in its internalized Romance phase," the tradition that gives Yeats his "true Mask," which for Bloom is the "Image of solitary wisdom in a natural context" (pp. 243–44). This image, Bloom says, an amalgamation of the youth in "Alastor" and the sage, Ahasuerus, in Shelley's lyrical drama, *Hellas*, becomes in Yeats "the simplification through intensity of a manifold of images, of everything in pastoral romance that is a vision of Innocence, of change without decay and the body's wisdom" (p. 244). In other words, our categories of chapter 1 continue to hold tightly here for this new Bloomian reading project, as Blake and Shelley become the arbiters for evaluating the various impulses of a poetic achievement coming a full hundred years to the decade after the death of the judges.

Bloom's central contention, of course, is that much of the later Yeats is unfaithful to its Blakean and Shelleyan heritage, and must be acknowledged to be a less profound and less humane poetic achievement than its Modernist critics had previously claimed. The polemical core of the last half of *Yeats* is its firm devaluation of poems formerly regarded as Yeatsian masterpieces, poems such as "The Second Coming," "Leda and the Swan," "Under Ben Bulben," and "The Circus Animals' Desertion," all of which Bloom claims are, in varying ways, unsatisfying in their imaginative import because they are too closely tied to the reductive categories of *A Vision* in their imaginative inception.

It is here, with Bloom's attempt to subsume Modernism at its putative strongest by his special version of visionary Romanticism and thereby to deliver a resounding blow against critical tradition, that we encounter the most troubling aspects of his reading method, and the most unsettling prophecy of things to come under the brilliantly one-sided Bloomian anxiety of influence. Bloom has a simple enough problem when evaluating the older Yeats: many of the poems he wants to condemn seem even to him to be masterpieces of poetic craft and rhetorical force. His argument against them is seldom a quarrel over their craft (though he does contend, in opposition to many other critics, that Yeats generally harmed his poems in the rewriting). In fact, Bloom is, as usual, simply not much interested in meter, rhyme, diction, or any of those other attributes of the poem as text, as a crafted object on a page, which have been the traditional concern of literary critics. Rather, he is concerned, again as usual, solely with that attribute of poetic meaning that most resists the imprisonment of existence as mere words on a page—that is, with vision—and his indictment of many of the established greatest poems of the later Yeats rests on the simple enough premise that, whatever their excellence as products of poetic *art*, they do not advance imaginative arguments that are acceptable within the tradition of Romantic vision. The same criteria, then, that we saw in chapter 1 to guide Bloom's method of reading the visionary company and of canonizing its neglected and derided avatars, Blake and Shelley, are now used to keep a distinguished latecomer within the House of Visionary Art, while at the same time confining him occasionally to the dungeon for willful disobedience of his several fathers' instructions. The only difference in Bloom's method of reading here in *Yeats* derives from the obvious difference in critical situation. While he seldom had to deal with transgressions when analyzing the primal prophetic words of the Romantic fathers, Bloom now, in his first encounter with what will prove to be an entire flock of disobedient sons, must do so, and the only way he can do so is always to read the sons' words in one light and one light alone: as deliberate distortions of the wisdom of the Romantic fathers. Thus, the "anxiety of influence" is born—and the tautologies of the narrow canonizing logic behind it.

Continually, in the latter part of *Yeats*, Bloom is forced to make a distinction between the rhetoric of the poem, a rhetoric that he usually concedes to be uncannily powerful, and the poem's argument, or *what it says*, which is seen to be all the more dangerous precisely because the poem's rhetoric is so strong. Even to make this distinction, of course, is to refute one of the central tenets of the New Criticism, with its insistence that the "content" of the poem could not really be separated in any fruitful way from the manner of its presentation. More important, though, is the further heresy that Bloom's paraphrases operate in service of, the heresy that sees in the imaginative arguments of Yeats's prized poems a Modernism that is no more than a disguised and diminished Romanticism—a Romanticism ruined by the failure in vision of the Modernist latecomer. Perhaps the key text in Bloom's discussion of Yeats's failings as a poet—and, by extension, the failings of an entire era—is that poem that, more than any other Yeats effort, had been celebrated by critics of virtually all persuasions over the last half-century as a true classic in the poetry of our language. Bloom, aware, of course, of the stature of "The Second Coming," and professing to maintain a properly "Johnsonian respect for the common reader" (p. 317), nonetheless condemns the poem, and he does so on the grounds that the poem's undeniable power finally is used for nothing more exalted than to persuade us "of our powerlessness" before the terrible grinding of a deterministic Gnostic history (p. 324). "The Second Coming," that is, communes too closely with the categories of *A Vision*, and like that longer flawed poem, succeeds only in making "explicit a cyclic necessity" that Yeats "implies the imagination must accept" (p. 261). Against the many critics who either evade the dire implications of the "rough beast, its hour come round at last," slouching "towards Bethlehem to be born" or prefer to see in the poem's concluding lines the profundity of true artful prophecy, Bloom aligns himself with Yvor Winters, a critic completely his opposite in literary taste but quite close in reading habits. Winters observes of "The Second Coming" that "we must face the fact that Yeats's attitude toward the beast is different from ours: we may find the beast terrifying, but Yeats finds him satisfying—he is Yeats's judgment upon all that we regard as civilized. Yeats approves of this kind of brutality."[16]

If Bloom's thesis on "The Second Coming" is "that our horror" is Yeats's "ecstasy" (p. 280), then the thesis in turn is based, as always, on a comparison with Blake and, to a lesser extent, Shelley. "As much as any other poem by Yeats, 'The Second Coming' bears its direct relation to Blake and Shelley as an overtly defining element in its meaning" (p. 317). Insofar as this involves merely identifying the many allusions in the Yeats poem to "Ozymandias," *Prometheus Unbound*, "The Book of Urizen," "Europe, A Prophecy," and other poems by Shelley and Blake, the thesis is nothing new and covers ground already mapped by previous Yeats scholars. But Bloom goes on to argue that the result of the allusion is, in almost every case, "deliberate" misinterpretation of the precursors' apocalyptic desires (p. 324), transforming their optimism about human potential into an ecstasy bordering on horror, taking their celebration of the freedom of imaginative man and changing it utterly into a willed capitulation before the inexorable gyres of history. "What Blake presents as disaster Yeats accepts as revelation," Bloom observes (p. 261), and there could be no greater condemnation of the inglorious latecomer than this. Furthermore, Bloom says, the poem's several basic inconsistencies and lacunae—its inappropriate and unmerited title hearkening back unto an irrelevant primary Christianity to intimate an antithetical new age, and its use of "surely" to welcome the "revelation" when no context has been established to justify such certainty—show that Yeats, unlike Blake, has a tendency to leap "too quickly past his own argument" in the fever of apocalypse (p. 170), and to undermine the authenticity of the prophetic voice itself.

"The Second Coming," as a test case for Bloom's theory of visionary reading as that theory metamorphoses into the anxiety of influence, reveals quite fully the Bloomian thesis that even the established masterpieces of Modernism must be read through the lens of visionary romance, if only to show that such romance is dying in our time from lack of confidence in its own visionary powers.

And yet, Bloom is much more successful at this point in telling us *how* such a transformation and a diminishing occur than he is in answering the even greater question his work poses: namely, *why* this falling away from Romantic knowledge and power is inevitable. In "The Internalization of Quest Romance," Bloom hazards the observation that "Modernist poetry in English organized itself, to an excessive extent, as a supposed revolt against Romanticism, in the mistaken hope of escaping" the inherent "inwardness" of the Romantic quest (RT, p. 16), but, while this helps explain the savagery of Modernist distortions, poetic and critical alike, it still does not account for the inevitability of the entire unhappy situation. In a brief essay on Walter Pater composed a year before "The Internalization of Quest Romance," Bloom perhaps comes closer to delivering an answer to our question, and, in the process, to revealing the full range of his assumptions about modern culture and the place of literature within it, which underlie everything he has written before or since. Pater, whose doctrine of the "privileged moment" Bloom feels to be an important bridge between Wordsworth's "spots of time" and the "epiphanies" of much modern and Modernist writing, "inaugurates, for writers and readers in English, the decadent phase of Romanticism, in which, when honest, we still find ourselves" (RT, p. 190). *Why* do we still find ourselves in this phase? Why is there no escape? What have we done wrong to earn the exile of our modernity? Bloom, in as vulnerable and forthright a passage as he has ever written, responds to these questions in a way that anticipates the fully elaborated theory of influence of his critical maturity.

> What Pater, and modernist masters following him, lack is not energy of apprehension, but rather the active force of a synthesizing imagination, so titanic in Blake and Wordsworth. Yet this loss—in Yeats, Joyce, Stevens—is only an honest recognition of necessity. Except for the phenomenon of a last desperate High Romantic, Hart Crane, the faith in the saving, creative power of the imagination subsides in our time. Here too Pater is the hinge, for the epiphanies of Marius only help him to live what life he has; they do not save him, nor in the context of his world, or Pater's, or ours, can anyone be saved. (RT, p. 190)

"An honest recognition of necessity": upon such bald (and Shelleyan) visionary despair, Harold Bloom will continue to build, in his many books of the seventies, a House of Visionary Art for our belated and unredeemable epoch. The ravages of time, especially its relentless destruction of imaginative confidence, will now become his central subject, and the battles against time's depredations by our century's greatest poets—Stevens, even more than Yeats, among the moderns, A. R. Ammons and John Ashbery among contemporaries—will now offer him his only hope and sustenance. That such a tale of literary history as Bloom now goes on to tell seems as completely deterministic as the history against which he rebels in Yeats should not surprise us. According to his own logic, Bloom, like Yeats, cannot "be saved"; the anxiety of influence to which we now turn, and the canon of modern literary history yielded by that theory, are quite self-consciously intended by their creator to deliver what is, at best, a protest against the very necessity that subsumes them.

Vision's Revision:
The Anxiety of Influence

Perhaps the best way into the labyrinthine complexities of Harold
Bloom's theory of the anxiety of influence is through the figure that
Bloom announces as the central emblem of his discussion, the
covering cherub.[1] We have already considered the Bloomian perspective on Yeats's reductive misreading of Blake's cherub, a misreading said by Bloom to involve Yeats's first "interpreting a dialectical figure as though it were cyclic," and then twisting Blake's
"demonic" into the "*daimonic*" of the Yeatsian mask (*Yeats*, p. 218).
Unlike Yeats, who interprets Blake's cherub as having two "aspects"
for everyone, serving not only as a "satanic hindrance keeping our
eager wills away from the freedom and truth of the Divine World"
but also as a potential road to imaginative salvation,[2] Bloom, at the
heart of his theory of poetic influence, conceives of the cherub as
a totally demonic or thwarting agent, and cites Blake, Milton,
Ezekiel, and Genesis against Yeats to support a definition of the
figure as "that portion of creativity in us that has gone over to con-
striction and hardness" (AI, p. 24). The cherub, standing for the
"creative anxiety" that afflicts all imaginative people (p. 36), thus
helps to demarcate the true enemy in all Romantic quest, an ultimate enemy now fully revealed to have its origins *within*, and
identified by Bloom as the spectre of the internalized poetic
precursor.

This Bloomian conception of poetic history as a tale of parricidal
battles between the Titans of the past and their increasingly desperate poetic descendants owes much to his extensive reading in
philosophy, psychology, literary scholarship, and Jewish theology.
Even a brief list of the thinkers appropriated by Bloom to contribute
insights to his map of the defensive rhetoric of Romanticism would
have to include figures as diverse as the second-century Gnostic,

Valentinus, the sixteenth-century Kabbalists Moses Cordovero and
Isaac Luria, the eighteenth-century Italian philosopher of rhetoric
Giambattista Vico, the early nineteenth-century Danish theologian
Sören Kierkegaard, and a host of more modern philosophers,
psychologists, and literary theorists, ranging from the Germans
Nietzsche, Schopenhauer, and Freud, to the French poets Stéphane
Mallarmé and Paul Valéry, to the American explorers Ralph Waldo
Emerson, Charles Sanders Peirce, and Kenneth Burke, to, finally,
academics of formidable recent achievement such as Angus
Fletcher, Walter Jackson Bate, Geoffrey Hartman, and Paul de Man.[3]
Many reviewers have complained of the rhetorical opacity that results from Bloom's penchant for dropping these names so licen-
tiously and with so little accompanying explanation—a penchant
particularly pronounced in the alarming seizures of the associative
sensibility that mark much of the almost impenetrably allusive van-
guard volume, *The Anxiety of Influence*.[4] Yet it is possible that
Bloom's forbidding erudition, coupled with his distinctively Emersonian refusal to deliver the expository grounds of his many assertions, has contributed to an air of almost gothic mystery about his
whole recent project that is not altogether warranted by what the
project itself presents. As Denis Donoghue, one of Bloom's most
distinguished reviewers, has noted, Bloom's recourse to masters
such as Vico, Nietzsche, Emerson, Pater, and Freud "is frequent but
opportunistic."[5] These and the other thinkers Bloom uses with
such profligacy in his recent work are models, Donoghue observes,
not sources. For the real source of the later Bloom's theories we
need only look to Bloom himself and to his early writings on his true
precursor, Blake, especially to the crucial chapter on *Milton* in
Blake's Apocalypse, which, Donoghue sagely observes, "could easily
be translated into the idiom of *The Anxiety of Influence*."

A brief summary of Bloom's approach to *Milton* in that early
study will show the acuity of Donoghue's point. Blake's *Milton* is
about the descent of John Milton from eternity in order to redeem
his works, cast off his spectre, and embrace his saving emanation,
Ololon. To accomplish all this, the character of Milton must confront Urizen, the false deity who, in Blake's world, stifles human
energy and imagination, and with whom Blake associates the historical John Milton in his Puritan orthodoxy. And yet, *Milton* is not
written, Bloom says, merely to "correct" *Paradise Lost* or the public
doctrines of its author; rather, as the union of Milton with Blake in
book 1 of the poem makes clear, Blake's epic is intended "to invoke
Milton as a savior for Blake and for England, and therefore for man-

kind" (BA, p. 308). Although Milton was for Blake "a prophet who had not subdued his own Spectre" and who had then contributed much toward the "Deist" culture that the bard of the apocalypse inveighs against one hundred years later, Blake's poem called *Milton* "does not exist to convert John Milton into being a Blakean." On the contrary, Bloom says, "Blake's part in the poem rises out of *his* desperate need for Milton's strength" (p. 322). By the end of book 1 of the poem, after the magnificent vision of time and space achieved by Los in the famous "Pulsation of the Artery" passage, it is apparent that Milton's descent has indeed answered Blake's needs, saving the later poet, Bloom says, "for the life of prophecy" (p. 341).

We have already approached, from several angles in chapters 1 and 2, a few of the more important moments of book 2 of *Milton*, including most notably the enunciation of the doctrine of the states by the seven angels before Milton. The action in this second half of Blake's brief epic is minimal; Milton, after descending to Blake's garden in all the revealed errors of his spectre, vanquishes his enemy with an assertion of prophetic power that secures for him Ololon, the saving contrary of his vision with whom he may find love, and thus, in Bloom's words, the "divine form of the human" (p. 356). The climax of book 2 is Milton's "great chant of prophetic dedication" (p. 357) in Plate 41:

> To bathe in the Waters of Life; to wash off the Not Human
> I come in Self-annihilation & the grandeur of Inspiration
> To cast off Rational Demonstration by Faith in the Saviour
> To cast off the rotten rags of Memory by Inspiration
> To cast off Bacon, Locke & Newton from Albions covering
> To take off his filthy garments, & clothe him with Imagination
> To cast aside from Poetry, all that is not Inspiration
> That it no longer shall dare to mock with the aspersion of
>   Madness
> Cast on the Inspired, by the tame high finisher of paltry Blots,
> Indefinite, or paltry Rhymes; or paltry Harmonies.
> Who creeps into State Government like a caterpiller to destroy
> To cast off the idiot Questioner who is always questioning,
> But never capable of answering.... (2.41.1 – 13)

This passage of great visionary affirmation delivers what Bloom sees as the central message of Blake's epic, which is that the ways of God are justified to man only insofar as "certain men have the courage to cast out what is not human in them, and so become Man," and, in becoming Man, thus "become God" (p. 363). For man to become fully Man, he must, of course, pass through the "Eternal Annihilation" of the twenty-eighth state, the state of Milton, and enter then that "Imagination" that is "not a State" but "Human Existence itself." Bloom, in *Blake's Apocalypse*, sums up the differences between the twenty-seven churches, representing the "demonic cycles of fallen history," and the twenty-eighth:

> The State of Milton, which is about to be created by the poet's self-purgation, is a state of self-annihilation, in which the Spectre is cast off by the awakened humanity in a man. To enter that state is to cast off also everything that can die, every mortal encrustation. . . . We verge for the first time in Blake on what will be the burden of *Jerusalem*, the distinction between mortality as the self's prison and immortality as the imagination's freedom. (Pp. 348 – 49)

Milton, who in his orthodoxy was "one with the Covering Cherub" (p. 353), is finally identified in Blake's epic with that state that purifies us to enter the sublimity of authentic imagination, in the process of casting off the "Idiot Questioner" of creative anxiety in whose shadow, Bloom says, we may discern "the Covering Cherub acting as barrier between creative desire and artistic completion" (p. 359).

The implications of all this for Bloom's later theorizing are obviously striking. The entire conceptual framework for the theory of the anxiety of influence is, in fact, here in embryonic form, along with many of the ruling emblems of the later Bloomian critical universe. Already in Bloom's early reading of Blake there is an emphasis on the relations between precursors and descendants as the central constituent of poetic meaning; already there is the acknowledgment, via Blake, of all the spectres, cherubs, and idiot questioners whose dualisms and whose doubtings may undermine the thrust toward imaginative immortality of the visionary impulse. Already, too, we have the germ of Bloom's contention that it is the later poet who, in every case, depends on the primal strength of the precursor, even as he may be amending the import of the earlier poet's life and work. What we do not have here yet is the key to that obsessive brooding over the inescapable *burden* of poetic influence which marks the later Bloom; what we do not have is the acknowledgment that the latecomer poet is necessarily *disfigured* as well as diminished by his relationship with his precursor—a dark recognition built into the very warp and woof of Bloom's later theorizing on the moderns.

Given that in *Milton* Blake summons his ancestor in order to profit from him, that Milton comes to awaken, not to thwart, the imagination of his descendant, why, then, does the later Bloom's theorizing take the dark turn we see to be so pronounced from *The Anxiety of Influence* onward? Why does Bloom, in his many books of the seventies, call Blake the "theorist of the saving or revisionary aspect of Poetic Influence" (AI, p. 41), but then proceed relentlessly to emphasize his own visionary despair over the final impossibility of any poet ever fully attaining a saving strength within the "vast visionary tragedy" of the Romantic tradition (p. 10)? We have already begun to answer these questions in the previous chapters. Blake, while himself undeniably a victim of the anxiety of influence,[6] nonetheless remains, by virtue of his remarkable conceptual powers and his equally remarkable confidence in the visionary imagination, a sort of grand exception in the Bloomian map, a great Romantic mythographer against whose visionary demarcations all other achievements in the tradition must be measured. *Yeats*, as a prolegomenon to the study of poetic influence, goes about this business of measuring the most celebrated modern poet against Blake and, to a lesser extent, Shelley, and finds Yeats wanting in almost every way. It is only when Bloom turns his visionary gaze to the modern and contemplates what he sees as the telling inferiority of Yeats in relation to his chief Romantic precursors that he comes to appreciate the grim implications of the theory of influence advanced by Blake. The intellectual shock of this new phenomenon is well revealed in Bloom's pithy summary at the conclusion of *Yeats*: "Blake was one of the Instructors who came down on Yeats's path, but he failed to do for Yeats what Milton had done for him" (p. 471). Blake fails to help Yeats because, as we have seen, Yeats misreads him on the very emblem of the covering cherub which marks the Blakean conception of stifling creative anxiety, a misreading so severe and, to Bloom, measuring matters from his strenuously Blakean vantage point, so perversely antipoetic in its implications, that it cannot be accounted for by anything other than an imputation of willful distortion. Thus, a hypothesis to cover the Blakean facts: Yeats's misinterpretation of the sublime wisdom of his instructor, and the body of poetry yielded by that misinterpretation, can only be functions of the motivated malignity of a latecomer poet who knows, with "deep self-knowledge" and "true imaginative inwardness" (p. 78), that his only hope for securing imaginative space in a cruelly belated time is ruthlessly and cunningly to assault the great ones who have come before.

The Anxiety of Influence and its several sequels of the seventies might best be seen as Bloom's attempt to account for the modern swerve away from the great Romantics by using a language and a map drawn largely from the master whose most powerful poems not only anticipate the swerves of influence relations in their choice of Miltonic subject but also demand, by the very force of their visionary confidence, that such a troping away from a primal instructor proceed inexorably from them as well, and in less benign fashion than their visionary instructions could ever have foreseen. What is in Blake a belief finally in the saving power of the visionary imagination, and in early Bloom a fervent hope that such a sublime power might at least be held out as a *possibility* for the poet in man, now becomes in the re-visions of the later Bloom a brooding over the inextricability of the "rotten rags" of memory and poetic desire, and an explicit refutation of the master insofar as memory is now seen "always" to be "the most important mode of thought" in poetry, "despite Blake's passionate insistences upon the contrary view" (PR, p. 30).

The swerve begotten by the memory of the latecomer facing his internalized poetic precursor Bloom now calls a *clinamen*, "necessarily the central working concept of the theory of Poetic Influence" (AI, p. 42), and a concept derived primarily, despite its nominal Lucretian origin, from Blake's account of the fall of Los under the baleful influence of the stifling Urizen in "The Book of Los," and from that greatest of all falls so often parodied by Blake, the casting out of Lucifer from Heaven in *Paradise Lost.* "The true history of modern poetry would be the accurate recording of these revisionary swerves," Bloom says of *clinamen* in *The Anxiety of Influence* (p. 44), and it is precisely this history that his many volumes of the ensuing decade seek to construct. As history, Bloom's enterprise is what the Miltonic inspiration of *clinamen* might suggest: an attempt to read Romanticism not only forward to our own time, but also *backward* to the time of its origins in the great age of Milton and, to a lesser extent, Spenser. Spenser's Gardens of Adonis in *The Faerie Queene* loom formidably as a source for all Romantic pastoral from Blake to Yeats to Ashbery, but the real focus of much of Bloom's theorizing in his anxiety of influence phase is Milton—specifically, Milton seen through the Blakean lens of a self-avowed "unreconstructed Romantic" (PR, p. 23).

Milton's powerful role in the tetralogy of books initiated by *The Anxiety of Influence* in 1973 derives not only from Bloom's reading of Blake's *Milton*, but also, just as important, from Bloom's response to the notorious Blakean and Shelleyan readings of *Paradise Lost* presented in "The Marriage of Heaven and Hell" and "A Defence of Poetry." Both poets, of course, see in fallen Satan a moral and imaginative energy far outshining the cold, authoritarian morality of Milton's God the Father; Blake, delivering an early instance of what M. H. Abrams has called "that radical mode of romantic polysemism in which the latent personal significance of a narrative poem is found not merely to underlie, but to contradict and cancel the surface intention,"[7] goes on to offer the famous thesis that Milton "was a true poet and of the Devils party without knowing it" (Blake, CP, p. 35). "Most modern scholarly critics of Milton sneer at the Blakean or Shelleyan temerity," Bloom observes, perhaps with C. S. Lewis in mind, "but no modern critic of Milton is as illuminating as Blake and Shelley are, and none knows better than they did how omnipotent an opponent they lovingly faced, or how ultimately hopeless the contest was" (RT, p. 97).

Bloom's own remarkably rigorous brand of Romantic polysemism is predicated upon a revisionary Blakean reading of Milton's conscious intent in *Paradise Lost*, and a consequent celebration of Satan as, variously, a "great rhetorician" (PR, p. 23), an "archetype of the modern poet at his strongest" (AI, p. 19), and "the greatest really Modern or Post-Enlightenment poet in the language" (MM, p. 37). In Bloom's diabolic Blakean allegory, Satan's salience for the modern poet and reader resides in the very nature of his falling, which is a curse transformed into a blessing only through Satan's "profoundly imaginative" refusal to "repent" before the harsh Miltonic God. To repent, Bloom contends, would be "to accept a God altogether other than the self," a God of "cultural history" and "dead poets," the oppressive God of "a tradition grown too wealthy to need anything more" (AI, p. 21). Against such a disastrous fate, what Satan manages, at least for a while, is a heroism and a poetry that Bloom professes to "respond to . . . more strongly than to any other poetry I know" (MM, p. 37), a heroism that is poetic precisely because it sets so grandly about the task that Bloom now thinks to be central to the motivation of all poetry: "to rally everything that remains" (AI, p. 22). Satan lapses later in *Paradise Lost*, retreating into merely facile rebellion with his formula, "Evil be thou my Good,"[8] but for a few brief books in Milton's epic he presents what is for Bloom the greatest heroism of all, one "exactly on the border of solipsism, neither within it, nor beyond it" (AI, p. 22), a heroism that "chooses . . . to know damnation and to explore the limits of the possible" within its necessary exile (p. 21). *Clinamen* for Bloom, then, is a central working concept of the theory of poetic influence because the swerve that it effects *away* from the blocking power of a previous creator is the only way *into* the possibilities for agonistic imaginative meaning that are manifest in the ensuing five ratios of the Bloomian map. "Poetic influence is the passing of Individuals through States," Bloom says, employing the Blakean distinctions of *Milton*, "but the passing is done ill when it is not a swerving." The strong poet, to attain his strength, must, in other words, cultivate the o'erweening pride that comes *after* a fall: " 'I seem to have stopped falling; now I *am fallen*, consequently, I lie here in Hell,' " the poet as Satan says, but even as he says so, he is thinking, " 'As I fell, *I swerved*, consequently I lie here in a Hell improved by my own making' " (p. 45).

We have by now examined Milton's importance to Bloom from two key Blakean angles—the principle of the relation between poets as a central constituent of poetic meaning featured in *Milton*, and the allegory of Satan as a prototype for the Romantic and modern poet derived from *Paradise Lost* via "The Marriage of Heaven and Hell." We now approach a third crucial Miltonic angle, one that is a product of the union of the first two. If in *The Visionary Company* Bloom had noted in passing that Blake and Wordsworth both sought "to emulate and surpass *Paradise Lost*" (p. 5), now, twelve years later in *The Anxiety of Influence*, he is able fully to elaborate the dark implications of such an observation, and declares that Milton is "the central problem in any theory and history of poetic influence in English" (AI, p. 33) precisely because *he* is the prior creator against whom *all* Romantic poets must lovingly rebel if they are to find their own imaginative strength. Keats's observation, "Life to him would be death to me,"[9] now becomes, in Bloom's view, the motto for all English poetry in the shadow of Milton, a shadow created not only by the simple fact of Milton's magnificent achievement as an epic poet—an achievement that many of the Romantics themselves confessed to find daunting—but also by the characteristic concerns that he displays in his calling as epic bard. Milton as the eloquent preacher of "the power of the mind over the universe of death" (AI, p. 34) in poems such as "L'Allegro," "Il Penseroso," and *Paradise Lost* is, Bloom says, the father of all post-Enlightenment and Romantic poetry, a poetry whose "obsessive theme" is what Wordsworth, Milton's ephebe, calls in *The Prelude* the extent to which "the mind is lord and master—outward sense / The obedient servant of her will" (12.222 – 23); Milton as a false prophet of orthodox religion, of the

triumph of God the Father over Satan, is, on the other hand, a covering cherub whose conscious commitment to doctrines that kill
must be confronted by a legion of lovingly defiant eighteenth- and
nineteenth-century descendants, all of whom *but Blake* will, like
him, fail for lack of ultimate faith in their own radically creative
visionary powers.

II

The remainder of Bloom's map for reading the anxieties of influence
attempts to chart the wrestling with the mighty dead made possible
by the latecomer poet's initial *clinamen* away from his precursor. As
we have seen in the introduction, Bloom calls the six revisionary
movements "ratios"—yet another term appropriated from that
master revisionist, Blake, who uses it to signify the uncreative
mechanisms of Newtonian reason. Bloom defines "ratios" as "relations between unequal terms," wherein "the later poet always
magnifies the precursor in the very act of falsifying ('interpreting')
him" (MM, p. 95). Besides *clinamen*, the ratios are, in order, *tessera,
kenosis, daemonization, askesis,* and *apophrades,* all with their own
psychic, rhetorical, imagistic, and topical components, all partici-
pating in the "dialectic of revisionism" that Bloom derives from his
study of the Kabbalist Isaac Luria, and from the Kabbalah's revisionist precursor, the Gnosticism of the early Christian era.[10] While we
do not want to get lost amid the gothic complexities of the fully
elaborated Bloomian terminology, we do need to examine Bloom on
and in his own terms here, even if, as some reviewers have complained, the profusion of terms reveals the critic finally to be
trapped within the prison house of his own critical language.

The terms themselves only mask—to use the characteristic language of this new phase of Bloom's career—their creator's anxieties
about the processes of poetic creation. The effect of Yeats's malignant reading of Blake was to shock Bloom into confronting more
strenuously several crucial questions that were only implicit in his
early incarnation as prophet of vision, questions having to do with
the nature of reading and interpretation, and with the relation
between the "re-visioning" that is reading and the origins of imaginative vision. To answer these questions, Bloom has been drawn
over the last decade to a close, if often elliptical and self-serving,
examination of writers from traditions as seemingly divergent as
biblical hermeneutics, nineteenth-century metaphysics, and
modern psychology. For all their differences—differences some-

times blurred by Bloom in the heat of his typically Romantic quest for similitudes and identities—what figures such as Valentinus and Luria, Nietzsche and Freud, have in common is a concern with the relation between origins and creation, whether religious, cultural, or psychological, and a radically nonnormative view of the nature of interpretation.[11] If we are to understand the terms of Bloom's map, and to appreciate fully the implications of his switch in midcareer from the master term of vision to that of influence, we need to assess his use of these theorists.

Bloom's appropriation of the Kabbalah is a suitable starting point, for it is the Kabbalah that stands behind the earliest presentations of the fully elaborated map of revisionism in *A Map of Misreading, Kabbalah and Criticism,* and *Poetry and Repression.* In his introduction to *A Map of Misreading,* Bloom announces that the story of creation delivered by Luria in the sixteenth century as a corrective to more normative kabbalistic readings of the Old Testament is "the best paradigm available for a study of the way poets war against one another in the strife of Eternity that is poetic influence" (p. 5). Why? What does an obscure centuries-old commentary on the Bible have to do with the processes of poetic creation? A brief summary here of Bloom's borrowings from Luria—borrowings typically mediated by Bloom's readings in the great modern scholar of the history of the Kabbalah, Gershom Scholem[12]—should help focus our discussion.

The central importance of the Lurianic Kabbalah for Bloom is in its rereading of the most powerful of the medieval Jewish commentaries on the Bible, Moses de Leon's thirteenth-century *Zohar,* the attempt of which to describe God through the tenfold images of the *Sefirot*[13] delivers what Bloom calls a "progressive" myth of the outward emanation of God's creation. Luria's creative interpretation over two centuries later of de Leon's own highly elliptical reading of Scripture transforms the smooth movement of Sefirotic creation seen by de Leon into "a startlingly regressive process, one in which an abyss can separate any one stage from another, and in which catastrophe is always a central event" (KC, p. 39). As such, Luria's account, strongly mixing an orthodox neo-Platonism with a darker Gnostic dualism and sense of evil, yields what is for Bloom a signal instance of Western revisionism—a revisionism engendered by the very wealth of tradition already accrued by centuries of kabbalistic commentary and by the grim historical fact of the expulsion of the Jews from Spain in 1492. Luria's story of creation, a story composed in a troubled exile against a massive and imposing body of rich prior interpretations of Scripture, is important to Bloom

chiefly for the implicit "psychology of belatedness" (p. 34) that it
develops in response to a cultural situation obviously quite similar
to the one Bloom envisions for poetry and for criticism in our own
time. This psychology of belatedness takes shape in Luria's rendering of the triple rhythm of a creation-in-exile from its too-strong
Creator, a creation based on "the beautiful necessity" of its own
need, *as meaning*, to protect itself from the stifling otherness of
prior meaning (p. 82). The triple rhythm, called by Luria "*zimzum*,"
"*shevirat hakelim*," and "*tikkun*," is the process whereby creation
endeavors first to contain the radiance of God's name through contraction, then is shattered by the primal force of the deity into a pattern of substitute vessels, and finally, at the last, is able to restore
itself in its by now fully human exile through acts of mediation "that
lift up and so liberate the fallen sparks of God from their imprisonment" in the fallen world (p. 43). Applied by Bloom to the situation
of Romanticism, Luria's creation myth of contraction, breaking-of-
the-vessels, and restitution becomes the pattern of all modern crisis
poetry as that poetry enacts a quest for visionary power against the
far greater visionary priority of its precursors, and, through the
triple rhythm of contracting or limiting itself, shattering or substituting meaning, and seeking the saving force of representation, fails
fully to secure such strength.

But it is difficult to discuss the importance of the Lurianic
Kabbalah for Bloom's theory without also considering the Gnosticism that, as Bloom has come to emphasize in several of the most
important essays of *Agon*, strongly informs it. And now we must
confront an apparent contradiction that perhaps contains the key
to Bloom's metamorphosis from celebrant of vision to belated
prophet of influence, for did not Bloom in his study of Yeats continually deride the Romantic latecomer precisely for presenting
a Gnostic vision of history, personality, and poetic creation? If
Bloom himself, only a few years later, now undertakes to assimilate
Gnosticism into his own mappings of the psychopoetics of influence, upon what grounds does he do so? Is there something in his
reading of Gnosticism that makes it different from the Gnosticism
represented by Yeats? Or has Bloom changed his mind about what
he saw as Yeats's vicious and reductive historicizing?

If a phenomenon as complex as heretical Gnostic Christianity
can be summarized, we might say that it features above all a relentless rereading of the chosen texts of the early Christian church, a rereading that focuses on fundamental questions of creation or
origin, purpose, plan, and end in the Christian universe. The "cardi-

nal feature of gnostic thought," as Hans Jonas, the preeminent scholar of Gnosticism, has put it, is a "radical dualism that governs the relation of God and world, and correspondingly that of man and world."[14] Against the developing orthodox Christian cosmogony, Gnosticism—and now we may speak in particular of the Valentinian Gnosticism especially important to Bloom—provides a reading of Genesis and of the world-artificer, Demiurge, in Plato's *Timaeus*, that sees the world of man as not only fallen but exiled, the residue of some primal catastrophe of creation in which the originating Fullness, or Pleroma, was shattered by the passion of one of the Aeons, the Sophia, to know the Fore-Father, or Abyss, more fully than she could.[15] Thus, a crisis within the godhead results in the creation of a world outside the Pleroma, a world presided over by the demiurge, whose main attributes as world-god are not, as in Plato, craft and knowledge, but, rather, in the Gnostic rereading, "ignorance and passion." Salvation in such a world can only be achieved through an inward turning to the inner spark, or *pneuma*, which, in contradistinction to the soul, or *psyche*, is "not part of the world, of nature's creation and domain," but is "as totally transcendent and as unknown by all worldly categories as is its transmundane counterpart, the unknown God without."[16]

In his famous epilogue to *The Gnostic Religion*, Jonas compares the world of Gnosticism to modern nihilism and to the existentialism of the early Heidegger, showing the affinities of Gnostic knowledge, which effaces the present before the eschatological momentum of the past and future, to the "radical temporality" of Heidegger in *Being and Time*, for whom "the present is nothing but the moment of crisis between past and future."[17] Bloom, who relies as heavily upon Jonas for his exegesis of the Gnostics as he does upon Scholem for his explication of the Kabbalah, dissents partially from this reading, acknowledging the existential alienation implicit in the Gnostic world view, but preferring to emphasize as always what endures beyond the existential: the frustrations and desires necessarily involved in any quest for transcendence when the very need for that quest presupposes an exile from origins. For Bloom, the central trait of the Gnostic vision of origins is that, like the Lurianic Kabbalah, it posits a creation that can also be said to be a catastrophe, a primal crisis that leaves people estranged from the divine and forced to encounter the many "echoing" crises of temporal beings who endeavor to "know" the primal power of origins while condemned to existence within the prison of merely natural history. The analogue to poetic creation is obvious; in the new phase of the anxiety of influence, latecomer poets such as Yeats are attempting to return to the greater power of their precursors, but are fated by the very forces of time, which have made them latecomers, never to be able to do so.

And yet the situation is more complicated than this, for, as the example of Yeats makes clear, the latecomer himself is afflicted by an almost debilitating *ambivalence* toward his precursors, a love that shades into jealousy and hatred because the later poet cannot stand to be suffocated or thwarted by such primal power as his precursors possess, but must choose, if he is to be a strong poet, to try to fight his way free of his poetic fathers with the arsenal of psychic and linguistic weapons known collectively as misprision. There is nothing in the cosmogony of either the Kabbalah or Gnosticism to provide Bloom a language for the specifically psychic aspect of such battles; for that we will need to turn to Freud. But in the very nature of the Kabbalah and Gnosticism as commentaries on Scripture there is a spirit, or a stand, that Bloom is able to apply to the situation of poetry and its criticism. That is, Gnosticism, like the Kabbalah, presents a psychology of belatedness not only in its vision of creation but also in its own characteristic mode of operation as a radical misreading of precursor texts. Just as Bloom was drawn in the early stage of his career to the renegade Romantic prophecy of Blake and Shelley, so now he is attracted to the nonnormative readings of canonic tradition presented by men such as Valentinus and Luria, embattled inheritors of traditions they mean to subvert.[18]

For Bloom, the interpretive stances of the kabbalistic commentators and of the even earlier Gnostic heretics, in demonstrating the problematics of tradition, reveal at the same time how closely related the workings of tradition are to the processes of meaning in the cosmogonies that their readings present. A tradition, for poets or critics, *is* an origin, and Bloom, combining the examples of the Kabbalah and Gnosticism with modern poetry, argues that it makes no sense to discuss a "new" creation as anything other than an attempt to remake—reread—the old. Especially interesting in Bloom's account of the relation between vision and re-vision is the way in which the rhythms of creation within tradition reflect the dynamics of the progression toward salvation in the exiled worlds of Luria and Valentinus. Gnosticism becomes an important topic of discussion for Bloom in his most recent work, not only because it extends his theory of revisionism backward in cultural time but also because the dialectic of creation that he derives from its cosmogony is even more compatible with his characteristic emphases when describing poetic revisionism than was the initial kabbalistic triad of limitation, substitution, and restitution.

The new dialectic, called by Bloom "negation," "evasion," and "extravagance," is a function of the Gnosis itself, the inward knowing of God that is the end of the Gnostic's quest for vision. As Jonas notes, such a "knowledge of God" in the deeply dualistic cosmos of Gnosticism, where the transcendent absolute is alienated from the demiurgical natural world, is necessarily the "knowledge of something naturally unknowable"[19]—a transcendence emptied of positives. Gnosis as a form of knowing thus resembles quite closely the vision celebrated by Bloom early in his career, a vision we saw in chapter 1 to exist ultimately by virtue of its contextlessness and nonreferentiality. If now, after the shock of Yeats's misreading of Blake and Shelley, and the ensuing exploration of the patterns of misreading informing all modern poetry, such vision is regarded by Bloom as a result of "the perpetual struggle of *becoming a poet*, and then remaining a poet, by continually becoming a poet again" (PR, p. 102), then the Gnostic triad of terms, with its air of agonistic melodrama, takes us closer to the core of visionary desire—the desire, as Bloom constantly puts it, "to be elsewhere . . . to be different" from the precursor (*Agon*, p. 59). In particular, "evasion" is a better term for the breaking-of-the-vessels of poetic creation than "substitution," because evasion implies darker truths about the lies or misreadings that the latecomer poet employs as he quests desperately for freedom from the origins of the precursor.

Of course, in one sense, the Gnostic commentator evades (misreads) his literary precursors—the Bible, Plato—only because he does *not* want to evade his ultimate origins—the unknowable God; likewise, the latecomer poet deeply loves the mysterious and powerful precursor—hence his ambivalence. But, in both cases, Bloom asserts, love is finally akin to hatred, insofar as the desire for origins in the belated imagination necessarily takes form not as a desire to return to the suffocating power of priority, but as the desperate need to usurp such power for the sake of one's own imaginative freedom. Bloom's summarizing point about Gnostic knowing is the now predictable one that such knowing must be seen as an attempt to evade, through its misreading of its precursors, time itself, and all that time implies. If Gnosticism eschewed the eschatology of orthodox Christianity, with its anticipated climax or fulfillment at the end of historical time, it did so, Bloom concludes, in the service of an "internalized pleroma" (*Agon*, p. 69), a pneumatic fullness within, which can stand for the desire of any belated visionary to be free.

Now perhaps we are able to situate the pattern of Bloom's own response to Yeats on the question of Gnostic determinism. Bloom's main divergence from Gnosticism consists of his recognition that the Gnostic cosmogony, while accurately dualistic, is not *dialectical* enough, and it is not dialectical enough because it holds out for the possibility of *pneuma*, or spark, or vision, existing *apart from* the natural order. What Yeats's own brand of Gnosticism has done—what his misreading of the Gnostic side of Blake in particular has accomplished—is to convince Bloom that the spark of vision cannot be idealized as Blake idealized it, but must itself be seen to exist within the activities of the psyche, within the many negations, evasions, and treacheries of the natural man whose internalized sense of time as tradition imprisons him even as it holds before him always the endlessly deferred possibility of escape.

Bloom is fond of quoting the famous Valentinian formula that announces that:

What makes us free is the Gnosis
   of who we were
   of what we have become
   of where we were
   of wherein we have been thrown
   of what we are being freed
   of what birth really is
   of what rebirth really is[20]

But, in Bloom's dialectical version of internalized Gnostic revisionism, such freedom—such a visionary desire, that is, to be elsewhere, to be contextless and different—is shown finally to be illusory, a grand enabling fiction, a "something evermore about to be" in the imagination of the poet when the imagination is seen to be what it truly is: "the faculty of self-preservation" (PR, p. 25). We observed in chapter 2 that Yeats's central misprision of Blake involved his placing of imaginative possibility within the "wrong" side of the Gnostic dualism, the tyranny of the natural and historical world. Now we can see that Yeats was only half wrong. His problem was not that he lied about his precursors—such lying, Bloom now recognizes, is necessary and inevitable—but that he lied about the wrong things. Yeats, in misreading Blake, lied out of obedience to a type of deterministic principle that is death to a poet, the determinism of the cycles of fallen history. The history of poetic warfare that Bloom has now developed is itself deterministic, of course, but the dread necessities it features are psychic, not external, not imposed from without in the orthodox historical sense. As such, Bloom's internalized history offers, along with an almost self-indulgent despair, a formidable array of bracing prophetic tones, all based on the now fully developed recognition that it is the poetic battle proper, the drive toward an illusory freedom, that is the great glory—indeed, the only remaining one—of strong poetry in a "belated" age.

Thus—to answer our earlier question—Bloom has not changed his mind in any essential way about the reductiveness of Yeats's historicizing; Bloom's values in this later phase of his career remain Blakean even as he is forced by the example of Yeats's generally malign relation to Blake and Shelley to the recognition that Blakean visionary freedom is only a guise for the deeper processes of poetic misprision. Yet, in an essay in *Poetry and Repression* entitled "Yeats, Gnosticism, and the Sacred Void," Bloom *does* moderate his position on Yeats, producing what he calls "a rather more sympathetic account of the Gnostic tendency" in the poet (p. 206). This essay is important for our purposes not only because it furnishes the first major discussion in Bloom's work of the relevance of historical Gnosticism to the psychodynamics of poetic creation, but also because, in so doing, it endeavors to apply the ratios of the map of misreading to several of Yeats's most famous poems, including the poem that served as a key example in our discussion in chapter 2, "The Second Coming." Perhaps we can use this later Bloomian treatment of Yeats, which is obviously a rereading not only of Yeats but of Bloom's own earlier critical self as well, as a continuing illustration in our assessment of the logic and the many defensive mechanisms of the map of influence.

Bloom's framing text for his treatment of Yeats in *Poetry and Repression* is taken from the Valentinian work *The Gospel of Truth*, where the aftermath of the fall of the Sophia is described: "It was this ignorance concerning the Father which produced Anguish and Terror. Anguish became dense like a fog, so that no one could see. Therefore Error became fortified. It elaborated its own Matter in the Void."[21] Arguing now that Yeats's Gnosticism was "finally a considerable aid to his poetry, however dubious it may seem in its human or social consequences" (p. 212), Bloom sees that aid operating, predictably, within the psychic arenas of influence. Yeats's central Gnostic trope, in this view, becomes his conception of the phases of the moon that represent the movement of the "primary" and "antithetical" cones of history in *A Vision*, a conception that Bloom identifies as a strong misreading of the image of the moons in the system of the Gnostic heretic Simon Magus. In Simon Magus, the waxing and waning moons symbolize, as Jonas notes, "salvation," with an especial connotation, however, of harlotry befitting "the depth to which the divine principle has sunk by becoming involved in the creation."[22] In Yeats, the hope of such a dubious "salvation" is thus identified with the cycles of history, as in the rhetorical question concluding "The Second Coming." Why is Bloom in *Poetry and Repression* any more receptive to, or forgiving of, this mistake than he was in *Yeats*? In fact, when speaking in particular of "The Second Coming," he is not; he is, he cautions, "at least as skeptical" about the poem as he was earlier, the only difference now being that, having explored in greater depth the implications of his earlier theorizing, he "can elucidate" his "reservations rather more sharply" via the terminological resources of the map of misprision (p. 216). His forgiveness, instead, takes the form of a more general dispensation. If "certain consequences" that Yeats "deduced" from his Gnosticism must still be regarded as reprehensible (p. 213), nonetheless his Gnostic tendencies as a whole enabled him more effectively to battle precursors such as Blake and Shelley whose "integrity" in confronting the fallen world of merely natural man "was finally a little too terrifying" for their less confident descendant (p. 234). Like the Error of the Valentinian *Gospel of Truth*, or like the Nietzsche of the *Genealogy of Morals*, whose influence Bloom also finds to be pervasive in Yeats's work,[23] Yeats "seeks . . . to elaborate his own matter in the Void"; if such elaboration— and such a creative swerving from the pneumatic core of the Valentinian Gnosis—is tantamount finally to a Nietzschean embracing of "the Void as purpose" (p. 234), it represents a sort of triumph nevertheless, for the very desperateness of its willful errors about the past reveals the self-preserving "splendor" of the poetic imagination at work (p. 222).

III

But it is time now to confront directly the mechanisms of this Romantic will as Bloom sees them working within—or, rather, constituting—the world of poetry. If the realm of anxiety and its twistings is largely derived from a resourceful reading of Freud, Nietzsche is an excellent guide into it, because it is Nietzsche who provides Bloom with both a key rationale for his conception of the poetic will and a stirring example of the dangers of such a will unless affixed to the ground of enduring Blakean and Shelleyan values. With his destruction of God and all other terms of essence, with his transvaluation of the values and structures of societal belief, and

with his assertion of the notorious doctrine of the "will to power"—
in short, with his embracing of "the Void as purpose"—Nietzsche is,
of course, a central forerunner of the school of deconstruction,
whose challenge to Bloom on questions of priority, origins, and
interpretation will be considered in chapter 6. Bloom, as suspicious
of Nietzschean ethics and heroism as he is of the values implicit in
Yeats's related cult of the hero, tends to be very careful and rather
sparing in his use of the antilogocentric Nietzschean philosophy,
contenting himself with brief citation, sometimes again and again,
of a few touchstones drawn from the large body of Nietzsche's
aphoristic writings. Among the most important of these borrowings
is the one from the second essay of the *Genealogy of Morals*, where
Nietzsche, in ruminating on the increasing anxiety, or "bad conscience," felt by societies as their past grows larger, richer, and
more oppressive, furnishes Bloom a framework for the specifically
diachronic part of his history of poetry: "the fear of the ancestor and
his power and the consciousness of indebtedness increase in direct
proportion as the power of the tribe itself increases, as it becomes
more successful. . . . we arrive at a situation in which the ancestors of
the most powerful tribes have become so fearful to the imagination
that they have receded at last into a numinous shadow: the ancestor becomes a god."[24]

A Nietzschean proclamation from *Thus Spake Zarathustra* on the
nature of our response to the past is even more important to Bloom.
Here is Zarathustra moved to meditation by the accusations of
a cripple:

> To redeem those who lived in the past and to re-create all "it
> was" into a "thus I willed it"—that alone should I call redemp-
> tion. Will—that is the name of the liberator and joybringer; thus
> I taught you, my friends. But now learn this too: the will itself is
> still a prisoner. Willing liberates; but what is it that puts even the
> liberator himself in fetters? "It was"—that is the name of the
> will's gnashing of teeth and most secret melancholy. Powerless
> against what has been done, he is an angry spectator of all that
> is past. The will cannot will backwards; and that he cannot break
> time and time's covetousness, that is the will's loneliest
> melancholy.[25]

When, a little later, Zarathustra defines revenge as "the will's
resentment against time and time's 'it was,' " he has delivered his
modern critic a serviceable aphorism for the agonistic processes of
poetic creativity. That the subject of Nietzsche's discussion at this

point is not specifically the *poetic* will does not alarm Bloom; his appropriation of Nietzsche shares with his borrowings from one of Nietzsche's imaginative heirs, Freud, the idiosyncratic and entirely typical premise that their "insights work better for poems than for people" (MM, p. 92). How, then, does this premise work itself out in Bloom's by now decade-long creative misreading of the Freudian account of the unconscious?

Freud, like the Gnostics, the Kabbalists, and Nietzsche, is important to Bloom as a theorist both of the wars of creation and origins and of the processes of interpretation necessarily involved in trying to construct an account of those wars. The first of many obvious differences between Gnosticism and the Kabbalah and Freud—that the two bodies of scriptural commentary have to do with cosmogony while the Freudian enterprise is concerned only with the internalizations of psychology—does not threaten Bloom, who instead seizes the difference to make a Blakean conflation of the worlds of cosmology and psychology, the body divine and the body human. Since, in Bloom's particular version of our many modern fables of Psychological Man, "we are our imaginations, and die with them" (RT, p. 32), any story of origins—that is, of tradition—whether religious or psychological, is necessarily a fiction, a tale, a trying to tell what cannot be literally told by virtue of the nonreferentiality of the imagination within tradition, the new god. "What the *Ein-Sof* or the Infinite Godhead was to the Kabbalists, or the Imagination was to the Romantic poets, tradition is now for us, the one literary sign that is not a sign, because there is no other sign to which it can refer," Bloom announces in *Kabbalah and Criticism* (p. 98); to this brief roster of correspondences we need only add two others, the primal abyss of the Gnostics and the primal repression posited by Freud, to see how the normally strong Bloomian quest for parallels becomes even more persistent as his thought advances upon the absolute.

But we are jumping ahead of the story just a little. Before getting to specifics in Bloom's reading of Freud on origins and creation, we need to characterize his treatment of Freud in more general terms, both as an unfolding tale in Bloom's own career and as another contribution to the rich tradition of literary critics' appropriation of ideas from psychoanalysis. Bloom's first extensive use of Freud in *The Anxiety of Influence* features an assimilation of the Freudian ideas of the family romance and of the primal scenes that, in *Totem and Taboo*, are seen to connect the developmental psychology of the individual to the origins of guilt in culture. At the center of

Bloom's early use of Freud are two crucial Freudian formulations: first, that "all the instincts" of the son are "gratified in the wish to be *the father of himself*";[26] and second, that tradition in culture is "equivalent to repressed material in the mental life of the individual."[27] Bloom translates the first dictum into the idiom of revisionary poetry under the aegis of Milton's Satan, who bristles in the darkness of poetic influence that "We know no time when we were not as now; / Know none before us, self-begot, self-rais'd / By our own quick'ning power" (*Paradise Lost*, 5.859 – 61). With the help of Freud, such boasting can be seen to be the necessary blindness of the poetic son questing for power against an oedipal father whose very priority establishes the conditions for meaning in the son's revolt. The second prescription, besides highlighting the internalization of tradition that we have already discussed, also features what is for Bloom the most profound of the mechanisms of defense posited by Freud: repression. The dialectical complexities inherent in this central concept taken from Freudian ego psychology have preoccupied Bloom in the many volumes since *The Anxiety of Influence*, even as the specifically oedipal cast to the drama of the poetic agon has tended to fade from his rhetoric.

What should already be apparent is that Bloom's use of Freud is a significantly self-conscious *and self-serving* exploitation of Freud's dense theorizing. For instance, the Freudian hypothesis of a family romance in the life of a biological son afflicted by the oedipus complex features two important principles that are boldly misread by Bloom. First, Freud tends to emphasize in such oedipal drama the sexual element, the desire of the son to rescue his mother by "giving her a child or making one for her."[28] Bloom, translating the Freudian mother into a poetic muse whom the poet longs to rescue from the "degradation" (*Yeats*, p. 5) of her conjugal alliance with the poetic father through the ultimately futile ploy of savagely misinterpreting the precursor, displaces Freud's emphasis on sexual impulses into his own agonistic affirmation of the primacy of *aggression*. Freud's two primal scenes, the oedipus complex in biological relations and the engendering history scene in the life of a culture,[29] thus become in Bloom a single primal scene of instruction, a scene that "strong poems must will to overcome, by repressing their own freedom into the patterns of a revisionary misinterpretation" (PR, p. 27).

Next, Freud's theory of psychoanalysis features a faith in the idea of a *second chance* in psychic relations, a chance to break free of the repetition-compulsions of one's oedipal youth via the psychic ad-

justments of sublimation and substitution. Although a theorist of
the "catastrophe" of influence, "of the giving that famishes the
taker" (MM, p. 11), Freud opts finally, as Bloom puts it, for the "qualified . . . optimism that happy substitution is possible" (AI, p. 8), that
"thought" can be "liberated from its sexual or dualistic past, by the
rare person capable of true sublimation" (MM, p. 66). For Bloom,
such an optimism with its principle of compensatory imagination,
while perhaps offering "pragmatic wisdom" for our lives as men (AI,
p. 9), is nonetheless hollow and vicious counsel when applied to the
life of poets, who "as poets cannot accept substitutions" (p. 8), and
who, if they accept sublimation, find that they have accepted as well
"the self's sense of its own diminishment" and the "precursor's
survival as the inevitable form of the other, as a dualism that never
again can be banished" (MM, p. 73). Against such capitulation,
Bloom, ringing a change on the famous Freudian formula, argues
that the prescription for every strong poet *as a poetic ego* must be
"*Where it, the precursor's poem, is there let my poem be*" (AI, p. 80).
The latecomer, Bloom concludes, *has no choice* but to confront his
father on the grounds established by the poetic equivalent of the id,
where he must fight for his creative life against not only the precursor poet himself, but against all those mediating forces within
him that would seek a reductive and *un*creative adjustment of the
tensions of the oedipal agon.

This, therefore, is the general outline of the early Bloomian reading of Freud. Since Bloom is at pains to reject even the slightest hint
of optimism in what he calls the "rationalized Romanticism" of
Freud (MM, p. 65), he would dispute violently the prophecy of
Thomas Mann in 1936, who saw in Freud's project "a humanism of
the future," a humanism that in taking a new stance toward "the
powers of the lower world, the unconscious, the id," would come to
liberate us into "a relation bolder, freer, blither, productive of a riper
art than any possible in our neurotic, fear-ridden, hate-ridden
world."[30] For Bloom, all strong poetry, since it is built upon the extremely powerful psychic ambivalences of the scene of instruction,
the mixed love and hatred of the poetic son for his poetic father, is
an affair precisely of neurosis, of fear, anxiety, and hatred, of forces
that the poetic ego of the poet must wrestle with, just as Jacob
wrestled with the angel, just as Satan grappled with the power of
God. And yet, despite the determinism of his own theory, Bloom will
not abide any of the recent continental readings of Freud, whether
Lacanian or Derridean, that reduce the psyche to yet another structure of signifiers at a loss for signification. Like Lacan and Derrida,

and like many of the new Anglo-American readers of Freud, Bloom, with his own principle of misreading, calls into radical question the status of Freud's texts as a privileged mode of discourse somehow apart from what they purport to be about: the workings of the mind. Like other recent theorists, then, whose interests, as Geoffrey Hartman has put it, center on "what kind of event in the history of interpretation psychoanalysis is proving to be,"[31] Bloom is quick to devalue the official rhetoric of Freud, the rhetoric of the biologist, of the scientist who upon occasion was given to fits of melancholy over the essentially speculative nature of his work. For Bloom, Freud's attempt to describe what is unknowable and ineffable, the origins of the unconscious, guarantees that his account is itself a fiction, just as the interpretations of creation by the Gnostics and the Kabbalists are fictions. And yet it is not *merely* an arbitrary fiction, not merely a commentary on, and an unintentional picture of, the problematics of signification. With his usual audacious and dubious blurring of distinctions between different types of imaginative activity, Bloom contends that his version of Freud, a darkly humanistic Freud whose greatest achievement is to have delivered in his own "figurative language" a "literary project of representing the civil wars of the psyche" (BV, p. 63), transcends ultimate reduction into the mere tropings of signification. How Freud becomes for Bloom the "strongest of modern poets" (MM, p. 90) and the one "inescapable mythologist of our age" (BV, p. 62) is the story of how Bloom himself uses Freud to build his own serviceable fictions of the map of misreading.

And so we arrive at our beginning: the psychic and rhetorical swerve, the *clinamen*, that initiates Bloom's chart of revisionary ratios. A ratio for Bloom, as an integral relation between psychic force and rhetorical deception, represents a sort of perilous balancing act between deep meaning and surface linguistic embodiment in the latecomer's misreading of the precursor. Bloom's use of Freud in this context can be seen to follow in the tradition of Lionel Trilling and Kenneth Burke, especially of Trilling's observation from the essay "Freud and Literature" that "it was left to Freud to discover how, in a scientific age, we still feel and think in figurative formations, and to create, what psychoanalysis is, a science of tropes, of metaphor and its variants, synecdoche and metonymy."[32] Like Trilling, Bloom has little use for Freud's speculations specifically on the creative psychology behind works of art, with both critics seeing Freud to be at his most reductive and rationalistic when confronting directly the subject of the imagination. Unlike

Trilling, and unlike Burke, too, Bloom in his application of Freud to the patternings of poetry is *not* concerned with the forces in the poet as a man, but rather solely with the poet as an embattled poetic ego—a nexus of forces within the patterns of force of an internalized literary history. Bloom's use of Freud to describe the processes of the questing poetic will has, in fact, perhaps its most important underpinning in some observations of Blake from the second series of "There Is No Natural Religion":

> VII   The desire of Man being Infinite the Possession is Infinite & himself Infinite
>
> Application. He who sees the Infinite in all things sees God. He who sees the Ratio only sees himself only. . . .
>
> Therefore God becomes as we are, that we may be as he is (CP, p. 3)

In his discussion of this passage in *Blake's Apocalypse*, Bloom notes that what Blake presents here is a "humanistic displacement of the doctrine of the Incarnation" (BA, p. 28), an incarnation, furthermore, whose desired fulfillments can come, as Blake says in his accompanying tract "All Religions Are One," only from the "true Man . . . the Poetic Genius" (CP, p. 1). As Bloom observes, however, there is also in every man the "ratio," and to confront this "bounded mental abstract" or "negation of the Infinite" is, for Blake, "to see only one's own divided self" (BA, p. 28). Over a decade later, in his theory of the anxiety of influence, Bloom combines this Blakean concept of the constricting ratios of a self exiled against itself with the equally Blakean valorization of infinite desire yearning toward infinite fulfillment to produce a theory of poetic meaning wherein poets attempt through misreading and distortion to make the human God of their internalized precursors become more as they are, in order that they might be as he was: powerful, proud, and *prior*. Freud fits in here because his figurations for the forces of the psyche divided against itself—his tale, that is, of instinctual drives and defense mechanisms within the fully elaborated ego psychology of his mature work—capture most powerfully the specific mode of exile of our secular age.

IV

Let us now get a brief overall view of the workings of the ratios. The swerving of *clinamen* initiating the process of misprision constitutes, in Freudian language, a reaction-formation, and, in rhetorical terms, an irony. After this opening, which itself represents a limitation, or contraction, or negation, of meaning according to Bloom's Lurianic and Valentinian paradigms, the poem shatters, or evades its precursor, in order to arrive at a *tessera*, a restituting representation of visionary desire whose psychic components are "turning against the self" and "reversal," and whose rhetorical trope is synecdoche. This tripartite rhythm is then achieved two more times with heightening intensity, as the poem moves toward the crises of poetic will that mark its ultimate battle with anteriority. *Kenosis*, with psychic components listed by Bloom as "undoing, isolation, and regression," and a rhetorical manifestation as metonymy, breaks into *daemonization*, whose trope of hyperbole and psychic force of repression combine to form the proper source of the literary sublime. *Askesis*, the resulting recoil into the mere perspectives of metaphor and the psychic dead end of sublimation, then shatters into *apophrades*, the final home—origin and end—of the revisionary imagination, whose rhetoric of metalepsis or transumption represents the deeper psychic troping of Freud's introjection and projection.

Why present the map in this skeletal form, outside the context of its applications to a poem such as "The Second Coming"? For one, we are enabled to see just what a symmetry, a self-sufficiency, it has as an imaginative critical construction—a self-styled Romantic myth for a belated age. More important, for our purposes here, presenting the map in isolation from its intended objects allows us more clearly to relate it to several of Bloom's other key sources in the Freudian vein. As a map of the mind, for instance, Bloom's chart manages to incorporate, albeit with radically different emphases, all ten of the defenses listed by Anna Freud in *The Ego and the Mechanisms of Defence*.[33] As a map of the tropings of the text, Bloom's ratios assimilate all four of Kenneth Burke's "master" tropes— irony, metonymy, metaphor, and his featured synecdoche—adding to Burke the two tropes, hyperbole and metalepsis, that reflect Bloom's narrowly defined Romantic interest in "successively more heightened representations" of visionary "desire" (PR, p. 253).[34] As a map of the crises of Romantic vision, Bloom's revisionist structures represent, of course, a cunning and subversive expansion of the paradigm delivered by M. H. Abrams in "Structure and Style in the Greater Romantic Lyric,"[35] a paradigm whose featured crises of Wordsworthian memory revolving around the interplay of mind and nature, subject and object, are internalized by Bloom via the much bleaker reading of memory advanced by Freud.

Memory for Freud is not the passive receptacle that it had been

in the tradition of mechanistic psychology against which he re-
belled; rather, as Philip Reiff has acutely summarized, it "embodies
a moral choice, a sequence of acceptances and rejections" whose
"false bottom" is repression, *below which* memory "really begins."[36]
The key to Freud's conception of the mind and of psychoanalytic
adjustment, says Reiff, is the notion that "forgetting is active." For
Bloom, borrowing this principle for the map of misreading under
his own guiding precept that "only the agon is of the essence" (DC,
p. 5), forgetting takes the form of a psychic warfare where the price
of any "acceptance" of the precursor, any "adjustment," is the ir-
retrievable loss of poetic power. It is precisely the latecomer's
refusal to accept the necessary priority of the precursor, and so
his refusal to accept the love he necessarily feels for his poetic
father, that initiate the lies and evasions of the poem. The opening
clinamen features reaction-formation, a primary mechanism of defense by the ego against the id in Freud's picture of the psyche,
because reaction-formation is the defense perhaps most directly
based on ambivalence—on the psychic opposites, in Bloom's reading, of love and jealous hatred.[37] Thus—to turn now to our illustration of Bloom's ratios—the first six lines of "The Second Coming,"
with their evocation of apocalyptic rending through the imagery of
gyres and falconry, are said by Bloom to mask Yeats's actual "emotional exultation" over his terrifying vision through "a deceptive,
only apparent emotional revulsion, a rhetorical irony that has been
canonically misread as a literal statement" (PR, p. 217). If this was
also the central import of Bloom's earlier reading of the poem—a
reading that aligned him with his temperamental opposite, Yvor
Winters, against most of the Modernist critical tradition—now
Bloom is in a position with his new critical terminology to explore
more fully the dynamics of such a meaning. For what has been made
clearer here is that the language of the poem is "lying" because the
deepest desires of the poet *will it to do so*—the desire of Yeats, in
this case, to swerve from Shelley, especially the Shelley who in the
climax to the first act of *Prometheus Unbound* has the last fury
announce:

> The good want power, but to weep barren tears.
> The powerful goodness want: worse need for them.
> The wise want love, and those who love want wisdom;
> And all best things are thus confused to ill.   (1.625 – 28)

In *Yeats* Bloom labels this "Shelley's central insight; an insight of
the left that Yeats proceeds to appropriate for the right" (p. 320). He
has not changed his position in *Poetry and Repression*; rather, he is

now simply able to see *how* such a perverse emendation came about. Yeats lies about Shelley's passionate and compassionate wisdom because he cannot stand to be smothered by his own awe for Shelley's integrity. And because this is so, because love must be changed utterly into psychic savagery within the imagination of the poet, nothing linguistic is what it appears, either. The image of man as falconer actually represents the image of man as a poet, observes Bloom, so that Yeats's "turning and turning" really means "troping and troping," and the discipline of falconry "represents not only a mastery of nature, but a mastery of language" (PR, p. 217). The first six lines of the poem constitute an irony not in anything like the New Critical sense of verbal or paradoxical wit, then, but in a darker rendering of the visionary sense that we noted in chapter 1. That is, a rhetorical irony occurs when we as readers see that the poet is lying to get started, saying other than what he means in order to appropriate some space from the precursor for his own vision (Bloom, who sometimes follows Quintilian in calling irony *"illusio,"* might be playing cleverly off the Latin root, *illudere,* to deride).

Of course, as Bloom's Lurianic and kabbalistic paradigms make clear, such negation of the precursor, such limitation of meaning resulting in a bewildering "dialectical interplay of presence and absence" in the images of the poem, cannot itself suffice, and must be shattered by a psychic evasion into the restoration of meaning delivered by the second revisionary ratio, *tessera.* To understand how Yeats's lines, "The best lack all conviction, while the worst / Are full of passionate intensity," represent the Freudian defense of turning against the self and the trope of synecdoche, we must remember that the real subject of the poem continues to be poetry. While Yeats in a superficial sense is commenting on the breakdown of the public order in Europe, he is actually on a deeper level grappling with his perception of an imperiled elitism "without which," says Bloom, Yeats knows that "poetry is not possible" (p. 217). This grappling takes the shape of a "part/whole image wholly turned against the deepest desires of his own *antithetical* self or Gnostic *pneuma,"* as Yeats, himself a worshipper of the "passionate intensity" at the center of the imaginative aristocracy of art, finds such intensity displayed only by the rabblement, not by those whom he admires, the elite.

In Bloom's new reading, the second movement of the poem, that featuring the progression from *kenosis* to *daemonization,* occurs in lines 9 – 17, with their evocation of the apocalyptic Sphinx image out of the *"Spiritus Mundi."* In *Yeats* Bloom had argued that Yeats's recourse to the Christian conception of the Second Coming is fraudulent, since the poem itself delivers not a Christian vision, but the grimly antithetical image of the male Sphinx. Now he calls Yeats's misleading device a *kenosis*, a "radical humbling" of the poem's own meaning via the metonymic "emptying-out substitution" of the Second Coming for what is really meant, the Gnostic Second Birth. But this Gnostic vision from the *"Spiritus Mundi"* itself is altered by Yeats, who, in a defensive act of isolation from his precursors, sees the Second Birth to involve not the Antichrist but the "mere Demiurge or god of the fallen world" (p. 218). There then follows the breaking into form of the ratio known as *daemonization*, whose psychic act of repression and restituting rhetorical hyperboles deliver the belated modern version of Bloom's cherished Romantic sublime. Bloom is clearest in his explanation of this central ratio in *Agon*, where he emphasizes that his project to merge misreading with repression involves identifying *"patterns of forgetting* in a poem" (p. 236), patterns that in language necessarily constitute *"the repression of quotation"* (p. 238). If the poem as a whole develops out of a primal repression of the precursor, an originating and continuing anxiety about priority, then the specific repression of the poem's first climax in *daemonization* represents not a *"true overcoming"* of the precursor—this is, of course, impossible—but a temporary *"outtalking"* of the rival text via the latecomer poem's "voiding and avoidance of its own tendency *towards quotation"* (p. 240). The task of the strong critic, himself caught in the same power play of vision and mastery in his reading of the poem as has existed between that poem and its precursors, is to identify "what is *almost* present" in the poem (p. 236; my emphasis), and thereby to determine *"how"* (Bloom's emphasis) the latecomer poet has managed the fine art of evasion in order to make his poem.

When Bloom's position is expressed this clearly—and it seldom is by Bloom himself—we can easily see how it provides a theoretical basis for the worst sort of the celebrated Bloomian critical arbitrariness. As we observed in the introduction, Bloom responds to his detractors by arguing that all reading, because it is inevitably misreading, is an exercise in the tautologies of the revisionary will. Yet it is possible that Bloom, characteristically enough perhaps, is showing himself too eager for battle here; the undeniably important theoretical point can be tempered by the purely practical one that "repressed quotation" in Bloom often is not far from the allusion of the orthodox critic, with the difference being, of course, the divergent conceptions of tradition within which the source, whether allusion or repression, is seen to operate. Simply put, in Bloom's mature phase tradition is to be battled, not joined; that is what makes tradition what it is. In this sense, a critic who began in the shadow of Northrop Frye has come to turn inside out Frye and one of Frye's mentors, the T.S. Eliot of "Tradition and the Individual Talent," delivering his own radical rereading of a history of "figural interpretation," which he now sees to have "allowed a curious overspiritualization of texts canonized by poetic tradition" (PR, p. 95).[38] But the cited source itself is often in the common realm, and has been cited by critics with predispositions and aims quite different from Bloom's own. Thus, the repressed quotation at the daemonic heart of "The Second Coming" is the vision of the tomb of Ramses II from Shelley's "Ozymandias," a literary influence noted by many readers of Yeats and by Bloom himself in his earlier reading. Where Bloom crucially departs from the canonical readings is to argue that Yeats represses Shelleyan quotation in order to distort. While the sculptor's hand in "Ozymandias" mocks the Sphinx image that it has created, Yeats's deepest intent, says Bloom, is to celebrate, a celebration that is the consequence of his repression of an overly violent personal sexuality and of "the return of his repressed Gnosticism, repressed in respect to its real hostility both to nature and to fallen human history" (p. 219).

What kind of sublime is this, though, envisioning as it does the terrible power of the demiurge, the "blank and pitiless" force of a deterministic history? This question will involve us in a discussion not only of *daemonization* but of the final two ratios, for these three culminating ratios in Bloom's map are alike in that they cannot be understood apart from their maker's continuing and increasingly subtle appropriation of Freud, especially the later Freud whose speculations on origins and the ego instincts emphasize themes dark and dialectical enough to open them readily for use in Bloom's agonistic world. The sublime in "The Second Coming," Bloom says, is an "uncanny" sublime, a sublime whose figurations reveal on a level deeper than their apocalyptic imagery the daemonic power of Yeats in pursuing his quest for imaginative independence. Bloom's text in Freud is the essay of 1919 on the *"Unheimlich,"* or "Uncanny," in which that concept is related to the daemonic:

> Our analysis of instances of the uncanny has led us back to the old animistic conception of the universe, which was characterized by the idea that the world was peopled with the spirits of human beings, and by the narcissistic overestimation of subjective mental processes (such as the belief in the omnipotence of

thoughts, the magical practices based upon this belief, the carefully proportioned distribution of magical powers or "mana"
among various outside persons and things), as well as by all
those other figments of the imagination with which man, in the
unrestricted narcissism of that stage of development, strove to
withstand the inexorable laws of reality. It would seem as though
each one of us has been through a phase of individual development corresponding to that animistic stage in primitive men,
that none of us has traversed it without preserving certain traces
of it which can be re-activated, and that everything which now
strikes us as "uncanny" fulfills the condition of stirring those
vestiges of animistic mental activity within us and bringing them
to expression.[39]

From this point of view, Bloom notes, "the daemonic is the survival of an archaic narcissism, which is defined as our faith that
mind can triumph over matter" (PR, p. 209). Indeed, for Bloom, interested as always in Freudian principles and not in Freudian cultural history, all Freud's defenses may be regarded as essentially
Romantic operations in the sense that they feature the attempt of
the mind to counter the reality principle, or the power of wounded
narcissism against all those forces that would constrict or delimit.
That Freud himself sought through psychoanalysis to adjust pa-
tients to the undeniable exigencies of the reality principle does not
trouble Bloom, who gladly admits of, and proceeds to discard, this
"reductive" side to the Freudian temperament. What *is* important
to Bloom is the despair of the late Freud over the efficacy of the
psychoanalytic transference in the face of various resistances, including those repetition-compulsions that Freud, in the notorious
speculative leap of *Beyond the Pleasure Principle*, finally identifies
with an instinct to *"restore"* the pure anteriority, or *"earlier state of
things,"* of death.[40] The daemonic is itself aligned with a certain type
of repetition-compulsion by Freud, who observes in his essay on
the "uncanny" that among certain cases of morbid anxiety, "there
must be a class in which the anxiety can be shown to come from
something repressed which *recurs.*"[41]

Bloom's own use of the concept of the daemonic, in assimilating
the Freudian insights to his continuing meditation on the meaning
of the daemonic in Shelley's "Alastor" and in Yeats's cosmogony,
enables him to place more accurately than he had in his earlier
theory of vision the psychology of the solitary Romantic quester. If
"Alastor" represents the "dark double" or "avenging *daimon*, the
Shadow or selfhood that stalks" the poet "until he wastes in death"

(*Yeats*, p. 15), then Yeats's willful misreading of that "daimon" to furnish his doctrine of the antiself or mysterious other that would complete him[42] shows the fate of the belated imagination to seek freedom through a violently narcissistic and self-conscious divisiveness that leaves the quester malformed and distorted, even as it allows him the only power really left in the age of Freudian anxiety: the power to battle the death-in-life of origins, the forces of the precursor, within one's psyche. The "glory of repression" for Bloom, "poetically speaking, is that memory and desire, driven down, have no place to go *in language* except up onto the heights of sublimity, the ego's exultation in its own operations" (MM, p. 100); the darkness of repression is that such an exultation, with its sublime knowledge and its power, is purchased by the latecomer at the high and "self-crippling" cost of making "the son more of a daemon and the precursor more of a man" (AI, pp. 109, 106).

Now we are in a position to assess the final two ratios of the Bloomian map, the "too happily dualistic defense" of the sublimating metaphors of *askesis* (MM, p. 100), and the metaleptic reversals of time in the final restituting movement of the Romantic crisis poem, *apophrades*. "The central argument" of the theory of the anxiety of influence, Bloom says in *A Map of Misreading*, "is that sublimation is a *defense of limitation* even as metaphor is a self-contradictory *trope of limitation*" (p. 99). Bloom greatly devalues metaphor, the central trope in the rhetoric of the New Critics, because the perspectivism it delivers, the inside-outside imagery following the heights and depths of the sublime in the Romantic crisis poem, only engenders "confusions," "polarities of subject and object" that "defeat" every attempt to "unify them" in their own terms (MM, pp. 100, 101). *Askesis*, that is, while necessary as a compensation "for the poet's involuntary shock at his own daemonic expansiveness" in *daemonization* (AI, p. 120), is nonetheless reductive and self-defeating in that it returns the poem to a problematical confrontation with that world of nature that, Bloom has told us all along, can never be the poet's home. Indeed, we are given a sense of the essential identity of Bloom's thought in all phases of his career when we find in *Poetry and Repression* that he explicitly associates the hopeless "dualistic imagery of inside consciousness against outside nature" (p. 19) featured in the fifth revisionary ratio of Romantic metaphor with that "secularized epiphany" whose precarious perch within the world of Blake's Beulah was a main subject of discussion in chapter 1.[43] If the poet does not secure his release from the upper gate of Beulah, he is doomed, Bloom says in *The Visionary Company*, to "the vision of eternal recurrence" (p. 30), a

vision whose confusions in perspective are fully elaborated fifteen
years later in *Poetry and Repression* via the Nietzschean nightmare
of a trope that sublimates in order to save, but succeeds only in stifling all that is strongest in the poet.

The *askesis* of "The Second Coming" occurs in the Yeatsian vision of "twenty centuries of stony sleep / . . . vexed to nightmare by a
rocking cradle," a vision whose "knowing," Bloom says, is a sublimation or condensation "of a greater desire or dream," specifically
to "become one" in a Gnostic knowing with the object of the vision,
the "antithetical beast." The terms of the metaphor are the inside-
outside dualism of the twenty Christian centuries, representing
"nature, the fallen object-world," and the "rocking cradle," standing, Bloom argues, "for the subjective consciousness that is aware of
the Incarnation" (PR, p. 220). But the key phrase is "stony sleep,"
which delivers a characteristic Yeatsian misreading of a central
source, the Blake of *The Book of Urizen*. In chapter 3 of that work,
Urizen falls amid the battle of the eternals that he has initiated—
"But Urizen laid in a stony sleep / Unorganiz'd, rent from Eternity"
(3.10.7 − 8)—there to lie for seven ages until emerging in another
birth as the deity of fallen man in a fallen world, the deity whose
"soul" has "sicken'd" (8.4.23) to the catastrophic creation of our
temporal and natural world. Yeats's use of the phrase "stony sleep"
associates Urizen with the Sphinx image and thus reveals to Bloom
once again the radical subversiveness of Yeats's reading of Blake,
since Yeats inwardly welcomes what Blake had reviled.

But this is only to say that in the most recent phase of Bloom's
career, the critic who once accepted Blakean vision on something
near its own terms and who still retains central Blakean values has
nonetheless won through to what he calls "a truly enlightened
Freudian perspective," a perspective from which he now sees how
"uncanny" and "curiously sympathetic" a figure Urizen is (*Agon*,
p. 87), since it is Urizen who presides over the only world, after all,
that we have, the world of our fallen and demiurgical condition. If
Bloom in *The Anxiety of Influence* and *A Map of Misreading* is moved
by the mighty revisionary willfulness of Milton's Satan, he is increasingly instructed in *Agon* and other recent writings by the predicament of Urizen in "The Book of Urizen," a predicament that is
itself an irony directed at Milton's conscious hero, the God of *Paradise Lost*:

> From the depths of dark solitude. From
> The eternal abode in my holiness,
> Hidden set apart in my stern counsels

Reserv'd for the days of futurity,
I have sought for a joy without pain,
For a solid without fluctuation
Why will you die O Eternals?
Why live in unquenchable burnings?

First I fought with the fire; consum'd
Inwards, into a deep world within:
A void immense, wild dark & deep,
Where nothing was: Natures wide womb

And self balanc'd stretch'd o'er the void
I alone, even I! the winds merciless
Bound; but condensing, in torrents
They fall & fall; strong I repell'd
The vast waves, & arose on the waters
A wide world of solid obstruction   (2.4 − 5.6 − 23)

The Urizenic perspective that Bloom finds in the late Freud, the
perspective that ties our deepest desires to an end that is an earliness, an origin boldly troped as death, is the perspective necessary
to understand Bloom's culminating ratio of restored power,
apophrades. For it is precisely Freud's "mature account of anxiety,"
what Bloom calls his "allegory of origins" (*Agon*, p. 111), that, in the
latest Bloomian meditations on poetic beginnings and ends, has allowed him to complete his own remarkable map—or tale, or prophecy—of Romantic revisionism. Urizen, in Bloom's reading, broods
over an abyss, and his passion, akin to that of the Gnostic demiurge,
gives birth to a catastrophe that *is* the creation. Blake, in seeing the
solitary terror of Urizenic creation—"self balanc'd stretch'd o'er the
void / I alone, even I!"—sees also, then, without admitting it, the
necessary "horror and solitude of all belated strong creativity"
(p. 89). This Urizenic tale represents for Bloom a perfect visionary
correlative to the allegories of Freud insofar as it dramatizes the
processes of creative narcissistic anxiety in natural man. Freud's
discussion of narcissism in "On Narcissism" and his later works is
an attempt to bridge the gap between autoeroticism and object
choice in the developmental psychology of the child.[44] Bloom's appropriation of Freud is his parallel attempt to explain what exists
initially in the poetic ego that can make up a scene of instruction
where the object choices of poetic vocation are determined. Borrowing loosely from Freud, Bloom posits an absolute, or primary,
narcissism, whose self-love, in effect, constitutes the poetic ego.[45]
In one sense, then, the agon of poetic creation occurs when this ego

is wounded by the threatening presence of anteriority, a presence both catastrophic and creative; but since, of course, we are dealing with what is internalized, it might be more accurate to say that the narcissism of the poetic ego *is itself an anxiety*, a preemptive anxiety establishing itself "prior to any stimulus" (*Agon*, p. viii) and thereby establishing the conditions for all the meaning of its anxious questing.

Authority for such a conception of preemptive anxiety can be found in Freud himself, who in *Inhibitions, Symptoms, and Anxiety* (1926), reverses a crucial earlier position to argue that it is "anxiety which produced repression and not, as I formerly believed, repression which produced anxiety."[46] From this point of view, Bloom observes, the daemonic might be defined as "an anxiety narcissistically intoxicated with itself, an anxiety determined to go on being anxious" (*Agon*, p. 114). "Catastrophic in their mutual origins," Bloom concludes, "Romantic and Freudian man amalgamate in an endless contraction from demiurgic injured narcissism," and this is as good a summary as he has provided of his view of poetic creation after the fall. And yet we must not forget the other side of the Urizenic equation either, the side drawn from the Freudian flight of *Beyond the Pleasure Principle*, which tells us that "where every agon has been internalized, as it was by Urizen," then "the drive for freedom becomes also the death drive" (p. 89)—a drive, in Urizen's words, for "a joy without pain."[47] For Bloom, executing his own bold misreading of a Freudian trope that merges origins and death, the death drive marks "the mind's limits" (p. 88) by marking the ground against which meaning comes to mean by coming to rebel: the figuratively impossible "literal meaning" of the precursors. Bloom's summary of the hidden formula of *Beyond the Pleasure Principle*—*"literal meaning equals anteriority equals an earlier state of meaning equals an earlier state of things equals death equals literal meaning"* (p. 107)—might very well stand as a formula for his own writings in *Agon* and *The Breaking of the Vessels*, as long as we add the complementary prescription that Eros, the power of poetic desire, must then equal "figurative meaning." Since one is not possible without the other, since figuration demands the "death" of origins against which to rebel, Bloom's most striking contribution to Freudian theory is finally to conflate the Freudian ideas of defense and drive, finding them to be "mutually contaminated" by virtue of their shared participation in the paradoxes and psychic ambivalences of origins.[48]

All these paradoxes have obvious implications for the final and the richest of Bloom's revisionary ratios. If anxiety in poetry is, as

Bloom says in another creative borrowing from Freud, an attempt to master anteriority by *"remembering"* it rather than *"repeating"* it (*Agon*, p. 110),[49] then the ratio of *apophrades*, "without which poems would not know how to end" (MM, p. 102), concludes the crises of revisionism by representing in essence what all strong poetry is about: time as tradition, time "remembered," and thus time troped via the dynamics of agonistic beginnings and endings. Psychically, the task of the poetic ego in this culminating act of aggression is to make of the earlier poem's earliness a lateness and of the later poem's lateness an earliness, with both reversals hoping to achieve, if only for one evanescent moment, the "greatest" of all poetic illusions, the "poetic immortality" of "having fathered one's own fathers" (PR, p. 20). Thus, Yeats in the final two lines of "The Second Coming" seeks to complete his misreading of his precursor texts in Blake and Shelley by asking a question that is not a question but a vision—and an implied answer to the "terrifying" integrity of his Romantic masters. The specific psychic mechanisms of defense involved are projection and introjection, united in their goal "to reverse anteriority by forsaking the evasions of mental space" featured in *askesis* for "those of mental time" (KC, p. 89). That is, Yeats with his final question projects, or casts out, the twenty centuries of the Christian past, and introjects, or identifies with, the upcoming "*antithetical* age, where the epiphany at Bethlehem will see the Second Birth of the Sphinx" (PR, p. 220).

It might be observed here that again Bloom's reading of this passage does not seem to be substantially different from the earlier treatment in *Yeats*. However, the new terminology derived from Freud does permit a more thorough exploration of processes of psychic warfare that were implicit in, but not developed by, the earlier theory. Since *apophrades* concludes the battle, it is not surprising that Bloom sees the defenses associated with it to be particularly strong ones; in *The Breaking of the Vessels* he announces that he wishes to emphasize the "psychic murderousness" of projection (p. 89) and the "violent narcissistic metamorphosis" that constitutes introjection (p. 66). What is most intriguing about these final defenses, though, is a feature that they share with their correlative rhetorical component, metalepsis. Bloom takes this latter term from Quintilian via a footnote in Angus Fletcher's *Allegory*, where it is discussed as a major stylistic device in Milton;[50] in Bloom's related usage, it is defined as "the trope of a trope," a "scheme, frequently allusive, that refers the reader back to any previous figurative scheme" (MM, p. 74). As such, metalepsis, more than any other of the tropes of the map of misreading, works directly off other tropes, and "is the largest single factor in fostering a tone of conscious rhetoricity in Romantic and Post-Romantic poetry." Similarly, the defenses of projection and introjection are said by Bloom to "trope most directly against other defenses, particularly of the obsessive or repetitive-compulsive kind." In "The Second Coming," the final two lines, featuring the murderous psychic casting-out of the Christian era, have the effect of *reversing* the psychic and rhetorical actions of *kenosis* in particular, where the poem had momentarily emptied itself of meaning through its metonymic substitution of the Christian Second Coming for the true Gnostic heart of Yeatsian vision. A metalepsis, Bloom observes, "can be called, maddeningly but accurately, a metonymy of a metonymy" (p. 102); the metaleptic representation of the conclusion of "The Second Coming," with its consciously rhetorical question, acts to restore meaning—to restore, that is, for one final moment, the poem's narcissistic desire to continue—by hearkening unto Bethlehem not as the future site of a Christian Second Coming, but as a place where the "antithetical" age shall truly begin.

Is there any cost to this final victory in the map of misreading, to this admittedly only temporary grappling of the mighty dead to an uneasy stand-off? The logic of Bloom's account of psychic origins suggests that there must be. If repression itself depends on an even deeper primal fixation, Bloom observes in *A Map of Misreading*, then the unconscious is in the language of poetic creation a "hyperbole, whose origins are in a more complex trope, indeed in the trope of a trope, the metaleptic or transumptive trope of a Scene of Instruction" (p. 56). The progression in the map of misreading itself, then, from the fourth to the sixth revisionary ratio is a fully necessary— indeed, a *deterministic*—one. Structured to show how the sublimities of vision themselves depend upon the deeper processes of internalized tradition in the metaleptic core of the latecomer's psyche, the map, in fact, presents a compelling emblem of the metamorphosis in Bloom's own thought from his earlier visionary Romanticism to his mature "prophecy" of the agon of influence. As such, it is designed precisely to highlight the peculiar manner of loss lurking behind *all* Bloom's envisioned ends for the poetic imagination, whether visionary or agonistic. Poetry, in this summarizing Bloomian perspective, because it is concerned solely with battling the past to secure the right to quest into the future, must be seen to have *no present tense, no psychic here and now.* The last revisionary ratio of "The Second Coming," with its distancing of the past and complete imaginative identification with the future, can stand for the end of all Bloom's charted patterns of misreading in the sense that the poet himself exists "in no time at the poem's close" (PR, p. 220)—a psychic force with no context save the force of his own continuing agonistic desires. If we recall here the "radical temporality" advanced by Jonas from his reading in Heidegger as an existential correlate to the darkness of Gnostic vision, we can see how Bloom's own tale of influence, in contriving to give us a more-than-existential salvation through the indescribable and nonreferential god of our mythopoeic imaginations, pays the high price of condemning us at the same time to a strikingly impoverished and alienated existence within the endless gap of the present. It is no accident that Bloom's favorite instance of metalepsis features a resourceful Shelleyan troping of the meanings of Christian redemption. When Shelley in "A Defence of Poetry" seeks to transcend the many human errors of the great poets by arguing that "they have been washed in the blood of the mediator and the redeemer Time" (SPP, p. 506), he is providing his later, and somewhat grandly less confident, critical prophet a rationale for maintaining his own paradoxical quest, in a faithless and "belated" age, to sacrifice the present for the sake of rallying what remains.

Influence and the Map of American Poetic History: The Emersonian Survival

Since the appearance of *The Ringers in the Tower* in 1971, with its important essays on the "Central Men" of American poetry—Emerson, Whitman, and Wallace Stevens—Harold Bloom has displayed an extraordinary critical energy in his quest to translate all modern and contemporary poetry into the idiom of an authentic, if belated, Romanticism, and, concurrently, to discredit all those critical traditions, especially the Modernist one, that would pronounce the gods of Romanticism dead. For Bloom the most salient feature of "strong" poetry in the twentieth century beyond Yeats is that it is almost exclusively American. Although he pays lip service to the poetry of Hardy and Lawrence, and has recently come to applaud the strength of the English poet Geoffrey Hill and the Irishman Seamus Heaney, Bloom has dedicated himself with almost oracular zeal in the last decade to delineating the strands of a modern poetic tradition that he sees as having veered via the gnomic rhapsodies of Emerson from its origins in the visionary company of early nineteenth-century England to its end, so desperate and so glorious, in the harsh religion of a distinctively American Orphism. The family romance of American poetry introduced by Bloom in *The Ringers in the Tower* in 1971 and portrayed in imposing depth through all his works since features Emerson as grand patriarch, both liberator and oppressor, before a host of powerful ephebes, including, most notably, Walt Whitman and Emily Dickinson in the nineteenth century, and Stevens, Hart Crane, A. R. Ammons, John Ashbery, and Robert Penn Warren in the twentieth. Conspicuously absent from Bloom's canon are, of course, many of the great names of modern and Modernist literary history. Pound, Eliot, Auden, Williams, and Cummings are largely ignored or derided; among more recent poets, Roethke, Lowell, Olson, Ginsberg, O'Hara, and Rich seldom receive Bloomian mention, and even more seldom Bloomian praise.

We have already examined Bloom's conception of Modernism in chapter 2. What we need to do now is to characterize the religion of American Orphism which he offers in its place, and discover for ourselves *why* Bloom has become such a relentless proselytizer for his extremist reading of twentieth-century American poetry as Romanticism revised. Bloom's writings of the last decade serve to make explicit what had been implied in all his earlier work on the English Romantics: canon formation, as a final defense against the oppressive richness of time and tradition, is an essential activity of the modern critical imagination. If, in Bloom's view, the Modernist canon, and the several post-Modernist ones as well, may best be seen as desperate attempts to escape the inevitable by lying weakly against their own essential continuity with Romantic tradition, then the canon of American Orphism that he has sought to define and uphold from *The Ringers in the Tower* through *Agon* and *The Breaking of the Vessels* continues to vivify precisely because the Emersonian tradition is the one that has told and continues to tell the darkest truths about the strong lies upon which our poetry is founded. For Bloom, the "Primal Lie" (PR, p. 287) at the origin of the Transcendental tradition of American Romanticism is Emerson's denial of belatedness and of influence, a denial summed up in his distinctively American prescription for an uncompromising "self-reliance" in the face of all the ties, social, personal, and literary, that might bind the individual imagination. Bloom, calling Emersonian individualism "the Supreme Fiction of our literature" and "our most troublesome trope" (MM, p. 172), generalizes from Emerson's oracular repudiation of anteriority to assert that the strength of all American poetry after him resides in its paradoxical resistance to influence, a resistance that, since it is much more vehement than what obtains between the poets in the English Romantic tradition, must also mask much more powerful defensive anxieties repressed beneath.

Analyzing the "peculiar *clinamen*," the "swerve or twist away from British and European study of the nostalgias, that has distinguished American poetry at least since the Age of Emerson," Bloom in *Figures of Capable Imagination* (and in a similar passage in *A Map of Misreading*, p. 52) provides a lucid summary of the paradoxes of the wealthy American agon of influence:

American psychopoetics are dominated by an American difference from European patterns of the imagination's struggle with its own origins. The literary psychology of America is necessarily a psychology of belatedness, in which the characteristic anxiety is not so much an expectation of being flooded by poetic ancestors, as already *having been* flooded before one could even begin. Emerson's insistence upon Self-Reliance made Whitman and Dickinson and Thoreau possible, and doubtless benefited Hawthorne and Melville despite themselves. But the Scene of Instruction that Emerson sought to void glows with a more and more vivid intensity for contemporary American poets, who enter upon a legacy that paradoxically has accumulated wealth while continuing to insist that it has remained poverty-stricken. (Pp. 272 – 73)

Any canonizer this late in time, living in what Bloom habitually calls, with borrowed hyperbole, "the great sunset of selfhood in the evening land" (PR, p. 244), must be especially attracted to a tradition that is characterized by a more acute sense of belatedness than any other in literature—and that has accumulated so much wealth in working out the anxieties of that belatedness.

Several obvious points can be made here before we move on to a closer analysis of Bloom's celebration of the Emersonian native strain. Bloom's reading of Emersonian individualism as a desire for pure vision unencumbered by ties to the past and his placing of that desire in a central position in American literature have affinities with a number of eminent earlier attempts by academic critics to define the quality of American literary language and experience. Roy Harvey Pearce's treatment of the Adamic poet in *The Continuity of American Poetry* engages many of the themes in Whitman and Stevens that will later preoccupy Bloom.[1] R. W. B. Lewis's classic discussion in *The American Adam* is also pertinent, with its definition of the archetypal American as "the poet par excellence, creating language itself by naming the elements of the scene about him."[2] Richard Poirier's examination in *A World Elsewhere* of the profound discontinuities of style in American literature as our writers struggle "with already existing literary, social, and historical organizations for power over environment and over language itself" clearly anticipates some of Bloom's major concerns as well. Poirier in particular could almost be speaking for Bloom with his central contention that "Emerson in many respects *is* American literature, both by virtue of the themes and images of which he is its storehouse and because of the exciting ways in which the impossible ambitions he has for his writing often fail, but only just barely, of being realized."[3] And yet there is good reason why Bloom in his own work very seldom alludes to any of these significant precursors, why he clearly feels that his reading of American literature departs radically from theirs. For Bloom is, as usual, busy translating the tale of Emersonian individualism into the paradigms of his own rather extreme critical prophecies. While Pearce, for example, can give equal time to the "mythic" poets such as Eliot who respond to the unlicensed freedom of the Adamic figures with a classical reliance upon order and authority,[4] Bloom must depose the pretenders to the canon on the grounds that their orthodoxies are barren and reductive when taken as counsel by latecomers desperate for what will suffice. And while Poirier's emphasis on the *verbal* world of American literature can provide insight into the liberating visions of our greatest writers, Bloom's continuing commitment to the Blakean spiritual forms underlying the actual words on the page permits him to examine only those visionary truths—now, of course, dark and repressed—that *alone*, in the Bloomian psychopoetic cosmos, determine and vivify the otherwise lifeless husks of "mere" language (WS, p. 394).

If Bloom's criticism may be distinguished from the work of other eminent commentators on American literature by virtue of its unabashed canonizing impulse and its corollary method of reading American poetry for "defenses" alone, we are justified in asking the question that Bloom himself says is crucial to canon formation: What is the *use* of the Emersonian strain as Bloom defines it? Why do our greatest poets of the last fifty years—Stevens, Ammons, and Ashbery—*need* to compose their work out of a massive internalized struggle with a precursor who lived, wrote, and died his creative death a hundred years before them? Given that, as Bloom acknowledges, only Ammons among the three is an obvious Emersonian while the other two are "involuntary," the question might very well be: Why does *Bloom* need Emerson to initiate and preside over his story of American poetry? What is Emerson's special power over his later critic, a power so strong that, by Bloom's own admission, it changed his "mind about nearly everything . . . in the middle of the journey" of his critical career (BV, p. 26)? In an essay on Emerson entitled "The Self-Reliance of American Romanticism," Bloom furnishes an excellent frame for answering these questions. "Romanticism, even in its most remorseless protagonists, is centrally a humanism," he observes, a humanism "which seeks our renewal as makers, which hopes to give us the immodest hope that we—even we—coming so late in time's injustices can still sing a song of ourselves" (FC, p. 57).

The first part of this pronouncement could easily have come

from Bloom's "visionary company" years; the second, with its rue over "time's injustices," is very much a part of the "anxiety of influence" phase. Bloom's love of Emerson, in fact, seems to combine the impulses of both stages of his career, the veneraton for pure moments of visionary mythmaking central to early Bloom, and the fear and trembling over what those moments are revealed finally to be in the Bloomian work of the seventies. In many ways, Emerson, despite the fact that he and Blake are said by Bloom to "disagree on most things" (FC, p. 91), serves as an American version of Blake in Bloom's schema. To Blake's "Exuberance is Beauty" (CP, p. 38), Emerson responds in kind, "The only sin is limitation."[5] To Blake's celebration of the "wonders Divine / of Human Imagination" (*Jerusalem*, 4.98.31 − 32), Emerson answers with his own glorification of the sublime transparencies of the "transparent eye-ball" (CW, 1:10), of "Imagination" as "a very high sort of seeing, which does not come by study, but by the intellect being where and what it sees; by sharing the path or circuit of things through forms, and so making them translucid to others."[6] To Blake's mixture of disappointment over the fallen state of man and visionary confidence that redemption into the fully human is possible through the imagination, Emerson delivers in his early "Nature" what Bloom calls "the closest American equivalent to Blakean myth ever hazarded" (RT, p. 223).

A man is a god in ruins. . . . Man is the dwarf of himself. Once he was permeated and dissolved by spirit. He filled nature with his overflowing currents. Out from him sprang the sun and moon; from man, the sun, from woman, the moon. The laws of his mind, the periods of his actions externized themselves into day and night, into the year and the seasons. But, having made for himself this huge shell, his waters retired; he no longer fills the veins and veinlets; he is shrunk to a drop. He sees, that the structure still fits him, but fits him colossally. Say, rather, once it fitted him, now it corresponds to him from far and on high. He adores timidly his own work. Now is man the follower of the sun, and woman the follower of the moon. Yet sometimes he starts in his slumber, and wonders at himself and his house, and muses strangely at the resemblance betwixt him and it. (CW, 1:42)

The famous moral of this story, drawn later in "Nature," expresses what is for Bloom a thoroughly Blakean conception of the elevating power of the visionary imagination:

The problem of restoring to the world original and eternal beauty, is solved by the redemption of the soul. The ruin or the blank, that we see when we look at nature, is in our own eye. The axis of vision is not coincident with the axis of things, and so they appear not transparent but opake. The reason why the world lacks unity, and lies broken and in heaps, is, because man is dis-united with himself. (cw, 1:43)

And, of course, there is the final and darker parallel between Blake and Emerson. If Blake posits in *Milton* an influence relation that could liberate and not oppress, and is once moved to note, after reading Wordsworth, "I cannot think that Real Poets have any com-petition" (CP, p. 665), then Emerson counsels throughout much of his work an even more radical self-reliance that will gladly dispense with any kind of influence at all. In both cases, the primal prophet's hope for visionary freedom is revealed finally by the drear tale of lit-erary history to be chimerical; in both cases, the harsh irony is that the very force of visionary confidence in the powerful patriarch serves not only to instruct but also to oppress all those who came after.

Perhaps it is already apparent that there is, as Denis Donoghue has observed, something adventitious about Bloom's highly selec-tive use of Emerson. Bloom himself, acknowledging that Emerson is "not our greatest writer but merely our only inescapable one" (RT, p. 301), sees such inescapability to inhere largely in the "Orphic, primary Emerson" (p. 226), the Emerson of yea-saying and visionary expostulation. In "The Central Man: Emerson, Whitman, Wallace Stevens," an essay written in 1965 and thus his earliest on these three key figures, Bloom is quite explicit about his curious use of the two nineteenth-century poets and about the need for seeing them in his chosen light if we are to understand their modern ephebe, Stevens:

> there is a universal and inevitable tendency among us these days to turn most readily to Emerson at his most apocalyptic and to Whitman at his most despairing. The Orphic, primary Emerson and the tragic, antithetical Whitman are what we want and need. The Emerson who confuses himself and us by reservations that are not reservations, and the Whitman who will not cease affirm-ing until we wish never to hear anything affirmed again—these poets we are done with, and in good time. If we are to understand Wallace Stevens, if we are indeed to follow Stevens in the difficult task of rescuing him and ourselves from his and our own ironies, then we need to have these two ancestral poets at their strongest, rather than at their most prevalent. (RT, p. 226)

We will approach Whitman and Stevens shortly. What is interesting here is Bloom's boldly announced tactic of treating the poets at their "strongest" rather than their "most prevalent"—the startling assumption being that the critic has the right, perhaps the obligation, to concern himself only with those aspects of any given writer that most fully engage the critic's sense of his own needs and the needs of his time. Since most of Bloom's criticism of the Emersonian line of American poets is built upon just this assumption, we will not be surprised to find that he either ignores or rather too quickly dismisses all those readings of American poetry that, on the one hand, would see in the works of the Bloomian elect something other than Romanticism or, on the other, would see in such Romanticism not glorious belatedness but lusterless puerility. Bloom's version of Emerson constitutes a pointed argument against the many critics who have condemned the New England poet and essayist as a questionable amalgam of Coleridge, Carlyle, Plato, and Lao Tse, or worse, in Yvor Winters's famous words, a "sentimentalist" and a "fraud."[7] Bloom hypothesizes that Emerson's development as a poet was stunted by the oppressive priority of Wordsworth and Coleridge, but this early defeat as a poet is seen by Bloom to clear the way for the grand triumph of Emerson's true calling as a lyrical essayist. In the essay form, Emerson is not, as his detractors claim, merely an orchestrator of themes given him by others, usually his English betters; rather, Bloom contends, he is the unfathered father, the prime mover, of all strong American poetry after him, surpassing even Nietzsche—and, by implication, Blake—in the depth of his confidence that he alone is the begetter of his superior, his transcendent, self. Emerson's Orphism "is very much his own," Bloom argues; "little is to be apprehended of Emerson by tracking him to any of his precursors, for no other Post-Enlightenment intellect, not even Nietzsche's, has set itself quite so strongly against the idea of influence, and done this so successfully, and without anxiety" (FC, p. 69). Of course, insofar as Bloom simply is repudiating all attempts to see Emerson as a Platonist, a neo-Platonist, or a Swedenborgian, the pronouncement is nothing new; ever since *Shelley's Mythmaking*, Bloom has passionately decried the reading of poetry as philosophy writ-into-verse. But Bloom also means here that Emerson is a first among American poets, a *cause* of himself, whose self-proclaimings have, in turn, caused—that is, created—in various complex and evasive ways, the other strong poetic gods in the shadowy embellishment of American Orphism.

Orpheus, man or myth, the poet of the enchanting lyre, became an oracle in his terrible death, a Thracian skull presiding over a religion whose frenzies intimate an immortality that Bloom characteristically chooses to see in his own somewhat circumscribed visionary light.[8] Central to Bloom's reading of Emerson's Orphism is a journal entry of 1836, in which Emerson, distinguishing "Orphic words" by their ability to "touch the Intellect & cause a gush of emotion," announces that "the Universal Man when he comes, must so speak" of "the whole nature."[9] Bloom extrapolates from this, and from other related passages scattered throughout Emerson's voluminous writings, a definition of Orphic man as that central man of the always receding future who will have the power to make of the mere recurrences of nature a visionary flowing, and who has such power because he has "priority" and is thus "free of the anxiety of influence" (FC, p. 71). Emerson's gnomic ecstasies, the many brief visionary flights that mark both his essays and his poetry, are viewed by Bloom as prophecies of the Orphic poet, foretellings of an ultimate Orphic man who, of course, can exist only as pure potential, as an American's dream of something evermore about to be. And yet the creative imagination that could even *foresee* such grandeur counts for more than the impossibility of its realization; the religion of American Orphism, Bloom says, "emphasizes not the potential divinity of man but the actual divinity already present in the creative spirit" (p. 94). The Orphic sublime in Emerson and his ephebes resides, Bloom affirms, "in that ecstasy when the axis of vision and the axis of things coincide, and we see into the life of things, we behold a transparency that is also ourselves" (p. 48). The most famous passage in all of Emerson presents an instance of such sublimity when the prophet, crossing "a bare common" at twilight on a New England winter's day, feels the influx of "a perfect exhilaration" and is transformed into a giant vision: "Standing on the bare ground,—my head bathed by the blithe air, and uplifted into infinite space,—all mean egotism vanishes. I become a transparent eye-ball. I am nothing. I see all. The currents of the Universal Being circulate through me; I am part or particle of God" (CW, 1:10).

Bloom's discussion of this passage in *Poetry and Repression* is rather tortured, since he wants to argue that the moment must feature the repression necessary to his sublime, while also feeling obliged to contend, as part of his featured problematics of Freudian origins, that Emerson's greatness inheres in the astonishing circumstance of his having no father really to repress. Thus, the metamorphosis into the "transparent eye-ball," regarded by most readers as signaling the absorption of Emerson's individual being into the oneness of the universe or the Emersonian Over-Soul, is seen by Bloom as a grand instance of "Emerson's bringing-forth a father-god out of himself" (PR, p. 247)—an observation that saves the "divinity" in Emerson at the cost of considerable patrimonial hanky-panky. Having saved the divinity, however, Bloom also saves the Emerson "who is to our modern poetry what Wordsworth has been to all British poetry after him; the starting-point, the defining element, the vexatious father, the shadow and the despair, liberating angel and blocking-agent, perpetual irritant and solacing glory" (RT, p. 269). And the particular glory of American poetry is precisely its Emersonian difference from the less exuberant Wordsworthian tradition on the issue of visionary divination.

If Wordsworth only hesitantly affirms such divination, if "British High Romanticism was either too commonsensical or too repressed to attempt" such an "enterprise" (FC, p. 75), then Emerson, the native American Orpheus who proclaims the sublime, solipsistic glory of that "which gives me to myself" (CW, 1:82), delivers the distinctively grand American affirmation of the human-making self willing to dare the crushing burden of anteriority, of prior priority, in order to seize a share of that visionary space held out as a sublime possibility to all imaginative people. That such pure visionary appropriation is not really possible, that the expansiveness of American visionary desires in the Emersonian strain only reveals an anxiety of influence more crippling than any that has ever before afflicted poets in the history of literature, does not deter Bloom from celebrating the impulse. In fact, there is in such an agon what he seems, above all else, to cherish: the grandeur of heroic defeat. In a journal entry made shortly after the death of his son, Waldo, in early 1842, Emerson provides Bloom with "the epitome of the glory and sorrows" not only of Emerson himself, but "of our American Romanticism, wildest and freest at last, most a giant of the imagination where it most confronts its own dwarf of disintegration" (FC, p. 63):

In short there ought to be no such thing as Fate. As long as we use this word, it is a sign of our impotence & that we are not yet ourselves. There is now a sublime revelation in each of us which makes us so strangely aware & certain of our riches that although I have never since I was born for so much as one moment expressed the truth, and although I have never heard the expression of it from any other, I know that the whole is here,—the wealth of the Universe is for me. Every thing is explicable & practicable for me. And yet whilst I adore this ineffable life which is at my heart, it will not condescend to gossip with me, it will not announce to me any particulars of science, it will not enter into the details of my biography, & say to me why I have a son & daughters born to me, or why my son dies in his sixth year of joy. Herein then I have this latent omniscience coexistent with omni-ignorance. Moreover, whilst this deity glows at the heart, & by his unlimited presentiments gives me all Power, I know that tomorrow will be as this day, I am a dwarf, & I remain a dwarf. That is to say, I believe in Fate. As long as I am weak, I shall talk of Fate; whenever the God fills me with his fulness, I shall see the disappearance of Fate.

I am *Defeated* all the time; yet to Victory I am born.[10]

If the Emerson who chants oracularly of visionary victory snatched from the laws of fated defeat is the only Emerson who intrigues Bloom, then the Whitman he wants and needs is, on the other hand, the anguished poet of visionary loss and imaginative despair whom we see in "As I Ebb'd with the Ocean of Life"—*not* the more prevalent and popular Whitman of *Song of Myself* and many other poems in *Leaves of Grass*. Whitman-in-the-affirmative, the multitudinous and all-embracing "Walt," does receive a sympathetic and discerning analysis in *Poetry and Repression*, where *Song of Myself* is adjudged to present "the most awesome repression in our literature" (of Emerson, of course), and "the greatest instance yet of the American Sublime" (PR, p. 259). But the Whitman closest to Bloom's temperament is the subdued seer who walks the shore of the Atlantic, musing upon his soul's wreck:

As I wend to the shores I know not,
As I list to the dirge, the voices of men and women wreck'd,
As I inhale the impalpable breezes that set in upon me,
As the ocean so mysterious rolls toward me closer and closer,
I too but signify at the utmost a little wash'd-up drift,
A few sands and dead leaves to gather,
Gather, and merge myself as part of the sands and drift.

O baffled, balk'd, bent to the very earth,
Oppress'd with myself that I have dared to open my mouth,
Aware now that amid all that blab whose echoes recoil upon me
    I have not once had the least idea who or what I am,
But that before all my arrogant poems the real Me stands yet
    untouch'd, untold, altogether unreach'd,

Withdrawn far, mocking me with mock-congratulatory signs and
   bows,
With peals of distant ironical laughter at every word I have
   written,
Pointing in silence to these songs, and then to the sand beneath.

I perceive I have not really understood any thing, not a single
   object, and that no man ever can,
Nature here in sight of the sea taking advantage of me to dart
   upon me and sting me,
Because I have dared to open my mouth to sing at all.[11]

This famous second section of the poem, enacting a *kenosis*,
a "defense of undoing the poetic self" which "is more direct than
anywhere else in the language" (MM, p. 181), is a microcosm of the
achievement of the poem as a whole; in fact, the *whole* poem for
Bloom "is remarkable as a version of *kenosis*, of Whitman undoing
the Whitmanian bardic self of *Song of Myself*" (p. 180), and thus of
Whitman undoing the source of that bardic self, his father and adversary, Emerson. But, of course, with Whitman as with Emerson
there is always victory in defeat—and Bloom, in a detailed and difficult treatment in *A Map of Misreading*, sees in the final stanza of "As
I Ebb'd" a quietly persistent Whitman succeeding in tempering his
visionary father's fabled optimism with the chastened knowledge
that the "sobbing dirge of Nature" (l. 67), the visionary ebb rather
than the Orphic flow, can also define us in our moments of imaginative need.

   Without engaging the intricacies of Bloom's many revisionary
analogues, we can see clearly enough the point that he is making
with his opposition of Emerson and Whitman, for the point is, in
fact, predictable in light of our exegesis in chapter 3. Emerson,
in what is to Bloom his central incarnation as a poet of shamanistic
frenzy, provides the "thesis" within "the historical dialectic of
American Romantic poetry," to which Whitman, in his "tragic"
mode, provides the "authentic antithesis" (RT, p. 226). Emerson as
the father of the visionary strain in American poetry initiates an internalized Orphic drama, a drama in which all subsequent major
poets must participate as they seek the divinity or liberating godlike
priority that would counter the ravages of time and save them for
the true life of unfettered poetic vision. They must all, however,
finally fail in this quest, since even to seek such creative influx is to
return inevitably to that visionary origin (that is, the scene of instruction) that contains the seeds of all the quest's possible mean-

ings. The paradox of poetical character sketched in chapter 3, with its illusory godlike freedom masking a fundamental visionary imprisonment, is once again worked out in the dialectic of American poetry; what is different—and the source of Bloom's pronounced preference for American wars of influence since 1850 over the English—is the ferocity of Orphic passion with which American poets, afflicted by an especially acute psychology of belatedness, aspire to godhood, and necessarily then, too, the unparalleled ferocity and the savagery with which they struggle to "rebeget" themselves at the expense of the Orphic fathers who remain always prior to them in the darkness of poetic origins.

II

And so we come to Wallace Stevens, the "largest" of the "Orphic inheritors in modern American poetry" (FC, p. 84). It seems rather odd to speak about the Orphic passion of a poet who has appeared to many of his critics to be an elegant, even detached, ironist of the austere fictions of our imaginative lives; so too did it seem odd to speak of the echo chamber that is Emerson as a fatherless father, a cause of himself. Yet such polemical audacity is at the heart of the revision of American literary history being attempted by Bloom, an enterprise whose main emphasis, since the publication of *Figures of Capable Imagination* in 1976, has been on securing for Stevens, and for A. R. Ammons and John Ashbery after him, their rightful places of preeminence within an Emersonian and Whitmanian tradition pertinent to their work. Nowhere is Bloom's adversary relation to the body of received critical opinion more pronounced than in his treatment of Wallace Stevens as "the authentic twentieth-century poet of the Sublime" (PR, p. 282), as "uniquely the twentieth century poet of that solitary and inward glory we can none of us share with others" (FC, p. 109). Dismissing most academic criticism of Stevens as inept and beside the point—that is, "weak"—Bloom enacts his own self-conscious *clinamen* away from a stultifying critical tradition by identifying as Stevens's greatest work the poems of his later years and by observing of these major poems, especially the triad, "Notes toward a Supreme Fiction," "The Auroras of Autumn," and "An Ordinary Evening in New Haven," that they are "themselves more advanced *as interpretation* than our criticism as yet has gotten to be" (WS, p. 168).

The Wallace Stevens favored by Harold Bloom, then, is not the
sensuous and witty Stevens of *Harmonium*, but the more difficult
and elliptical Stevens of the later and longer poems. For an especially sensitive expression of the traditional view of Stevens against
which Bloom is responding, we might turn to Randall Jarrell, who
admired the lush imagery and the sensuous tones and timbres of
the meditative sensibility in *Harmonium* but was disappointed
enough with *The Auroras of Autumn* in 1950 to complain, "As one
reads Stevens' later poetry one keeps thinking that he needs to be
possessed by subjects, to be shaken out of himself, to have his subject individualize his poem; one remembers longingly how much
more individuation there was in *Harmonium*." Jarrell's conclusion
—"the habit of philosophizing in poetry—or of seeming to philoso-
phize, of using a philosophical tone, images, constructions, of having quasi-philosophical daydreams—has been unfortunate for
Stevens"[12]—represents the conclusion of many readers of poetry
from the thirties through the early sixties, as they tried to unravel
the aberrant ambiguities of the later Stevensian vision, often with
the inappropriate exegetical tools of the New Criticism. Perhaps the
first major break in this tradition of what Bloom perceives as genteel
misunderstanding of Stevens came in 1961 with the publication of
Roy Harvey Pearce's *The Continuity of American Poetry*. To those
who had complained of the abstractness and the desiccation of the
later "philosophical" Stevens, Pearce answered with the argument
that Stevens, unlike Eliot, was compelled to write in an "egocentric
tradition" that, in effect, denied itself as tradition, and that, because
it was egocentric, forced the poet as an "ultimate Adam" to justify
the demarcations of his poetry without having recourse to the a priori guides of religion, history, and culture, which Eliot and the other
"mythic" poets were privileged to use.[13] If the later poems of Stevens, as "elaborate apologies for poetry," sometimes escape the
bounds of poetry altogether, if in "looking so compulsively toward
the decreative, they fail to be creative, fail to sustain themselves as
self-contained works of art," nonetheless, Pearce asserts, in a curious tone mixing one part wistful concession with an equal part con-
tentious approval, "we must attend closely" to them, to the wisdom
achieved by their passage "beyond poetry" into that exalted region
that Emerson foresaw as the meeting ground of poet, philosopher,
and priest. In Pearce's view, then, Stevens's mature poetry is valuable precisely because it *is* philosophical, because it does present
"ideas"—ideas about poetry, ideas about order—which "demand
of us . . . that we absolutely believe or disbelieve in them"; Stevens is

thus rescued from his detractors by the elegantly direct expedient of celebrating, albeit with grave qualifications, what they had typically lamented.

While it is predictable that Bloom's reading of Stevens as the foremost modern ephebe of Emerson and Whitman would routinely dismiss Jarrell, it is perhaps surprising, at least at first glance, that his reading also dismisses the type of approval of Stevens represented by Pearce. In Bloom's view, Stevens is not what either his detractors *or* his admirers have claimed him to be. The Stevens of *Harmonium* is not a Symbolist, a dilettante, a painter *manqué*, or any other kind of Frenchman-in-disguise; "French colorings in Stevens," Bloom observes, "invariably are evasions of more embarrassing obligations to Anglo-American literary tradition" (WS, p. 51). More important, Stevens beyond *Harmonium* is neither the "desiccated and mock-philosophical" poet lamented by Jarrell (FC, p. 104) nor the profound metaphysician of the Adamic imagination celebrated by Pearce. To present either view of Stevens is, for Bloom, to endorse a theory of poetry that effectively denies the power and integrity of the creative poetic act. Strong poets, Bloom never tires of asserting, write poetry, not philosophy, and Stevens is for him the strongest poet of the twentieth century. Stevens then also cannot be the essentially comic poet that other critics have described;[14] the good humor, acceptance, and final serenity that mark comic modes of perception can only guarantee premature poetic demise in the belated and increasingly baleful poetic cosmos envisioned by Bloom. The poetry of Wallace Stevens belongs fully to just such a world, Bloom contends, for Stevens, early or late, is above all the poet of "the solitude at our center" (FC, p. 109) where we feel ourselves to be "mortal gods," not only unable but *unwilling* to reduce our solipsistic glory by finding "companionship in one another" (p. 119).

Of course, we have characterized so far only a part of the context for Bloom's response to other critics of Stevens. In the years since the publication of *The Continuity of American Poetry*, a huge Stevens industry has developed. As the Age of Eliot and of monolithic Modernism has waned, the countering Age of Stevens has been erected, codified, and often fashioned into constricting dogma. Bloom's work on Wallace Stevens falls within this new age insofar as it too celebrates Stevens at the expense of Eliotic orthodoxies and sees in Stevens's poetry of the imagination and reality a fit emblem for the obsessions of our time. Yet Bloom's reading of Stevens over a seventeen-year period, from the essays in *The Ringers in the Tower* which originally appeared in 1965 through the massive *Wallace Stevens* of 1977 to the supplementary comments of *Agon* and *The Breaking of the Vessels* in 1982 departs from other powerful recent commentaries on the poet in a fashion so self-conscious and so extreme that we might profitably use it as a cutting edge to help define Bloom's whole enterprise as a "belated" critical prophet of influence.

Basically, and at risk of oversimplification, post-Modernist readings have taken two related forms, both based upon a repudiation of the view of Stevens as a sort of philosopher-in-verse which, for good or ill, had influenced the reception of his work for much of this century. The first, brilliantly represented by Helen Vendler in *On Extended Wings*, seeks to examine closely the language of Stevens's manifold hesitancies and qualifications,[15] and finds in that language the ironies of a poet whose vision tends toward the minimalist extreme of the "total leaflessness"[16] seen by an old man in an ordinary evening amid the world's poverty of New Haven. Such a Stevens is a master of the bare minima of what we—our minds and the rock of our lives—are, transmuting the austerities and "dilapidations" (CP, p. 476) of imagination's reality into a sophisticated protean rhetoric of what will suffice. The second Stevens, the Stevens of J. Hillis Miller in his phenomenological *Poets of Reality* and of Miller and several others in the deconstructionist readings of the seventies, shares with the first a preoccupation with the metamorphic flux of Stevens's rhetoric, but goes beyond the first in identifying that flux with the virtual nihilism of either consciousness or language in "decreation," returning always upon the origins of utterance in search of a Being that, as the logic of deconstruction ultimately would have it, is available only as an abyss promising the richness of other and endless abysses. In this view, Stevens, with his remarkably persistent equivocations and improvisations, becomes the presiding American master of the problematics of poetic origins as those problems and their fertile nonsolutions have been elucidated in recent years by a host of theorists gifted in the difficult ascetic arts of Derridean linguistic play.[17]

I shall examine the revealing quarrel between Bloom and the school of deconstruction in chapter 6. For the moment it is important only to note that Bloom's dispute with the Vendler and Miller readings of Stevens is at heart a dispute over how to read poetry —over, that is, the value and the use of poetry in our time. If Bloom repudiates the Pearce position on the grounds that poetry is demeaned when read in a naïvely straightforward manner as philosophy, he counters Vendler and Miller, opponents whom he regards as much more formidable, on the grounds that poetry also is undermined when viewed as entirely an exercise in reductive ironizing, or as an enterprise that relinquishes all truth-claims whatsoever through the force of its self-consuming rhetoric. Whether the ironies of poetry feature the careful crafting of perspectives of reference—thirteen ways of looking at a blackbird—or whether they be the virtuoso ironies of the prisonhouse of language-bound rhetoric, to limit poetry solely to their world of hesitancies and qualifications is for Bloom to condemn the imagination to the endless relational regress that we have seen him associate with all the revisionary movements of limitation, but most strongly with the metaphoric confusions of the final limiting ratio, *askesis*. The country of mere perspectives is no country for visionary men, Bloom warns; the imagination in search of its proper glory cannot long abide in a region where it feels itself abased before either the dull, inert dross of reality or the frustrating, elusive absences of its figurations apart from that reality.

Bloom's obvious problem in making his case for the redemptive Emersonian humanism of Stevens is that Stevens's poetry seems to be pervaded by exactly the sort of qualifications that should, in Bloom's schema, rob it of its visionary authority. Indeed, in *The Anxiety of Influence* Bloom is moved to label the sum of Stevens's poetry "an *askesis* of the entire Romantic tradition" (p. 135)—an observation that, were it abstracted from the idiom of Bloom's dramatic Freudian agon, might very well amount to saying what Vendler and Miller, in their own ways, have so often asserted: that Stevens, as the most distinctive modern poet of our being in "a place / That is not our own" (CP, p. 383), leaves us with many more qualifications than he does visionary assertions. Bloom's dialogue with Vendler and Miller in his many essays on Stevens is characterized by this curious tactic of conceding what finally, by virtue of his Freudian and his Orphic paradigms, he will not allow to be lost. Thus, we are told that Stevens, or, rather, that "the Idiot Questioner in Stevens" (FC, p. 108), "developed a tendency to speak more reductively than he himself could bear to accept," but the reductions are redeemed, at least partially, when we learn that they are the issue of the anxiety of influence, which "malformed" Stevens's "primary passion," the "Orphic aspiration of Emerson and Whitman, the quest for an American Sublime" (AI, p. 134). We are told that Stevens *does* feature "endless ironies" (RT, p. 220), that he does "endlessly" qualify "his sense of his own greatness" (FC, p. 113), but that nonetheless "he still endlessly returns" us to just such a sublime and near-solipsistic sense. We are told that, despite "the constant irony of diction and syntax" in Stevens's poetry "as well as the more obvious irony of Stevens's personae and of his imagery," his rhetoric delivers affirmations that *are* visionary, that not only survive, but prevail over their manifold qualifications. "A qualified assertion remains an assertion," Bloom instructs in *The Ringers in the Tower*, responding specifically to Vendler and Miller; "it is *not* an asserted qualification" (p. 228). "There is indeed a Stevens" as seen by his two prominent critical adversaries, Bloom acknowledges, a Stevens who is "a venerable ironist" and a poet "of a cyclic near-nihilism returning always upon itself" (FC, p. 110). But these are "aspects only," he goes on to affirm, "darker saliences that surround the central man, shadows flickering beyond that crucial light cast by the single candle of Stevens' self-joying imagination."

From the standpoint of the Bloomian logic of canonization that we sketched earlier, Bloom's determination "to follow Stevens in the difficult task of rescuing him and ourselves from his and our own ironies" is a sign of his own strong desire to appropriate—that is, to canonize—a somewhat recalcitrant poet by using the only method that Bloom himself thinks to be available to a critic this late in Romantic tradition: that most cunning of revisionary ratios, transumption. A metaleptic troping of Stevens's own tropes battles the adversary, time, to an uneasy stand-off by casting the unsettlingly pervasive ironies of the Stevens canon into a new and restorative light, which is really the old light of the Romantic sublime as that sublime in turn has its source in the deeper daemonic grounds of Emersonian tradition. Such is the complicated formula for Bloom's canonization of Stevens in his several studies of that poet since 1965, studies that, not surprisingly, present many and serious obstacles to the reader untutored in the mature Bloomian terminology and critical method. In particular, readers of *Wallace Stevens* who approach that volume with no background in Bloom's theory or who are interested only in quick illumination on individual poems will find that the exegesis of Stevens granted Bloom by the "strength" of his critical principles and paradigms is an especially arduous and elliptical one, often more difficult and self-referential than the poetic corpus it seeks to explain. If Bloom's analysis of Emerson suffers from the logical conundrum of the founding father's own singularly fatherless state, then his examination of Stevens's poetry as "an *askesis* of the entire Romantic tradition" must confront a patrimonial embarrassment, a plethora of fathers that includes not only the central American patriarchs, Emerson and

Whitman, but all the other beloved Romantics of Bloom's past, Blake, Shelley, Wordsworth, and Keats.

Wallace Stevens presents the same sort of difficulty that we saw Robert Preyer note in *The Visionary Company*, only now the difficulty is amplified, perhaps at times to a state beyond the bounds of intelligibility, by the increasing sweep of the literary history that Bloom endeavors to tell, and by the increasing theoretical resourcefulness of his elaboration of an intricate map out of the logic of Romantic revisionism. Even Bloom himself is impelled to acknowledge, in the midst of one especially forbidding early disquisition, that his "multiplication of terms is more than a little maddening" (p. 4); the volume as a whole represents, in fact, an apex of Bloom's analogizing sensibility, of his ability (recalling Preyer's words) to "throw down on the page hot slabs of melded relationships rather than paragraphs." Since the meld of relationships that Bloom is trying definitively to establish in this most ambitious of his studies is the complex family romance of American Orphism as that tradition finds its modern locus in Stevens, we must return to Emerson for a moment as a necessary preliminary to the thorny matter of his poetic descendant.

The crucial first and last chapters in *Wallace Stevens*, "American Poetic Stances: Emerson to Stevens" and "Coda: Poetic Crossing," rename much of what we have already discussed in Emersonian Orphism, and thereby establish the conceptual basis for a framework of almost programmatic equations that Bloom uses to connect the works of Emerson, Whitman, and Stevens in the middle chapters of the volume. The situation that Bloom needs to explain in one sense is fairly simple: his great Orphic yea-sayer and prophet of the central man, Emerson, is, at other times and in other moods, the chastened proponent of a reconciliation with things-as-they-are who denies the visionary impulse and seeks to make a dishonorable peace with the cruel laws of experience and fate. As early as *The Ringers in the Tower*, with its important essay, "Bacchus and Merlin: The Dialectic of Romantic Poetry in America," Bloom had attempted to map the many moods of Emerson, seeing the two key poems of Emerson's collection of 1846, "Bacchus" and "Merlin," as visionary poles staking out the contours not only of Emerson's work but also of the entire tradition to which he is father. According to Bloom, "Bacchus" is the great chant of the central Orphic in Emerson, a frenzied gnomic appeal "for a renovation as absolute as Blake's vision sought," a renovation that would "free man from his own ruins, and restore him as the being Blake called Tharmas, instinctual innocence triumphantly at home in his own place" (RT, p. 301). "Merlin," on the other hand, represents Emerson's departure from "Blakean affinities when, in his extraordinary impatience, most fatedly American of qualities, he seeks terms with his Reality Principle only by subsuming it." The Emersonian worship of Merlin, whose "blows are strokes of fate" (EW, 9:120), signals for Bloom the dark side of American poetic vision, the "American poetic disaster" wherein the poet is duped by a "Muse" who masks herself "as Necessity" (RT, pp. 302 – 3).

In the essays on American Orphism in *Figures of Capable Imagination*, Bloom designates presiding deities for this dialectic of Bacchus and Merlin. Eros is the latent divinity within us, the godhood at our origins "who brings us our souls by literal inspiration, by prevailing winds" (p. 81). To reach this "Time's firstborn," however, "we need" the "Dionysiac enthusiasm" invoked by Emerson in his central Orphic mood, the "influx" or frenzy that can propel us into vision. When influx fails us—and fail it must, as the generally downward curve of Emerson's own career as a prophet suggests—"when we are left with only the sinful Titanic elements in ourselves, then truly we fall into Time, and finally into Hades." In the "intervals left" to us as "failed Orphics," Bloom concludes, "our religious sense grants us visions of only one deity: Ananke," or the "bodiless" serpent (Stevens, CP, p. 411) of necessity and of death whose formless figure quite appropriately looms before Stevens in "The Auroras of Autumn," an aging poet at the end of tradition.

The intricate mythography of the opening chapter of *Wallace Stevens* performs four important operations. First, it explicitly and elaborately correlates the dialectic of Bacchus and Merlin and its accompanying Orphic deities with the rhythm of Lurianic creation presented by Bloom in *A Map of Misreading*, *Kabbalah and Criticism*, and *Poetry and Repression*. Bloom's favorite Emerson, the Emerson of "Bacchus" and of the exuberant moments in "Nature," "Circles," and "The Poet," is now called a prophet of visionary restoration-through-substitution. Eros is now aligned with the restitution of the second, fourth, and sixth revisionary ratios in the map of misreading, while Dionysius becomes the deity of that breaking-of-the-vessels that marks divine creative influx. The Emerson who frightens and appalls Bloom, the subdued seer who so often invokes, in essays such as "Experience" and "Fate," the dread serpent Ananke, the reality principle that Emerson as Merlin calls "Justice" and "the rhyme of things" (EW, 9:124), is now identified with the ratios of limitation or contraction, the initiating *clinamen*, *kenosis*, and *askesis*.

This first operation marks a significant expansion in Bloom's use of the Lurianic theory of creation. If previously it had been employed largely as a barometer of the revisionary rhythm of given *poems* in the tradition of the Romantic crisis lyric, now its paradigmatic power is generalized to apply to visionary development over entire careers and to the structure of the visionary psyche at any point within a career. While both these applications were implicit in Bloom's earlier theorizing on the anxiety of influence and had occasionally been broached by him, his use of them in *Wallace Stevens* to chart not only the Emersonian psyche and career but also then the entire visionary mode that is Emersonian tradition, is much more precise and fully realized than it had ever been before, indicating the seriousness of Bloom's desire to construct a thoroughgoing rhetoric of Romanticism in which the synchronic is completely subsumed by the diachronic, in which the timeless forms of vision manifest on any level of poem, psyche, or career, are revealed finally to be engendered by the temporal struggles of revisioning that combined constitute tradition.

The second operation in *Wallace Stevens* involves imposing yet another paradigm upon the mixed kabbalistic-Freudian-Emersonian-Orphic model already established. As part of his effort to deliver a complete rhetoric of the Romantic vision, Bloom now attempts to tie the tropology of the Romantic crisis poem to the traditional appeals and topics of Aristotelian and Ciceronian rhetorical theory. He aligns his own terminology for describing the visionary strife in the Romantic crisis poem, psyche, and career, with the conventional language of the rhetorician who speaks of the appeals of *logos, ethos,* and *pathos* in an oration, and of the commonplaces, or *topoi,* which that oration employs. As usual, little is to be learned by comparing Bloom to his originals; his "misreading" of Aristotle and Cicero is characteristically deliberate and audacious. *Ethos,* used by Aristotle to describe the "character" of the orator as he presents himself to an audience,[18] is translated by Bloom, via a complicated analysis of the role of recollection in Wordsworth, into "the spirit of place revealing its character, with or without incident, through images of voice" (WS, p. 383).[19] Since, in Bloom's reading, the spirit of natural place in Wordsworth serves as "a contraction or withdrawal of meaning, that opens the way for a rethinking that is necessarily a remeaning" (p. 385), then *ethos* might be said, "in more Freudian terms," to result from that "successful translation of the will into an act" (p. 382), which Bloom already has offered as definition for the revisionary ratios of limitation. And if *"ethos* or character or natural action is converted into a poet's fate,'' then necessarily, by the logic of Luria, there will follow the "re-cognition" or breaking-of-the-vessels of fate which signifies "imaginative freedom,'' and this leap, in turn, will allow the restitution of meaning now called by Bloom "the power of self-recognition" and "the ultimate *pathos* of wonder" (p. 385). *Pathos*, used in traditional rhetoric to denote the arousing of transient emotions in the audience by the orator, becomes for Bloom the power of the poetic psyche in its representations of what, after all, cannot be represented: pure vision. And *logos*, often translated in traditional rhetoric as "logic" but encompassing all the means of representing the proof proper of an argument, is, in Bloom's rhetoric of Romanticism, the gap between the two modes of poetical thinking where the psyche breaks from one type of figuration to another.

If this were all Bloom hoped to accomplish with his introduction of the terms of traditional rhetoric into his map of misreading, we would certainly be justified in regarding it as one of his weakest discussions—a strained and entirely nugatory elaboration of terminology for terminology's own sake. But Bloom is maneuvering into position to present one of the most charged concepts of his career, a concept that might be regarded as delivering a culmination of several of the central strains of his theorizing over the last twenty years on the nature of poetic meaning. For Bloom's appropriation of the *ethos-logos-pathos* paradigm is inextricably bound to his redefinition of the Aristotelian and Ciceronian *topos*, or topic, a redefinition that allows him to assess more fully the nature of the process of substitution or breaking-of-the-vessels that has figured prominently in his work since the publication of *A Map of Misreading* in 1975. For Aristotle, a *topos* is a commonplace or line of argument—a conceptual place where arguments, either universal or particular, may be found. For Bloom, again pondering the relation between memory and voice in Wordsworth, a *topos* is conceived as "not so much a commonplace or a memory place as more nearly *the place of a voice*, the place from which the voice of the dead breaks through" (WS, p. 399). "Hence," Bloom says, "a *topos* is an image of voice or of speech, or the place where such an image is stored." These places can be charted, of course, and Bloom goes on to incorporate sixteen classical *topoi* into his map of misreading, citing as most important those topics of representation—definition and division, comparison, and temporal effect-and-cause—that may be associated with synecdoche, hyperbole, and metalepsis, respectively.

Even more salient than this marshaling of *topoi* is what Bloom does with the leap *between* the places and the figures of poetry, for it is here, in this nomad's land between the contractions and the restorations of desire, that Bloom finally locates the "meaning" of a poem, or a psyche, or a career. This meaning or *logos* he now calls a "Crossing"; the three crossings in the rhythm of Romantic creation are labeled crisis points of election, solipsism, and identification, respectively.[20] The crossing of election in a poem occurs between the ratios of *clinamen* and *tessera*. In it the aspiring poet confronts "the death of the creative gift," and seeks an answer to the crucial question, "Am I still a poet, or, perhaps, am I truly a poet?" (WS, p. 403). The crisis of solipsism moves between the reductions of *kenosis* and the great expansion of the Romantic sublime, as the poet "struggles with the death of love, and tries to answer the fearful query Am I capable of loving another besides myself?" The final crisis of identification, addressing the "dilemma" of "death" itself, chooses introjection over the weaker psychic defense of sublimation, and thereby identifies so strongly "with something or someone outside the self that time seems to stand still or to roll back or forward." All three crossings indicate a movement from "mimetic" to "expressive" modes of representation, Bloom says (p. 404), using the language of M. H. Abrams to authorize his own passage beyond the subject-object dualisms of Romanticism as seen by the author of *The Mirror and the Lamp*. Each of the three crossings also then marks "an even greater degree of internalization of the self," as the poet moves from striving to correct or complete the dead to an attempt at repressing them, and finally to the match proper over the laurels of time.

Why is this theory of the crossing so important? And what explanatory power does it have when applied to Emerson and Stevens? The concept of the crossing accomplishes several crucial tasks for Bloom. First, it helps to make sense of the conflicting demands of writing and speech in poetry. Bloom's theory of poetic vision has always valued "eloquence, the inspired voice" (MM, p. 176), over the figures of writing, a predisposition evident in Bloom's own perhaps excessive use of the orotund tonalities of prophecy. The logical problem that then presents itself—that poetry typically exists as figures on a page—is now ameliorated by the importation of the *topoi* into poetic "argument," and by Bloom's oxymoronic definition of these topics as *images* of the *voice* of the dead. The *logos* of the crossing, the "dynamism of the substituting process . . . which tells us that meaning in a poem is itself liminal, transgressive, a breaking as much as a making" (WS, p. 401), necessarily then is "tropological *and* topological"; as such, it is "always a crisis because it is a kind of judgment or criticism between images of voice and between the different kinds of figurative thinking that opposed topics generate" (p. 399).

The consequent definition of poetry as "a debate between voicing and writing, an endless crossing between topics *or* tropes, but also an endless shuttling between topics and tropes" (p. 401),[21] subtly expands long-standing Bloomian conceptions of the nature of poetic "argument" and poetic vision by first conceding the quiddity of the tropes of language, but by then identifying the ruling or generating essence of vision as those *topoi* whose power as voices of the dead sets into motion the patternings of the poem and the poetic psyche. "Crossing" is an especially apt term for the creation-by-catastrophe of poetic meaning insofar as it reminds us within this appropriately American context of one of the key lessons of chapter 3, the lesson of Bloom's kabbalistic and Gnostic paradigms that all poetic meaning is at the same time a quest *and* a wandering *in exile* from a visionary godhood which, since it can never exist in language, can be incarnated by humankind only through the spiritual forms of frustrated desire burdening the belated visionary psyche. A crossing in ordinary usage is an attempt to get somewhere, often at great peril and against great odds; in Bloom, that somewhere is the origins of tradition, and since those origins can no more fully be recaptured—that is, remade in one's image or voice—than they can ever finally be escaped, the quest is doomed from the start, its only possible victory the perilous triumph of *continuing to achieve* the anxiety necessary to cross again.

It is precisely because the crossing is such a strong emblem—at once capacious and appropriately dramatic—of Bloomian preoccupations that it serves him so well as a tool for investigating the tradition that Emerson inaugurates and Stevens massively redefines. For the idea of a crossing, like the rest of Bloom's terminology in this latest stage of his work, is applicable not only to specific poems but to the structure of a psyche, a career, and indeed an entire tradition. Bloom's last major operation, then, in the crucial opening and closing chapters of *Wallace Stevens* is to chart the psyche and the career of Emerson in a far more elaborate way than his previous master terms, "Bacchus" and "Merlin," would allow, and to map the dialectical rhythm of the crossings in Emerson's work as a basis for establishing the visionary contours of Stevens's own poetry. Emerson, as the greatest American prophet of the "stubbornly . . . logocentric" voice of vision (MM, p. 176), reveals through his dialectic of limitation-substitution-restoration the movement of imaginative need to imaginative re-creation which Bloom says is central to Stevens. If the most famous "crossing" in Emerson's work is that on the "bare" and wintry "common" (CW, 1:10), which yields the Dionysiac rhapsody of the "transparent eye-ball," then perhaps the deepest Emersonian wisdom about the nature of the intensely private vision thereby gained is delivered in an essay much bleaker than the blithe "Nature," the rumination of the early forties called "Experience." Bloom does not deny the very real skepticism in "Experience," but sees Emerson's "power over us" in this "grandest" of his essays (MM, p. 169) to reside in the "astonishing recovery from skepticism that suddenly illuminates" the anguished oracle late in his meditation (p. 171): "And we cannot say too little of our constitutional necessity of seeing things under private aspects, or saturated with our humors. And yet is the God the native of these bleak rocks. . . . We must hold hard to this poverty, however scandalous, and by more vigorous self-recoveries, after the sallies of action, possess our axis more firmly" (EW, 3:81).

The crucial term for Bloom in this passage is "poverty," which he says is "one of the most dialectical of tropes" in Emerson (WS, p. 9) in that it signifies "imaginative need" while at the same time establishing the dynamic for that imaginative re-conception that is poetic power and vision. In other words, "poverty" is the Emersonian master trope for limitation, for that Ananke that, in the form of fate or necessity, Emerson sometimes worships. The temptation "to join" the "natural process" that one has "failed to assert his power over" is great, Bloom acknowledges (p. 10). But the seduction of cyclic process can be mastered through influx, which redresses imaginative need by crossing into a realm that *seems* momentarily beyond the stultifying imperatives of all that is merely natural within and around us. According to Bloom, the key word in Emerson for such visionary moments is "surprise," which connotes the proper Orphic ecstasy at feeling temporarily free of the ties of anteriority.[22] "Surprise" is only one term, however, from an almost embarrassing bounty of terminological counters staking out the lines of Emersonian vision in Bloom's most elaborate map. The remarkable tissue of correspondences and equivalences offered by Bloom in *Wallace Stevens* as a synoptic representation of Emerson's life and poetic vision displays in especially graphic form the final logic of Bloom's historicism, a logic that, despite its diachronic trappings, is directly opposed to conventional notions of history and psychobiography. Here is the "full list" for Emerson as "father of us all," a list that we are justified in seeing as a sort of echo chamber of most of Bloom's own ideas, themes, and values as he has elucidated them in his work since *Shelley's Mythmaking* in 1959:

> *Ethos*: Fate, Destiny, Necessity, Fortune, Race, Powerlessness, Experience, Limitation, and Nature, but Nature only in its most alienated or estranged aspect. *Logos*: Freedom, Wildness, Nature (in its humanized or redeemed aspect), Vocation, Temperament, Self-Reliance, Solitude, Reason, Transcendentalism, Thought, Subjectiveness, Wholeness. *Pathos*: Power, Potential, Will, Vitality, God, Greatness, Salvation, Vital Force, Victory, Inspiration, Surprise, Mastery, Ecstasy. (P. 5)

When we add to this list the Gnostic terminology of *Agon* and *The Breaking of the Vessels*, with the new dialectical counters negation, evasion, and extravagance, and when we remember that the apparently still expanding roster is meant to serve not only as a description of Emerson, but as a skeletal summary of the entire tradition of American Romantic poetics culminating a hundred years later in Emerson's visionary heir, Wallace Stevens, we can see that Bloom's "history" of American poetry, like his previous history of the visionary company, does not constitute history—"diachrony"—as we commonly speak of it, but, rather, represents an especially thoroughgoing *Romantic geometry*, a temporal unfolding of essentialized Romantic principles that have been formulated a priori by the critic and that are seen by him to individuate themselves in quite predictable patterns over the span of our culture's poetic history. Bloom's interest does not focus, in the manner of the orthodox historical critic, on the meeting of local quiddities of language, culture, and personal experience in the imagination of the poet; rather, for Bloom, as we have seen time and again, the imagination exists only in the depths of its internalized relations to itself—exists, that is, only as *what remains* after all the local accidents of personality, language, and culture have been burned away.

III

It is this conception of the creative moment as an essentially timeless incarnation of deep Romantic *topoi* that allows Bloom to furnish a central formula for all American poetry, a formula not only for the individual "strong" poems of American poetic history, but for all the psyches and careers that comprise that history. "Emerson wanted Freedom, reconciled himself to Fate, but loved only Power, from first to last," Bloom asserts, "and I believe this to be true also of the central line of American poets coming after him" (WS, p. 8). In the remaining few pages of this chapter, I would like to examine Harold Bloom's canonization of Wallace Stevens according to this formula, a canonization that is notable for the fearfully symmetric network of analogies, correspondences, and visionary parallels that it establishes between two poets a century apart in order to save the authentic if diminished American Romantic humanism represented by the later writer. To begin with, Stevens's career divides fairly neatly for Bloom into the three crossings of poetic vision, with the crisis of election falling in 1915 when Stevens wrote his first strong poems, the crisis of solipsism coming to a crux in 1921 — 22 but not resolving itself until 1934 — 36, and the crossing of identification occurring in 1942 and determining the vision of Stevens's poetry for the last thirteen years of his life. We have noted earlier that Bloom does not value the poems of *Harmonium* as highly as he does those of the older poet's confrontation with mortality in the final phase initiated by "Notes toward a Supreme Fiction" in 1942. Since the early edition of *Harmonium*, which covered poems written from 1915 to 1923, represents not only the complete negotiation of the first crossing in Stevens's career but also a crux of the second, we might very well ask: What has been crossed in the earlier poems, and what remains for the later period to resolve?

Bloom's handling of this question is a key to his entire discussion of Stevens, and, as we might expect, it involves yet another transformation of terms, this one from the Emersonian dialectic of fate, freedom, and power to Stevens's paradigm for the first idea. Emersonian fate becomes in Stevens the "metonymic reduction" of the first idea itself; Emerson's Transcendental freedom becomes the later poet's "refusal to bear so dehumanizing a reduction"; power or will in Stevens's "mature poetry is the reimagining of a First Idea," with the fruits of pleasure that only such a supremely reimagined fiction can give (WS, p. 27). For Bloom, there is an "impasse" at the end of Stevens's luxuriant "poetry of earth" in "Sunday Morning" and "Peter Quince at the Clavier," a "dilemma" (p. 47) that the poems of the crisis years, 1921 — 22, must confront. Stevens has found his muse, but she presents herself to him as both "mother and fatal woman," and he must answer this confusion by turning for the first time to those metonymic reductions of the spirit and the place that were to engage his vision for the rest of his life. Although Stevens himself does not introduce the term "first idea" until the composition of "Notes toward a Supreme Fiction" twenty years later, Bloom contends that this is precisely what the poet is formulating in his important poem of 1921, "The Snow Man," and precisely what he transcends, in a manner paradigmatic for all his later poetry, in the sublime counterpart to "The Snow Man" of that same year, "Tea at the Palaz of Hoon." Between the two poems, Bloom asserts, between the reduction to the first idea in the wintry vision of the first and the reimagining of that idea through the self's compassing of the sea in the second, there lies a crossing or a freedom that is exactly the freedom of "Notes toward a Supreme Fiction," Stevens's great poem of the Emersonian and Whitmanian Orphic center, and the poem whose crossing of identification establishes the "imaginative formulations" (p. 3) for all of Stevens's great crisis poetry in his final volumes, *The Auroras of Autumn* and *The Rock*.

Bloom's concern with the poems "central" to the Stevens canon, especially with "Notes toward a Supreme Fiction," features an almost obsessive pattern of reading and rereadings. Bloom devotes twenty-one pages of explication to "Notes" in his essay of 1965 in *The Ringers in the Tower*, five more in *Poetry and Repression*, and an imposing fifty-two pages of revision of his earlier emphases in *Wallace Stevens*. "Tea at the Palaz of Hoon" receives five pages in *Wallace Stevens*, while the one sentence of "The Snow Man," already the beneficiary of a lengthy analysis in *Poetry and Repression*, is given ten pages of explanation in terms of its many precursors. Fortunately, we do not need to rehearse the exhaustive details of these discussions in order to capture the Bloomian logic of canonization operating within them. Whatever his subject may be, Emerson or Stevens, Freud or the Kabbalah, influence or vision, Bloom's message in the later phase of his career is essentially the same. The symbology and the hot slabs of influence relations that he offers by way of reading any given poem do not exist horizontally as explorations across a fluid or inductive conceptual horizon, but, rather, vertically, as self-conscious and theoretically resourceful exfoliations of the rather rigid central principles that we have seen to catalyze his work from the start.

"I think that what Blake and Wordsworth do for their readers, or can do, is closely related to what Freud does or can do for his," Bloom says in a straightforward moment at the beginning of his decade-long rumination on the anxiety of influence, and that "is to provide both a map of the mind and a profound faith that the map can be put to a saving use" (RT, p. 13). In Bloom's analysis of "The Snow Man," "Tea at the Palaz of Hoon," and "Notes toward a Supreme Fiction," the mind of the poet whom he views as the greatest of our century becomes a battleground for visionary priority within a tradition whose ruling symbols, patterns, and arguments already have been overdetermined by the great patriarchs of the century past. Thus, "The Snow Man," as "a lyric monument to belatedness" and "Stevens's most crucial poem" (PR, p. 269), presents a "bare place" and a wintry "nothing" (Stevens, CP, p. 10) which trope against the main empty place in American literature, the "bare common" of Emerson's metamorphosis into a "transparent eye-ball," by reducing the transcendent nothing of the all-seeing Emersonian sublime into the bleak metonyms of the wintry mind living amid the poverty of barest figuration. Thus, "Tea at the Palaz of Hoon," with its picture of the sea change of the poet into something "more truly and more strange" (p. 65), represents a sublime and saving transumption of the already powerful Whitman of *Song of Myself*, who chants of his ability to "encompass worlds and volumes of worlds" with the "twirl" of his tongue (WW, sec. 25, p. 213). Thus, "Notes toward a Supreme Fiction," as a powerful modern version of an earlier central man's *Song of Myself*, must be seen as a massive and appropriately exuberant fulfillment of Emersonian Orphic prophecy, a promise kept, and a world redeemed, by an "ephebe" of the visionary center whose work encompasses and clarifies an entire tradition.

Behind such a revisionary mapping of the "central" poems of our "central" poet is the Bloomian position that the first idea in Stevens's dialectic of the imagination is itself a *necessary fiction*, a swerve away from the dross of mere reality which enables the imaginative act of Stevens's poetry to begin. And if the first idea is a fiction, then necessarily, according to the immutable laws of influence, it is a fictional idea not of nature or of language but of a precursor—a precursor whose prior visionary achievement menaces the latecomer poet and determines his acts of belated vision. Bloom is well aware of the audacity of this argument when advanced within a contemporary critical tradition that has tended to follow Stevens himself in seeing a poem such as "The Snow Man" as a meditation on "reality" or "mere being" which not only forsakes but implicitly repudiates the vision at the heart of Romantic tradition. Bloom knows that if his map of Stevens is to be put to a "saving use," then at the very least it must save Stevens from himself, from pronouncements of the sort that he makes on "The Snow Man," which he cites, contra his later critic, "as an example of the necessity of identifying oneself with reality in order to understand it and enjoy it."[23] If the poem were only this, if early Stevens were authentically the poet of the nothingness of pure being that J. Hillis Miller de-

scribes in *Poets of Reality*,[24] then there would be for Bloom no possibility of saving the rest of the canon, with its magnificent assertions, "however self-qualified, of the imaginative fable of the Central
Man" (RT, p. 228). Bloom is willing to concede that Stevens at the
very last gives himself over to the "Sublime chill" (WS, p. 374) of the
abyss "Of Mere Being," albeit still as a poet of the vision that tropes
"fire-fangled feathers"[25] into transumptive power. But the first idea
of Stevens's formative vision is not and cannot be for Bloom a concession to the rock of mere desiccated and recalcitrant reality; the
Snow Man cannot be what a critic as acute as J. Hillis Miller (in his
phenomenological phase) says he is: a being totally "free of mental
fictions."[26] The first idea, however it dehumanizes, must itself be
seen as what Stevens at one point in "Notes" calls it: an "imagined
thing"; the "nothing" that the Snow Man is and that he "beholds,"
while it may be "the most minimal or abstracted of fictions," nonetheless must be a "fiction" itself (WS, p. 63). In *Poetry and Repression*, Bloom summarizes "this difficult matter in Stevens" by saying
that "the reductive act of wintry vision, the Snow Man stance, is not
imaginative in its *impulse* and yet is imaginative in its effect" (p. 287).
And the effect of the poverty or the imaginative need of the Snow
Man, Bloom goes on to say in *Wallace Stevens*, is to catalyze that
crossing into the power of the supreme fiction upon which all
strong poetry in our only tradition depends.

The "saving use" that Bloom has in mind for Stevens, the use that
will rescue the poet from his own more skeptical moods and secure
his poetry from the depredations of many of his best critics in our
skeptical time, is nowhere better stated than in the final sections of
"Notes toward a Supreme Fiction." Here Bloom sees Stevens himself, as the supreme creator of his supreme poem, vaulting over his
own creation, the Canon Aspirin, a "High Romantic fallen angel"
(WS, p. 205) whose leap into the transcendent has degenerated into
the bane of the Romantic mind, the imposition of arbitrary "orders"
and the meaningless frenzied building of "capitols" and "corridors." Against the visionary lapse of the Canon Aspirin, Stevens
poses a series of questions that are their own answers, culminating
in a question that takes him to the center of Emersonian prophecy:

> Is it I then that keep saying there is an hour
> Filled with expressible bliss, in which I have
>
> No need, am happy, forget need's golden hand,
> Am satisfied without solacing majesty,
> And if there is an hour there is a day,
>
> There is a month, a year, there is a time

In which majesty is a mirror of the self:
I have not but I am and as I am, I am.   (CP, pp. 404 – 5)

In this, in what is for Bloom the "greatest moment" of Stevens's poetry (WS, p. 206) and "the supreme achievement of post-Romanticism" (RT, p. 254), Stevens overpowers a host of visionary precursors throughout the Romantic tradition, Wordsworth as well as Emerson, Coleridge as well as Whitman, "in order to proclaim his own momentary incarnation of a supreme fiction, which will turn out not to be poetry or a poem but, as in Emerson and Whitman (and Wordsworth), to be a poet, to be a fiction of the self, or the poetic self as a transumption, an audacious trope undoing all previous tropes" (WS, p. 206). Thus, the tradition begotten by Emerson with his sublime trope of the "transparent eye-ball" which is "nothing" and yet sees "all," receives a glorious final embellishment in the proclamation of a belated Orphic seer who has "not" and who yet rebegets within himself that godlike power that is the "majesty" of the central man.

Of course, Stevens's poetry does not end with this assertive and Romantic moment; for thirteen years afterward, he continued to write other, often less confident poems, poems that confronted the auroras of autumn and the rocks of being in the bleaker moods of the poet's own encroaching mortality. In one of the most serenely chastened of these final meditations in the shadow of death, there is a passage, ushered by our mapmaker through now predictable crossings into the central sublimity of the map of misreading, which might yet have a chilling resonance that Bloom could not admit, both for the vision of Stevens within the world of its own making, and for the "saving use" to which Bloom puts his unsettlingly recalcitrant subject:

These leaves are the poem, the icon and the man.
These are a cure of the ground and of ourselves,

In the predicate that there is nothing else.   (CP, p. 527)

When *Wallace Stevens* was published in 1977 to a reception whose extremes of praise and censure fittingly fulfilled Bloom's own prescription for a critical language of hyperbolic intensity, it seemed that the real issue was whether, indeed, there *was* anything else, any way of reading Stevens beyond Bloom's own, which could "cure" the ground of our conception of this now most celebrated of modern poets, and thereby cure ourselves of the skepticism engendered by our culture's wintry post-Romantic self-reflexiveness. To a surprising extent, even critics unpersuaded by Bloom's oracular style and put off by his incessant proliferation of paradigms were moved to accept his definition of Stevens as an embattled inheritor of the Emersonian strain in American poetry. Frank Kermode, for instance, while complaining of the "horrible and ugly obstacles" presented by Bloom's excessive allusiveness, nonetheless championed Bloom's "placing" of Stevens in relation to his "great predecessors," Emerson and Whitman, as "extremely authoritative."[27] Phoebe Pettingell acclaimed Bloom's study as "the largest and most generous interpretation we have had yet" of Stevens, an interpretation—and a "contribution to poetics"—so rich that it could stand as "the greatest tribute to Stevens's inspiration."[28] It remained for the most provocative reading of Bloom's summarizing volume to be offered not by an enthusiast but by an ideological opponent, a newly converted deconstructionist whose own earlier canonical treatment of Stevens Bloom's book implicitly repudiated. I refer to Joseph Riddel, the author of *The Clairvoyant Eye* (one of the most influential studies of Stevens appearing in the sixties), who published two reviews of *Wallace Stevens*, one in the *Wallace Stevens Journal* and the other in *Diacritics*.[29] Both of these reviews argued that the real drama in Bloom's often highly dramatic rescue of Stevens from the nothingness of mere language and being resided not so much in the saving of Stevens himself as in the larger attempt to salvage an enduring meaning for the language of modern poetry, even if that meaning appeared to have as predicate only the groundless grounds of our modern linguistic faithlessness.

Dissenting from his previous explication of Stevens as a poet whose polar terms of "imagination" and "reality" participated in a "coherent" post-Kantian "system of aesthetics and philosophy," Riddel now advanced in response to Bloom the notion that Stevens, especially the late Stevens prized by Bloom, was a poet singularly preoccupied with the figurality of all language, including the deep language of Romanticism which Bloom had endeavored to secure against all assault through his assimilation of Stevens's crucial first idea into the dialectic of Emersonian creation. For Riddel, the characteristic Stevensian poem would now have to be seen as "a fictional fold, a new construct to house an old fiction of presence," a construct, that is, endlessly imagining and relentlessly pursuing what it just as endlessly deferred via the language of the poem's own "arche-tectonics." Thus, Riddel argued, the featured crossings of Bloom's map could never actually fight free of their exile to arrive at the ground of determinate and determining Romantic meaning so passionately envisioned by Bloom; according to the logic of deconstruction, such crossings would necessarily remain in transit forever.

We do not need to endorse Riddel's own critical position in order to appreciate his concluding assessment of the significance of Bloom's work. Above all, Riddel observes, Bloom's canonizing project, with its remarkable accretions of terminology, is an attempt to "recuperate, perhaps for a final time, the primordial power that western poetry and criticism celebrates in the form of loss." And above all, he says, what we cannot do, if we wish to counter the manifold assertions and appropriations of that operation, is to settle for offering a simple "point-by-point refutation" of Bloom's treatment of any given poem or poems. Such a tactic will not work, Riddel cautions, in the face of a critical fable designed precisely to resist "anyone's reading or breaking it."[30] What *will* work, then? What *can* we do, if we wish to penetrate the carefully contrived tautologies of Bloom's audacious map? In the next two chapters, I shall try to approach Bloom's contribution to poetics and to the rhetoric of Romanticism in perhaps the only way really possible—through a direct confrontation with the assumptions about poetry, language, and culture that govern his radical revision of our literary history.

The Poems at the End of
The Romantic Mind:
A. R. Ammons and John Ashbery

The previous four chapters have concentrated almost exclusively on providing an exegesis of Harold Bloom's theories of visionary Romanticism and the anxiety of influence, and on examining the crucial principles and assumptions behind those theories. We have looked closely at what might be called the internal logic guiding Bloom's development as a self-conscious and self-consciously extreme critical prophet for our "belated" time. Our analysis of Bloom's many determined "misreadings," not only of poets but of other critics and literary theorists, has taken shape largely and perhaps inevitably as an expository mapping of Bloom's own maps. While such a charting operation is certainly necessary when dealing with a theorist of Bloom's almost uncanny resourcefulness and methodological excess, it also must be seen as just a beginning, a prerequisite to the larger project of assessing the significance and the appeal of Bloom's theories of vision and literary influence within our contemporary intellectual climate.

That Bloom's theories are not only appealing to many but that they translate their appeal into critical "power" we can hardly doubt. The Bloomian desire to arbitrate in matters of poetic canonization has earned him fame both in the academy and in the popular press (witness the *Newsweek* essay of 1981 on the Yale School.)[1] On the other hand, Bloom has also received his share of criticism, even ridicule, for everything from his Romantic nostalgia to his elliptical and sometimes rather sententious oratorical style. He has been condemned as a false prophet, a solipsist, a determinist, a willful obfuscator, a male chauvinist, and, worst of all, a poor reader. His canon making has been denounced as an egregious abuse of the role of the critic, while the canon thereby made has been excoriated by competing canonizers as wrongheaded, reductive, narrow, and foolish.[2]

It is no doubt a mark of Bloom's own uncompromising claims for the act of criticism as he conceives it that work as difficult and as erudite as his has been met with such passionate approbation and censure not only by critics of Romanticism but by rhetoricians, scholars of Jewish theology, readers of modern literature, and poets themselves. The fierce polemics of Bloom's own position and the extreme critical response that his project has inspired suggest by their very extremity that any assessment of Bloom's significance and appeal necessarily will involve a probing of the ways in which his fundamental principles and assumptions either meet, or fail to meet, the needs of our time. Mining the extremes of critical censure for the deep clash of conceptions about the nature of reading, of poetic meaning, and of literary history that they imply, we might play devil's advocate for a moment to Bloom's own demonic/daemonic allegories, and ask some questions about the import of his entire enterprise.

First, why is a theory that sees all the poetry of our time as a progressive and inexorable falling-away from the riches of past poetic tradition so appealing to so many readers? Why does Bloom as "kakangelist" (MM, p. 39) to the Evening Land of Western culture command so much allegiance when his tidings reveal little hope for "a cultural situation of such belatedness that literary survival itself seems fairly questionable" (p. 39)? What sort of exigency is there within our cultural situation to recommend Bloom's Freudian and Gnostic determinism as a style fit for our despair?

Second, is the "vision" featured by Bloom's conception of poetry as a relentless agon a vision and a sublimity that we want or need? Bloom's cherished Romantic sublime is a strange and empty darkness at the heart of this vision, a darkness that exists only by virtue of the psyche having grappled savagely and, for a brief moment, successfully, with the grim phantasms of the regenerate and non-referential Romantic mind. What is there in such a sublime that captures the spirit of our age? Bloomian vision in turn is wed to Bloomian ethics, as in the trenchant observation of *Wallace Stevens* that the *use* of strong poetry is to "strengthen us by teaching us *how to talk to ourselves,* rather than how to talk to others" (p. 387). What is there in Bloom's forthright praise of poetry as a *"restitution of narcissism"* (DC, p. 17) that speaks to us rather than merely, as its own logic might suggest, to its author? Why should we *need to be* what all strong poets and readers, according to Bloom, are: solip-

sists, albeit imperfect solipsists living with and within the miserable
dualisms of the everyday world?

Third and finally, what sort of "necessity" resides in the method
of reading that Bloom gives us? Because a poem has meaning for
Bloom only insofar as it is *not itself*, only insofar as it engages, twists
askew, and attempts to replace other poems, and because poetry
and criticism are for Bloom activities different only in degree and
not in kind (AI, p. 95), then Bloom's method for "misreading" in his
mature phase is really a method for fashioning his own "defensive"
tropes in order to combat the endless and debilitating swerving of
significations that he calls "tradition." The ruling tropes of Bloom's
system, "tradition" and "influence," master the wanderings of
poetic meaning by mapping them into highly determined poetic
ratios, thereby allowing Bloom to furnish a mythographic chart of
what, by definition, is unchartable: the mythopoeia of visionary
desire. The implication of this manner of mastery is the Nietzschean
one that strong readers must exercise a will-to-power over their
chosen text (or the text that has chosen them) if they are to survive
and flourish.[3] The implication of this in turn is the thoroughly uncommon one that when we are reading Bloom on Blake, or Bloom
on Yeats, or Bloom on Stevens, what we really are reading in some
final sense is Bloom on Bloom, Bloom going about the savage and
sublime business of troping toward a restoration of his own imper-
fectly solipsistic imagination.

On a practical level, Bloom's hermeneutic encircling of texts
within himself results in readings dense with details—analogues,
correspondences, parallels—which purport to chart what is
"there" in the poem, while recognizing at the same time that the
poem, as a convenient defensive starting point into the manifold
swervings of poets and other readers that constitutes tradition,
really is not "there" at all. Thus, while we may quarrel with the many
seemingly arbitrary connections and perceptions of visionary
resemblance contributing to a typical Bloomian "misreading"—a
reading of the sort that we have seen him give Emerson, for example,
or Stevens's great crisis poems, or Yeats's "The Second Coming"—
we will find it very difficult, if not impossible, to refute Bloom on his
own terms, since those terms are designed precisely to present the
irrefutable circle of Bloom's own highly self-conscious solipsism.
What is the appeal of a critical method such as this, a method that
claims to follow Emerson in its logic of the "deep tautology—of the
solipsist who knows that what he means is right, yet that what he
says is wrong" (AI, p. 96)? And how can we cope with a critic who

tells us portentously that he reads only for the deep Romantic essences that can be used by his belated Romantic will, and then goes on to intimidate us with the "power" and the "strength" of such an exercise in apparent extremity?

The three sets of questions in this lengthy roster obviously are related. The first set concerns the ends or the "uses" of reading when guided by the visionary and finally ethical precepts advanced in the second. We will consider at length in chapter 6 the issues raised by Bloom's philosophy of rhetoric and Romanticism. In this chapter, however, we would do well to prepare for that discussion by exploring more thoroughly the questions in the third set, the questions concerning Bloom's *method* for arriving at his avowed goals. The advantage to examining the "means" of Bloom's misreading of Romanticism at this time is that in taking us to the drama of choice necessarily underlying any rhetoric, it will take us also to vantage points from which we will be able to map more precisely not only the featured "triumphs" of Bloom's revisionist reading of poetic history but the final *costs* and *effects* of that enterprise as well. As Kenneth Burke, a rhetorician with considerable "influence" over Bloom, has observed, a rhetoric, or a "terministic screen," necessarily selects and deflects as it spins out the possibilities inherent in its terminological structure.[4] The canonizing project operated by Harold Bloom under the related master principles of "vision" and "influence" is so brilliantly aware of the entelechial nature of its own systematizing logic that those interested in criticizing the project often are left feeling defenseless before it, hurling charges of reductive Bloomian selections and solipsistic Bloomian deflections which say as much for their own principles as they do for the difficulties of Bloom's map.

And yet, one of the services of Bloom's critical prophecy has been to remind us forcibly that the reading of criticism as well as the reading of literature is not and cannot be a value-free activity, whatever the ruses we employ to convince ourselves otherwise. As Bloom instructs by both precept and example, all reading, including the most impersonal decoding stratagems of the most grimly ascetic semiotician or linguist, is fully fraught with *human* meaning (in Bloom's own case, peril), and charged with the passionate morality of selection, of human-making choice. Therefore, while it may not do much good to engage in the typical detractor's gambit of calling Bloom names—"solipsist," "determinist," "misreader"— that he has already, at least in effect, called himself, nonetheless the fact that these names can be summoned, and in the spirit of ill will, indicates that Bloom's choices might be examined profitably for what they *fail to do* in the very act of accomplishing their nearly perfect solipsistic symmetry. What is *left out* of a typical Bloomian misreading? What choices does Bloom make as a self-conscious proselytizer for the "psychology of belatedness" when he confronts a poem or a poetic career? Is there any price to be paid for the Romantic "freedom" of agonistic visionary desire that Bloom values above all else in post-Enlightenment poetry?

Obviously, these questions will involve us in a consideration of Bloom's ends and assumptions; just as obviously, since they are value-laden questions, they will entail as well a presentation of conceptions of poetic meaning and the role of criticism in culture different from Bloom's own. In the final part of this study I would like first to present a counterreading to Bloom on two of the most important poets in his revisionary canon, and then in chapter 6 to use the questions raised by that conflict of readings to probe the larger issue of the significance of Bloom's entire enterprise as a Romantic humanist living in a fragmented and faithless age.

The crucial appropriation of Bloom's as a canonizing critic that we have not yet examined is his selection and subsequent misreading of A. R. Ammons and John Ashbery as the greatest of our contemporary poets. The canonization of Ammons and Ashbery within the Emersonian line of American poetry is an especially intriguing Bloomian maneuver for several reasons. First, it represents the only instance in Bloom's personal history of revisionism where he is not so much revising earlier canonizing "errors" of others as he is staking out new and relatively uncharted territory for the fatherland of his belated Romanticism. Past Bloomian readings of Blake, Shelley, Yeats, Emerson, and Stevens have relied for much of their impact on the audacity of their repudiation of an adversary literary tradition, usually that associated with T. S. Eliot, Modernism, and the New Criticism. With Ashbery and Ammons, on the other hand, Bloom is writing the literary history of figures of his *own* generation, of men who, like him, began their publishing careers in the fifties and did not rise to real prominence until the middle to late sixties. The consequences of Bloom's characteristically hyperbolic evaluation of these two poets cannot easily be dismissed. In particular, the developing interest in Ammons through the late sixties and into the mid-seventies, culminating in his winning the National Book Award for his *Collected Poems* in 1973, is inextricably tied to Bloom's powerful championing of him as "the wisest" and "most enduring" poet of his generation (FC, p. 137). Although Bloom did not come to Ashbery until several years after a tentative reputation already had been established, his authoritative placing of the author of *Some Trees, Rivers and Mountains, The Double Dream of Spring*, and *Three Poems* as an authentic inheritor of the vision of Wallace Stevens quickly subsumed other less concentrated readings, and brought many readers to Ashbery who might otherwise have dismissed him as just another poet of the New York School.

If Bloom's largely successful canonization of two key contemporary poets as belated American Romantics represents a striking display of his considerable power as a cultural commentator, it is intriguing also for the way in which it crystallizes the issues implicit all along in the Bloomian logic of misreading. Precisely because Ammons and Ashbery are contemporaries and are at a further remove from Romantic origins than any other major figures previously placed within the map of misreading, Bloom's attempt to rescue them via the metaleptic reversals of time that constitute canonization is an especially bold one, and especially revealing, too, then, of the costs necessarily accompanying the map's indubitable visionary "triumphs." The contours of Bloom's mapping of Ammons and Ashbery that I want now briefly to sketch should be quite familiar in principle, if not particulars. Both poets are seen as spent seers, fruitfully burdened by the ineluctable belatedness of their visionary desires. Ammons, "the most Emersonian poet we have had since Whitman's petering out after 1860" (FC, p. 160), is described as especially so in his quest to come to a unity of being where he will "be possessed fully by the Transcendental Self" (RT, p. 259). In Bloom's reading, the Emersonian dialectic of fate, freedom, and power governs the entire career of his visionary descendant, ranging from the "transcendental waste places" (p. 263) of *Ommateum* in 1955 through the grand Romantic crisis poems of the crucial *Corsons Inlet* period in the mid-sixties to the mature achievement of *Briefings, Sphere, Diversifications*, and *A Coast of Trees* in the seventies and eighties. Ammons's "largest flaw" (p. 270) as a poet, Bloom says, is his Emersonian tendency to identify himself with Ananke, with that natural process from which he is estranged simply by being human; Ammons's proper power and greater glory reside in his equally Emersonian desire to overcome the fated temptations of nature, and to transcend the limitations of vision recognized in the most famous line of his most celebrated poem, "Corsons Inlet": "Overall is beyond me" (CP, p. 148).[5]

Against the "stoic acceptance of bafflement" (RT, p. 276) in "Corsons Inlet," Bloom offers as central to Ammons at his best what

he calls the "imaginative reassurance" of the poem's companion
piece, "Saliences," a poem that returns to the other's littoral " 'field'
of action" (CP, p. 150) driven by, Bloom says, "the need not to abide
in a necessity, however beautiful." The vision in "Saliences" of the
"mind feeding out" (p. 151) over the lines of Atlantic dunes and moving toward the solacing wisdom that "where not a single single
thing endures, / the overall reassures" (p. 155) is praised by Bloom
as a "renovative fresh start" (RT, p. 277) for the imagination that
breaks the ground for all of Ammons's great poetry of the seventies,
a poetry in which Ammons's "obsessive . . . longing for unity" is
transformed into a more patient and profitable "assertion of the
mind's power over the particulars of being, the universe of death."
Of course, the bafflement of earlier visionary aspiration implied by
such a turn to the "saliences" and "radiances" along the "periphery" of being marks Ammons's belatedness, his distance from originating Emersonian strength. Ammons has discovered very early in
"Guide" that "you cannot come to unity and remain material" (CP,
p. 79); this "primordial romancing after unity" (RT, p. 283) must give
way, according to Bloom, to the "more possible quest" of an "unmediated telling" of the mind's out-leapings over particulars, a telling realized with rarest perfection in the many poems "small and
easy" of Ammons's volume of 1971, *Briefings*. "Emersonianism, the
most impatient and American of perceptual traditions, has learned
patience" in the latest phase of Ammons's career, Bloom asserts (FC,
p. 163). If such a patience is centered in a visionary area which
Ammons himself calls "transcendental only by its bottomless en-
tropy" (CP, p. 316), and if the transcendental moment is for him
a "destruction" to be "blessed by" (p. 161), a visionary "Purgatory"
(FC, p. 229) rather than an Emersonian Eden, nonetheless that
patience and that radiant evanescent vision remain worthwhile—
remain, that is, a compensating "residue" of the "primordial
strength" of the American sublime (p. 147).

While Bloom sees Ammons as primarily Emersonian, Ashbery's
"true precursor" is said to be "the composite father, Whitman-
Stevens" (FC, p. 131), though in the actual working out of his thesis
Bloom tends to emphasize Stevens. The Stevensian dialectic of the
first idea has its analogue, Bloom contends, in the muted reductions and equally muted restitutions of visionary power featured in
Ashbery's "self-curtailing" poetry of "visionary sublimation"
(p. 199). Stevens reduces to the first idea, "an imagined thing"
(Stevens, CP, p. 387), and "then equates the poet's act of the mind
with the re-imagining of the First Idea"; Ashbery, his chastened

ephebe, "reduces to a First Idea of himself, and then re-imagines himself" (FC, pp. 200 – 201). From Bloom's perspective, Ashbery in his first volume is too intimately an ephebe of Stevens. He has found already his "largest aesthetic principle, the notion that every day the world consented to be shaped into a poem" (p. 170), but this "antithetical completion" of the wisdom of Stevens's *Adagia* proves oppressive.[6] Not knowing yet how to re-imagine his father fruitfully, he is impelled to the dead end and the "fearful disaster" (FC, p. 172) of his second volume of poems, *The Tennis Court Oath*, in 1962. The "egregious disjunctiveness" (p. 174) and outrageous ellipticality characterizing most of the poems of this volume, poems such as "Leaving the Atocha Station" and the long collage "Europe," signify for Bloom "too massive a swerve away from the ruminative continuities of Stevens and Whitman" (p. 171). But Ashbery returns to the mainstream of his imaginative inheritance with *Rivers and Mountains*, whose long masterpiece, "The Skaters," is said by Bloom to be Ashbery's most Whitmanian poem and "the largest instance in him of the revisionary movement of *daemonization*, or the onset of his personalized Counter-Sublime, as against the American Sublime of Whitman and Stevens" (FC, p. 180). "The Skaters" inaugurates what is in Bloom's reading the most brilliant phase of Ashbery's career, a phase marked by the production of scintillant long poems such as "Fragment," the prose meditations of *Three Poems*, "Fantasia on 'The Nut-Brown Maid,' " and Ashbery's greatest achievement, "Self-Portrait in a Convex Mirror." All these, Bloom says, are, like Stevens's "Notes toward a Supreme Fiction," "versions or revisions" of *Song of Myself* (DC, p. 22), whose ecstatic internalized romance of consummated self and soul is troped by Ashbery via Stevens as "the imagination of a later self questing for accommodation not so much with an earlier glory (as in Wordsworth) but with a possible sublimity that can never be borne, if it should yet arrive" (FC, p. 175). While Ashbery is doomed to write "the history of someone who came too late," as his poem "As You Came from the Holy Land" puts it (SP, p. 7),[7] the great "resource" of his poetry is his ability "to make a music of the poignance of withdrawal," and thereby to transform what should be a "perpetual self-defeat" into an altogether "heroic" resistance of the lengthening shadows of time (MM, pp. 205 – 6).

Even this skeletal summary of Bloom's reading of Ammons and Ashbery sufficiently demonstrates the internal *coherence* of his extension of the religion of American Orphism into the realm of the contemporary. But what price does Bloom pay for such an extension? Perhaps the most common charge against him since the very start of his career has been, in the diplomatic words of James Benziger on *The Visionary Company*, that he displays "a certain one-sidedness" in his treatment of literary texts, a propensity grown more problematic with Bloom's subsequent advance upon the great moderns Yeats and Stevens. Now, deeper into the wilderness of modernity with his readings of Ammons and Ashbery, Bloom at the very least is paying the price of a more circumscribed selection of the works that "will suffice" to prove his theories of poetry and of life, and consequently, is forced into a more intractable denial of all that that would not be open to a "saving use" in the poet's vision. Bloom's campaign to save Ammons from himself involves ignoring the wide range of subjects, tones, and activities in Ammons's work, the language games, the bouncy humor, the tales of home and hearth and heartburn, the Cornellish ambiance of poet-as-profes-sor. It involves slighting the influences of Pound's metric and Williams's voice on Ammons, Bloom claiming not to hear the latter "anywhere in Ammons's work, despite the judgments of several re-viewers" (RT, p. 257). And even more important, it involves neglect-ing the influence of Coleridge's theories of the imagination and poetic creation on the central visionary Ammons, although Ammons himself pronounces just such an indebtedness.

The rescue operation for Ashbery is similarly strenuous and, not surprisingly, quite reminiscent of the operation to save Stevens. Ashbery too cannot properly be described as a painterly poet, de-spite his avocation as an eminent art critic and his many personal and professional ties to the Abstract Expressionists in particular. Ashbery too is no "French poet writing in English" (FC, p. 183), despite his years in France and his obvious fondness for avant-garde French writers and artists such as Pierre Reverdy. The Ash-bery volume with the heaviest connection to the French and to the world of avant-garde music and painting, *The Tennis Court Oath*, is dismissed by Bloom as "calculated incoherence" lacking any real "necessity." "Poems may be like pictures, or like music, or like what you will," Bloom instructs, "but if they *are* paintings or musical works, they will not be poems" (p. 174). Finally, too, Ashbery is the beneficiary of the same intriguing Bloomian rhetoric of near-con-cession that we saw applied to Stevens; in Ashbery this rhetoric takes the form of statements as puzzling as the one on Ashbery's sublime, which, we are told, exists, and yet can never "be borne," even "if it should yet arrive."

In my own analysis of Ammons and Ashbery, I would like to fol-

132

low up on what I see as the most important "deflections" in Bloom's misreading of the two poets—the lack of interest in Ammons's borrowings from Coleridge, and the postulating of a strangely self-effaced quest in Ashbery—in order to probe the consequences of Bloom's visionary Romanticism for reading and the role of poetry in the intellectual climate of our time. If in the process it becomes clear that my analysis is based on principles and assumptions about the nature of poetic meaning somewhat different from Bloom's own, it should be apparent also that the purpose of the analysis is not to refute Bloom as such, but rather, to place or to "locate" the powerful Bloomian conception of Romanticism by suggesting qualifications and moderations that, in my reading, need not be and should not be so estranged from the visionary intensities and the agonistic extremes of Bloom's eloquent map.[8] My analysis is not intended to suggest that Bloom is simply wrong on the poetry of Ammons and Ashbery; again, even if one wanted to make that judgment, it has been rendered already nugatory by Bloom's featured contention that critical strength inheres precisely in the savagery and the cunning of the critic's misreading. Rather, what I intend to address are questions that I think to be implicit in Bloom's powerful but claustrophobic narrowing of focus on the work of two of our most important contemporary poets. How far can such narrowing go before it admits, in effect, that the terrain not mapped and seldom even acknowledged by the critic also offers strong poetic argument to our belated time? And what perspectives does that uncharted land suggest on Bloom's own work and on the visionary logic of misreading behind it?

II

Geoffrey Hartman furnishes a suitable framework for our discussion of the laudatory reception afforded the poetry of A. R. Ammons when in his essay "Romanticism and Anti-Self-Consciousness," from *Beyond Formalism*, he wonders if "the modern poet, whom Schiller called 'sentimental' (reflective) and whom we would describe as alienated, [can] achieve the immediacy of all great verse, whatever its personal or historical dilemma."[9] The questions with which Hartman concludes his broodings on Romantic art and the problem of self-consciousness—"Is visionary poetry a thing of the past, or can it coexist with the modern temper?"—have been answered in the affirmative by a formidable body of commentators on Ammons, all of whom see a precarious "visionary strain" (FC,

p. 123) as indeed still available to poets strong enough to grapple with the many burdens of the Romantic visionary lode. Bloom praises Ammons for being a poet of true Emersonian power, a seer whose greatest "ambition . . . is an unmediated telling, a purely visionary poetry" (RT, p. 283). A similar thirst for the unmediated may be seen to animate Richard Howard's celebration of Ammons in *Alone with America*[10] as well as the many enthusiastic reviews of Ammons's poetry that appeared in the special issue of *Diacritics* devoted to his work in 1973.[11] Even Hyatt Waggoner, a critic quite removed from the Bloomian pale, cannot resist praising the poet of "Corsons Inlet," "Raft," and "Poetics" as a kind of Emerson for the modern reader, a poet of ultimately "religious vision" whose poems transcend the solid realities of earth from which they spring.[12]

The analyses given Ammons by Bloom, Howard, Waggoner, and others constitute a rich and rigorous placing of his poetry within the tradition of American Romanticism. And yet, reading the poetry, one must account for one's feeling—a feeling voiced by Denis Donoghue and Alicia Ostriker, too—that Ammons, as impressive as he is, is curiously unmoving. One must explain how poems whose intent, as Ammons himself puts it in *Sphere*, is to refresh and release "energies of the deeper self" through a rendered flux of "organized motion" (p. 40), can strike one frequently as not refreshing, but stale and "relentlessly dry, bloodless, unemotional."[13] And, ultimately, one must confront the possibility that Ammons's poetry is particularly appealing to critics, especially to critics of Romanticism, precisely because the world it provides *is* an *engagingly* ossified Romantic universe, a verbal world hardened into often self-conscious and *determinedly* belated posturings vis-à-vis the dialectics of a distinctively Romantic, and, by now, in the last quarter of the twentieth century, distinctively *conventional* cosmogony.

Virtuosity in handling the counters of Romantic dialectic is perhaps the central trait of Ammons's poetry. Overt allegiance is affirmed to the theories of Coleridge, whose conception of the creative imagination in chapter 14 of the *Biographia Literaria* as "the reconciliation of opposite or discordant qualities" has been said by Ammons in a rare prose piece to be the "greatest statement in our language" about poetry.[14] While Coleridge is attempting to describe the entire spectrum of creative fusion in the poem, however, Ammons tends to appropriate the doctrine of opposites solely as *subject matter*, as an excuse for rehearsing the paradoxes of Romantic metaphysics. One-Many is the generating opposition; others are motion-permanence, center-periphery, peak-base, mind-nature, and line-sphere. Here are the first two stanzas of the poem called "One:Many":

> To maintain balance
> between one and many by
>> keeping in operation both one and many:
>> fear a too great consistency, an arbitrary
> imposition
>> from the abstract *one*
>> downwardly into the realities of manyness:
>> this makes unity
> not deriving from the balance of manyness
> but by destruction of diversity:
>> it is unity
>>> unavailable to change,
> cut off from the reordering possibilities of
>> variety: (CP, p. 138)

This passage is quite characteristic of Ammons. It is a lecture, really, a re-creation of the architectonics of Coleridge's essay on "method." Bloom speaks of the visionary intensity of Ammons as his poetry tries "the impossible task, beyond a limit of art, in which language seeks its own end to the one:many problem" (FC, p. 215). Yet others may find it difficult to see anything visionary in lines such as these, though we may be tempted, indeed, to view the passage as a *prolegomenon toward* a vision—and as such, a problematical fulfillment of Coleridge's prescription, in a letter to Sotheby of 1802, that "a great Poet must be, implicitè if not explicitè, a profound Metaphysician."[15] "I know / . . . that I am / holy in amness," Ammons announces elsewhere in "Come Prima" (CP, p. 52), and the echo of Coleridge's famous definition of the primary imagination is obviously quite deliberate, another one of Ammons's self-conscious ploys. It is also troubled, however, for there is one essential distinction between Coleridge and Ammons, a distinction that has considerable consequences for the enterprise of Ammons's dialectic. It may very well be articulated as the distinction between the metaphysics of Kant and the antimetaphysics introduced by the Nietzschean palace revolt. Coleridge's theory of the dialectical imagination is founded firmly on what Derrida would call a "transcendental signified," an absolute One that stands outside of language as the chimerical origin and end of all linguistic desires.[16] Ammons, on the other hand, is extremely equivocal in his treatment of "finite mind" in relation to "the eternal act of creation in the infinite I AM," some-

times affirming, as in "Hibernaculum," a faintly Wordsworthian
faith that "there is one mind and one earth" (CP, p. 367), but at other
times resolutely facing the unconditioned world of "god" or "essence" in the best modern manner, seeing it as a function of the
transcendental mountings of our symbol systems. "Only the foolish
think [the] gods have gone away," Ammons says in *Sphere,* and then
he tells us why and how:

> . . . the mechanics of this have to do with
> the way our minds work, the concrete, the overinvested
>   concrete,
> the symbol, the seedless radiance, the giving up into
>   meaninglessness
> and the return of meaning. . . .   (Pp. 48−49)

If we have to recycle metaphysical commonplaces here, it is
because Ammons is so preoccupied with them—and not without
reason, since an epistemological mode obviously has great consequences for the linguistic and rhetorical strategies of its presentation. With his belief in a transcendent One, Coleridge could present
a theory of language based firmly on one kind of Romantic dilemma
of "multëity in unity." The basis is firm because Coleridge's brand of
Romantic frustration, his restless scheming, as Walter Pater put it,[17]
to arrive at the absolute, is focused with synecdochal singleminded-
ness on the impossibility of words ever being able to say the originating and now endlessly deferred Word. As Coleridge observes, "A
fall of some sort or other—the creation, as it were, of the non-
absolute," is the "fundamental postulate" before us.[18] The situation
is frustrating because the initiating Word cannot be put back together again with all the little words, the mere metonyms and opposites of our fallen or mortal meaning; it is comforting because there
is, after all, an essence to aspire to—and the fact that this essence *is*
there confers upon language, for all its inadequacies, the power of a
stable dialectical hierarchy. Thus, synecdoche, related to but much
more powerful than metonymy, becomes the central figure in Coleridge's symbolist theory of poetry; thus poetry, like philosophy, inevitably works through series of vibrant binary oppositions—*split
synonyms*—with the main distinction being that philosophy proceeds downward from sameness to difference,[19] while poetry
proceeds esemplastically upward toward the energy of the Logos,
propelled by words as "living Things."[20] While at its best the Romantic symbol in the various ensuing Coleridgean traditions perhaps enacts what Murray Krieger has called, in frankly metaphori-

cal language, a "miracle" of imaginative fusion,[21] at its worst, the
very conditions of its theoretical formulation seem to invite the in-
trusion of the programmatic, the abstract, the formulaic counters of
dialectical logomachy, into a poetry that is actually meant to feature
the appeal of the intuitive, the immediate, the natural:

> fear a too great consistency, an arbitrary
> imposition
> from the abstract *one*

The great failing of the poetry of A. R. Ammons is to fall into the
traps that it recognizes and habitually discusses. Although Ammons has generally removed from his poetry the possibility of a
strategically absolute signified, although he tells us time and again
that he is the poet of process, the singer of a reality "abob" with not
just one but many Emersonian "centers" (CP, p. 299), he finally is impelled to use as a strategy for his presentation of process all the tired
conventions and by now stale formulas of an essentializing Romanticism appropriated directly from Coleridge. This tension in
Ammons's work can result in quite unintentional comedy. "Look:
it's snowing: / without theory / & beyond help," he announces in
Tape for the Turn of the Year (p. 99). By the time of *The Snow Poems*,
however, it seems to have begun snowing theory, as we are given descriptions of snow like this: "histories of past / motions thawing
away into motions, / runlets and trickles, / histories of redisposi-
tions .. " (p. 164). Ammons at his most tiresome barrages us with
"natural" descriptions of this sort, despite the fact that in his
"Poetics" he has announced his task in this manner:

> I look for the forms
> things want to come as
>
> from what black wells of possibility,
> how a thing will
> unfold:
>
> not the shape on paper—though
> that, too—but the
> uninterfering means on paper:
>
> not so much looking for the shape
> as being available
> to any shape that may be
> summoning itself
> through me
> from the self not mine but ours.   (CP, p. 199)

This presents itself as a poetics of process, of the poet attempting to disperse himself among the burgeonings of things-in-the-world. And surely there is often a solid excellence in Ammons based on his talent for nicely observed natural detail, for capturing in the rhythms of poetry the "lowly" things he prizes (CP, p. 140), the "mold under the leaf" (*Sphere*, p. 65). But there is also the seemingly relentless compulsion to see in nature the world all too programmatically according to Coleridge and Emerson—with perhaps a touch of the latest in post-Einsteinian scientific thought. So, although Ammons says "the symbol won't do," that "it differentiates flat / into muffling fact it tried to stabilize beyond" (CP, p. 329), his poetry is, in fact, full of symbols, as the world is quite consciously read as a *book*—"nature's message . . . for / the special reader" (*Snow*, p. 241)—as an exercise in the dialectical problems of One-Many. And the natural phenomena subjected to the troping shapes of this "too great consistency" that Ammons has warned himself against tend to be, predictably, all the musty old Romantic symbols: ocean, shore, mountains, wind.

Wind predominates in the early poetry—"My subject's / still the wind" (CP, p. 214)—where it is seen as a "guide," because it has "given up everything to eternal being but / direction" (p. 80). Ammons uses the pathetic fallacy—again, as he has said in an interview, quite consciously[22]—as the wind constantly lectures him "to stop not-being and break / off from *is* to *flowing*" (p. 79). The pun on "flowing" is typical of Ammons's symbol-mongering, and effectively undercuts whatever visionary power the passage might otherwise have had. By the time of the crucial *Corsons Inlet* period, Ammons has fully assimilated his readings in science, for the wind now involves "variables / of position and direction and sound" (p. 152) amid the dunes of the New Jersey shore. "Guide" or "variable," the "message" of the wind is the same; it preaches flux, "leaves no two moments / on the dunes the same" (pp. 152 – 53). Wind, in other words, is a *symbol* of process, of the dispersed Many—a scientific cousin to the vivifying correspondent breeze. It is, as "Saliences" tells us, a symbol of "the open, / the unexpected . . ." (p. 153)—and a most predictable symbol it is.[23]

Mountains figure heavily in Ammons's early poetry as well, and like the wind, they tend to talk a lot. Bloom notes acutely the place of Ammons's garrulous peaks within a tradition of talkative mountains in Blake, Shelley, and Emerson, without remarking at the same time that the advantage in the comparison seems to belong entirely to the precursors.[24] Emerson's Monadnoc, "Anchored fast for many an age," awaits "the bard and sage, / Who, in large thoughts, like fair pearl-seed, / Shall string Monadnoc like a bead" (EW, 9:70). What in Emerson is quiet dignity and unpretentious invention becomes in Ammons coyness and unintentional bathos on the one hand, and pompous metaphysical posturing on the other. For an example of the first, here is a poem called "Mountain Liar":

> The mountains said they were
> > tired of lying down
> and wanted to know what
> > I could do about
> getting them off the ground
>
> Well close your eyes I said
> > and I'll see if I can
> by seeing into your nature
> > tell where you've been wronged
> What do you think you want to do
> > They said Oh fly
>
> My hands are old
> > and crippled keep no lyre
> but if that is your true desire
> > and conforms roughly
> with your nature I said
> > I don't see why
> we shouldn't try
> > to see something along that line
>
> Hurry they said and snapped shut
> > with rocky sounds their eyes
> I closed mine and sure enough
> > the whole range flew
> gliding on interstellar ice
>
> They shrieked with joy and peeked
> > as if to see below
> but saw me as before there
> > foolish without my lyre
> We haven't budged they said
> > You wood   (CP, pp. 54—55)

For an example of Ammons's pompous metaphysical tone we may turn to "Whose Timeless Reach," in which Ammons as Ezra, the favored persona of his early poetry, climbs once again toward

the top of the mountain, this time to discourse on Eastern wisdom
and on death. The dialogue between prophet and mountain is
rendered with near biblical solemnity:

> I Ezra the dying
> portage of these deathless thoughts
> stood on a hill in
> the presence of the mountain
> and said wisdom is
> too wise for man it
> is for gods and gods have little
> use for it so I do not know what
> to do with it
> and animals use it only when
>   their teeth start to fall and it
> is too late to do anything
> else but *be* wise and stay
> out of the way
> The eternal will not lie
> down on any temporal hill
>   The frozen mountain rose and broke
> its tireless lecture of repose
> and said death does
> not take away it
> ends giving halts bounty and
>   Bounty I said thinking of ships
> that I might take and helm right
> out through space
> dwarfing these safe harbors and
> their values
> taking the Way in whose timeless reach
> cool thought unpunishable
> by bones eternally glides   (CP, p. 33)

In both instances of Ammons's peaking, the mountain as a
familiar place of Romantic invention poses a problem for a poet too
self-conscious really to be able to *believe* in his vision, his symbol.
Wanting to present deep wisdom drawn from the wells of the imagination, Ammons himself is yet unable to accept his invention as
anything other than an instance of "the overinvested concrete"—
proof of the mechanics of our minds' workings. With what seems
like almost deliberate self-destructiveness, he then endeavors to

solve his personal problem of imaginative belief by presenting his visions in tones so alternately arch and melodramatic that no one else could possibly embrace them either.

The ocean and its shore become the dominant symbols of Ammons's poetry from *Corsons Inlet* through *Sphere*, and they too are invested almost programmatically with significance. The ocean, "multiple to a blinding / oneness," is for Ammons a "total expression," a wordless statement far superior to any of man's knowing (CP, p. 288). "Essay on Poetics" explicates:

> ... genius, and
>
> the greatest poetry, is the sea, settled, contained before the first
> current stirs but implying in its every motion adjustments
> throughout the measure: one recognizes an ocean even from a
> dune and
>
> the very first actions of contact with an ocean say ocean over and
> over: read a few lines along the periphery of any of the truly
> great and the knowledge delineates an open shore:
>
> what is to be gained from the immortal person except the
> experience
> of ocean: take any line as skiff, break the breakers, and go out
> into the landless, orientationless, but perfectly contained, try
>
> the suasions, brief dips and rises, and the general circulations,
> the wind, the abundant reductions, stars, and the experience is
> obtained.... (CP, p. 309)

These lines from Ammons could be viewed easily enough as a workmanlike disquisition—indeed, an essay—on the obverse, or redemptive, side of the great passage from Whitman cited in chapter 4:

> O baffled, balk'd, bent to the very earth,
> Oppress'd with myself that I have dared to open my mouth,
> Aware now that amid all that blab whose echoes recoil upon me
> I have not once had the least idea who or what I am,
> But that before all my arrogant poems the real Me stands yet
> untouch'd, untold, altogether unreach'd....
>
> I perceive I have not really understood any thing, not a single
> object, and that no man ever can,
> Nature here in sight of the sea taking advantage of me to dart
> upon me and sting me,
> Because I have dared to open my mouth to sing at all.

Thus, "As I Ebb'd With the Ocean of Life" delivers an anguished Romantic acknowledgment of the failure of human song before the "total expression" of nature (troped by Bloom, of course, as the Emersonian precursor). Ammons, who constantly reminds us of this old lesson that "everything but our understanding / is flawless" (*Snow*, p. 205), turns the expansive anguish of Whitman into a tired text—ocean as book, ocean as clever conceit with a predictable message, man as ocean on the model of the hoary metaphor. As Bloom notes, what Ammons presents here is an expression of "Emersonian Self-Reliance . . . severely mitigated by the consciousness of latecoming" (FC, p. 142). Yet the mitigation perhaps derives from a failing that Bloom, with his valuation of deep Romantic *topoi* at the expense of the mere significances of language on the page, cannot afford to notice. It is Ammons's *strategy* that lapses here, and it lapses because Ammons's reliance on symbols, on oceanic equations, lacks conviction within a verbal context characterized above all by self-conscious discursiveness, not by Romantic feeling.

Arguing eloquently that the "central American poems are houses founded on the sea" (MM, p. 177), Bloom sees Ammons's "visionary strain" taking its power from its intimate relation to Whitman's littoral tradition. But what is powerful or visionary about a passage such as our ocean essay? Is it not but an irritatingly mechanical working out of a Romantic terminology already brittle with age? Abstractions proliferate: "motion" is here, and "adjustments" and "periphery," and "suasions" and "circulations" are riding on the waves too. Even casual readers of Ammons know these words well by now, for they have seen at least one of these phrases, or their brethren, in virtually every poem that he has ever written, and they have seen that these counters of Ammons's terminology are always introduced with regard to the same old conundrums of dialectical philosophy—the One-Many problem and its various epigones. Indeed, by the time of *Sphere*, Ammons is so awash in the jargon his poems have generated that he is forced to render explicit the programmatic relations of his dialectical thought: "Actually," he confesses, "the imagination works pretty / diagrammatically into paradigm," and we feel that, for once, Ammons has given us an accurate accounting of the actual practice of his poetics, as opposed to its theory. An exegesis of paradigms follows:

> . . . for me, for example, the one-many problem figures
> out as an isosceles triangle (base:diversity and peak:unity)
> or, even, equilateral, some rigor of rising: and this is

not to be distinguished from the center-periphery thing, in
that if you cut out a piece of pie from the center-periphery
circle, you have a triangle, a little rocky, but if you

cut off the arc, it sits up good, as (peak:center:unity)
and (base:periphery:diversity): actually, one could go even
so far as (peak:center:symbol:abstraction), etc.... (P. 12)

In this intimidating passage, which reads like a philosopher's
notes to himself, Ammons succeeds finally in realizing one of the
essential directions of his work—that of rendering academic criticism of his poetry supererogatory (well, almost!)—by, in effect, writing that criticism himself. Forced to be a "profound Metaphysician"
by his definition of his enterprise in the not entirely applicable
terms of Coleridge, Ammons in a passage such as this delivers
neither interesting philosophy nor the fresh poetry of unmediated
reality that both he and his critics have announced as the destination of his work. Instead, what we have here is a sort of exercise, an
earnest charting of virtually the entire geometry of Ammons's ossified Romantic universe in something like Bloomian fashion, performed with an almost painful awareness of the potential for
mechanical symbolic equations therein.

And yet Ammons does make one crucial split with Coleridgean
strategies, a split forced on him by his recognition that, whatever
the stable mountings of his poetic thought, he cannot have recourse
to that transcendental signified that is the Coleridgean Logos. This
split is important, for it will show us why Ammons, despite his consciousness of the place of his work within the Romantic tradition, is
finally not liberated by his belatedness, as Bloom has argued, but
imprisoned by sets of strategies and modes of perception that are
simply incongruent with the poetry of "possibilities" he feels he
should be presenting. Ammons, trying to dedicate himself to presenting the "motions" of a "reality abob with centers" through the
"motions" of his language, is moved to say in *Sphere*:

             ... I don't know about you,
     but I'm sick of good poems, all those little rondures
     splendidly brought off, painted gourds on a shelf: give me

     the dumb, debilitated, nasty, and massive, if that's the
     alternative.... (P. 72)

Having discovered in "Corsons Inlet" that "Overall is beyond
me," the poet, then, is presumably free to discard as well the equivalent of "Overall" in poetry—that organic wholeness of form that

makes of the poem its own tidy, self-contained universe: hence, the longer, linear poems of the mature Ammons; hence, too, all the talk about openness to "black wells of possibility."

But what results from the collision of process with essence is a tension, and an effect of insincerity, that Ammons simply cannot explain away. His long linear poems, for all their exuberance and cleverness, fail, and they fail because their openness is finally a sham. They fail because the poet is not training strategically "for / inadvertency" in them (*Snow*, p. 286), but, rather, is constantly battling, and generally succumbing to, the de-terministic imperatives of his essentializing, paradigmatic imagination. Ammons's art in poems such as *Sphere* and "Hibernaculum" still is congealing into abstractions and formulaic symbols as it reads nature like a grand book of dialectical wisdom. His art in these poems still is running incessantly through the quasi-narrative formula of the Wordsworthian/Coleridgean crisis-poem format as defined by M. H. Abrams, a format, derived from a central mind-nature opposition, wherein the presentation of a natural scene is followed by moral reflection stimulated by that scene.[25] His art, too, still is plagued by empty Romantic posturing, the expressive correlate to formulaic symbolism, as the poet tries to sing of things visionary, but ends up parodying himself and the entire tradition he loves and cannot escape.[26]

Why can't Ammons resist these tendencies? Perhaps a passage from *Sphere* reveals an answer:

> . . . one terror mind brings on
> itself is that anything can be made of anything: if there are
> no boundaries that hold firm, everything can be ground into
>
> everything else: the mind making things up, making nothing
> of what things are made of: scary to those who need prisons,
> liberating to those already in. . . .   (P. 61)

Ammons's secret terror, a terror that actuates the strategies of much of his poetry, is that things can collapse into each other, if the mind cannot sustain the flux of its motions that somehow are correlative with the motions of reality. "The mind making things up, making nothing / of what things are made of" (with the pun on "making nothing" as both an emptiness and a mimetic inaccuracy): Ammons may seem Wordsworthian in his refusal to go beyond the doctrine of mind as half-creator, half-perceiver of the external world. Yet closer to his philosophical roots we may find, as usual, the twin ghosts of Coleridge and Emerson, both of whom envision the infinite regress of the Many as a terrifying consequence of the loss of the absolute One. If "the Invisible be denied," Coleridge observes in the work on "method," then "the component parts can never be realized into an harmonious whole, but must owe their systematic arrangement to accidents of an ever-shifting perspective."[27] Emerson reminds us that "without identity at base, chaos must be forever" (EW, 12:20); in another context, confronting the dangers of a thoroughgoing idealism, he makes this equation: if idealism "leaves God out of me," then "it leaves me in the splendid labyrinth of my perceptions, to wander without end" (CW, 1:37).

Ammons's secular version of this dilemma focuses on the need for hierarchy. The "human mind cannot get away from" it, he said in an interview in 1980.[28] "We cannot handle all the million bits of information that we receive every day except by subgrouping them under controlling suborders and symbols." An incontestable point about cognitive and linguistic psychology thus is taken up as a rationale for Romantic metaphysics—a particularly perilous rationale because the hierarchy Ammons delivers is at times *multi*-centered, a "systematic arrangement" based on "accidents" of "ever-shifting perspective." Perhaps it is the very perilousness of the enterprise that makes Ammons desperate. "Hell is the meaninglessness of stringing out / events in unrelated, undirected sequences," he observes in "Hibernaculum" (CP, p. 361). Faced with this dark destination as a possibility of his postmodern predicament and his announced poetics of flux, Ammons opts for the prisons of essentializing Romantic strategies, forgetting that the fearful either-or of absolute identity or absolute chaos is itself salient only so long as we accept the dubious premise that the human mind is constituted in its best moments by isolation and by the desire to know essences.[29] That the mind might be defined elsewhere—that cognitive hierarchy might be seen to serve merely as form to the richer, individuating content of shared social, political, economic, and rhetorical structures[30]—seldom occurs to Ammons, and never engages his attention in language other than the aridly metaphysical.[31]

Why so much critical praise for a poetry so compromised in its intentions, so frequently stale in its effects? Perhaps J. Hillis Miller's famous discussion, in the introductory chapter to *Poets of Reality*, of the three stages of growth in and beyond Romanticism, remains instructive after all these years. Romanticism proper gives us, Miller says, a Cartesian dualism in which "man as subjective ego opposes himself to everything else."[32] This dualism can only fall in upon itself until man "the murderer of God and drinker of the sea of creation wanders through the infinite *nothing*ness of his own ego" (p. 3; emphasis mine). But a relinquishing of the strenuous Romantic ego can transmute nothingness into the feast of the world, as "the mind is dispersed everywhere in things and forms one with them" (p. 8).

The poetry of A. R. Ammons seems to me to be important—and to be appealing to so many sophisticated readers—as an emblem of the *attempt* to negotiate this three-stage progression from Romanticism to the poetry of reality. It is a poetry not of process, of motion, of an always tantalizing and never achievable unmediated vision—a poetry not of stage three, as the poet often would have us believe—but, rather, a poetry *about* trying to leap from dualism into visionary immanence. At its most powerful, as in "Corsons Inlet," it remains a poetry that serves largely to remind us of characteristic Romantic frustrations, of the impossibility of seeing into the life of the Other through language. It remains a poetry of the assertive and frustrated Romantic "I," the wanderer, the solitary consciousness confronting nature and the sublime abyss of the self. The wooded glens in Ammons's poetry may be of Ithaca, not Cumberland; the landscapes may be suburban backyards and meadows, not lonely English valleys; the littoral imagination may be founded on a different shore of the Atlantic. But the crises that arise from the poet's egoistic recognition of his limitations as a seer in language are the same old crises; they come to us from 1798, and so do many of the strategies for their presentation. We should not be misled by the new flavor to the poetry, by its sophisticated science derived from the biologists and the physicists, by the marriage of this science to the counters of dialectical philosophy. The dialectic bears the aegis of Coleridge; the science, as Ammons himself has noted, has the blessing of Wordsworth, and is, at any rate, the logical culmination of a dualistic Romantic cosmogony rendered immanent, not transcendent.[33] The poetry of A. R. Ammons is simply belated, often *determinedly* so. This is the source of its appeal to those who are inclined to see the world as the great Romantics saw it; this belatedness is also the source of its failure for those who do not choose to feel bound by shapings of the now unregenerate Romantic mind.

If we are in a position to see that perhaps the poetry of A. R. Ammons is praised beyond all reason by Bloom precisely because it yields such a resourceful review of the visionary essences and the symbolism of the isolate Romantic imagination that Bloom so values, then we are able to see also that the cost of Bloom's narrow focus on the "deep meanings" of languageless Romantic will and transcendental Romantic desire is a reluctance to engage the language-bound conventions of a poem that necessarily constitute a significant part of the reading (and the composing) process. In some sense, Bloom reads Ammons correctly in the manner of the more orthodox literary critic. He sees Emerson where demonstrably there *is* Emerson, Whitman where Whitman is "posed," and symbols where the translucence of the symbolic transparently is offered. And yet Bloom is not bothered by the frequent tiredness of Ammons's language and strategies, just as he is not concerned with those aspects of Ammons—humorist, linguist-at-play—that depend upon the quiddity of verbal forces on a page. Ammons's many trite, jargon-drenched lectures on dialectical metaphysics in *Sphere*, for instance, are said by Bloom only to deliver "a curiously discursive Sublime" (FC, p. 220); the larger propensity of Ammons for quickly wresting pregnant theory out of the most cursory observation of natural phenomena is summarized—but not criticized—as the issue of "a Transcendental belief" shared with Emerson "that one can come to unity, at least in the pure good of theory" (p. 147). Ammons in his central incarnation as a visionary quester in the American vein ultimately is seen by Bloom to remain, "somewhat despite himself, the least spent of our seers" (p. 149).

If against such narrowness and deflection it has seemed appropriate to invoke Abrams, whose description of the structure of the Romantic crisis poem as an intricate interplay of natural scene with moral reflection defines perfectly the characteristic movement of Ammons's work, the point is not to favor Abrams's map over Bloom's, but to argue that Ammons's quest really does not appear "internalized" in the proper Bloomian fashion *except through* the fail-safe lens of Bloom's own logic of misreading. The strain in Ammons that is closest to Bloom's desires presents us with a time-honored and now rather weary Romantic poetry of the isolate Romantic "I" wandering about nature's " 'field' of action" in search of vision, somber and sublime, into the life of things. Bloom *sees* the empty posturing and the stale strategies marking the language of this most self-conscious and coy of belated Romantic poets, but true to the terms and the needs of his Romantic prophecy, he reads beyond such language-bound failings to the languageless vision that alone, he argues, gives us life.

III

We may point to the cost of this Bloomian logic of misreading, and yet, of course, we are faced with the question that Bloom's work

poses. Is there a way *out of* Romanticism as Bloom conceives it,
a way to break beyond the circumference of the Romantic circle? Or
must we agree with Bloom when he tells us that "the vitality of
Romantic tradition appears to inhere in its universality," that "we
are, all of us, largely involuntary Romantics, however intensely we
proclaim our overt beliefs to be anti-Romantic" (RT, p. 324)? Given
his assumptions, Bloom naturally enough sees the work of John
Ashbery as constituting another extension of Romanticism. Ashbery, Bloom instructs, is "the most legitimate of the sons of Stevens"
(AI, p. 143), a major poet in the tradition of the American sublime
whose poems tend, like Stevens's, to follow the "crisis-poem paradigm" at the heart of Romantic revisionism (MM, p. 205). However,
there are indeed all kinds of evasions and veiled concessions in the
Bloomian critical universe on the question of Ashbery, just as there
are on Ashbery's poetic father. Ashbery is "at his best," Bloom cautions, only "when he dares to write most directly in the idiom of
Stevens" (FC, p. 172). Ashbery "attempts a profound and beautiful
misinterpretation of all his precursors" only "*in his own best
poetry*" (FC, p. 185; Bloom's emphasis), only, that is, when he is
"most himself . . . most ruefully and intensely Transcendental"
(p. 131). And if Ashbery's domain is narrowed considerably by strictures such as these, the poetry still is not saved entirely, for even
within this diminished realm there is much that remains problematic, as is made evident by the rueful nature of Ashbery's transcendence, and the subdued self-effacing quality of his quest for a
Stevensian "beyond." Ashbery, like Stevens, tends to write and rewrite *Song of Myself*, but Ashbery's versions, Bloom notes, are even
more prone to qualifications and vanishing or thwarted epiphanies
than "Notes toward a Supreme Fiction" and "An Ordinary Evening
in New Haven." Ashbery's songs of himself are all self-curtailing versions of the central manner of our poetry; Ashbery may be summed,
in fact, as "a kind of invalid of American Orphism, perpetually con-
valescing" from his "strenuous worship" of the gods of the native
strain (FC, p. 131).

   If we have a sense that Bloom in praising Ashbery is granting to
his opponents as much as he is taking for himself, our suspicions
are confirmed when we find him summarizing the power of Ashbery's most celebrated poem, "Self-Portrait in a Convex Mirror," as
"a lesser pathos . . . an uneasiness, however Sublime, rather than a
transcendence" (DC, p. 31). When he goes on, at the conclusion of
his mapping of "Self-Portrait," to observe that the cherished "restitution" of the poem's final ratio features only an "achieved dearth"
of meaning (p. 37), we are left wondering if the habitual Bloomian

rhetoric of visionary battle has not undercut itself completely in one of its most elaborate attempts to save contemporary poetry from itself, and for our time. And the question is suggested: How far can a rhetoric of near-concession go before it *does* concede important issues to its opponents?

Bloom's problems do not end here, either. Saving Ashbery from himself is made even more difficult by the fact that Ashbery, somewhat like Ammons, "wishes to be more of an anomaly than he is, rather than the 'central' kind of a poet he is fated to become, in the line of Emerson, Whitman, Stevens" (FC, p. 206). This perversity is discovered by Bloom not only in the "fearful disaster" of Ashbery's elliptical mode, but also in the opposite pole of his defense against tradition, the "dialectical extreme" (p. 171) of his "re-vitalizing" of "proverbial wisdom." Both rhetorics are meant to defend primarily against the ellipses, the proverbial knowing, and the central sublime of Stevens; both rhetorics, according to Bloom, display Ashbery at much less than his best, risking the "disasters" (p. 172) of the totally disjunctive on the one hand and the blandly truistic on the other.

Considering the pervasiveness, frequently noted by other commentators, of the elliptical and proverbial poles of discourse in the work of Ashbery, perhaps we are justified in questioning the appropriateness of Bloom's decision to leave them largely unexamined. I would like now to concentrate on those areas excised by Bloom to see if there is in his selectiveness a revealing relation to the crucial deflections we have noted already in his reading of Ammons. If Ammons, from the perspective of the particular Coleridgean theories that he admires, is revealed in his own designs to be a highly conventional and decidedly mediated poet of *ostensibly* unmediated and intensely private vision, then Ashbery from the standpoint of his propensity for the proverbial can be seen only as a determined practitioner of the low arts of culturally engendered and entangled mediacy, and as such a proponent of a solacing *communal* wisdom whose serene sharings implicitly repudiate the darkly assertive vision of the solitary Romantic quester. An examination of the interplay in Ashbery's work between the modes of the elliptical and the eventually triumphant proverbial may show a way out of the solipsistic circle of Bloom's belated Romantic strategies, and may deliver to us then, as well, a helpful way of assessing the quality of the choices that Bloom has made.

A serious reader of Ashbery must sooner or later confront the apparent anomaly of the poet's second volume, *The Tennis Court*

Oath. The book is a grotesquerie, an elaborate exercise in unre-
claimed neosurrealistic pandemonium whose most celebrated and
characteristic efforts, "Europe" and "Leaving the Atocha Station,"
succeed only in pushing language beyond the bounds of *any* kind of
intelligibility. Here is a passage from "Leaving the Atocha Station":

> The worn stool blazing   pigeons from the roof
>   driving tractor to squash
> Leaving the Atocha Station   steel
> infected bumps the screws
>   everywhere   wells
> abolished top ill-lit
> scarecrow falls   Time, progress and good sense
> strike of shopkeepers dark blood
> no forest you can name drunk scrolls
> the completely new Italian hair . . .
> Baby . . .   ice falling off the port
> The centennial   Before we can   (P. 33)

These twelve lines yield an indeterminate number of constitutent
phrases, most nominal, some adjectival, some finally ambiguous.
And, of course, we cannot be certain of connections between any of
the phrases. They collide with each other in a baffling array of possible syntactic combinations, most of which will not mesh completely. And then we are confronted, too, with the frustrations of the
variegate semantic field, which deliberately mocks our attempts to
formulate an equivalence chain that would give the passage coherence. We are forced to agree with Bloom that what we have here
is indeed "calculated incoherence," but perhaps we can discern
a "necessity" in this spectacularly perverse extreme of Ashbery's
elliptical art that Bloom is loath to acknowledge.

   The Tennis Court Oath represents Ashbery's attempt to pass beyond the hierarchies of language altogether. In the Coleridgean
terminology of Ammons, Ashbery's second volume is an emblem of
the poet's desire to wed himself entirely to diversity, to the Many,
while ignoring the unity that diversity—no matter how much it is
dramatized as a matter of strategy—demands, if we are to make our
world intelligible by naming it. That Ashbery's aesthetic in *Some
Trees* would take him to the cul-de-sac of *The Tennis Court Oath*
was predictable by principles other than Bloom's logic of influence,
and was in fact predicted by W. H. Auden in his equivocal introduction to the earlier volume. "The danger for the poet working with the

subjective life," Auden cautions, is that "he is tempted to manufacture calculated oddities, as if the subjectively sacred were necessarily and on all accounts odd."[34]

"Calculated oddities" abound in *The Tennis Court Oath* because Ashbery in his first two books is forcing himself to face the "curse of mediacy"[35] afflicting modern writers, while not having fully marshaled the strategic resources to contend with it. Implicit in the elegant Stevensian evasions of the best poems of *Some Trees*—"Some Trees," "Two Scenes," "Le Livre Est sur la Table"—is an acknowledgment that the poet cannot, and furthermore should not, attempt to name an essentialized Romantic One, a point Bloom himself makes of Ashbery's poetry as a whole in another of his puzzling near forfeitures of his own position.[36] But there is also in Ashbery's poetry from the start an even more important move beyond Stevens. As Marjorie Perloff has noted, Ashbery turns his inherited "mode on its head by cutting off" entirely the residual "referential dimension" in Stevens's work.[37] That is, Ashbery's poetry, even as early as *Some Trees*, "doesn't have subjects," as Ashbery himself puts it, and it does not have subjects because it has *given up already, as a matter of strategy*, that quest to pin down and to wrest symbolic significance from the discretely other things-of-the-world that perplexes an isolate Romantic wanderer of the Ammons variety. In a review of Gertrude Stein's *Stanzas in Meditation* appearing in *Poetry* in 1957, the year after the publication of *Some Trees*, Ashbery praises Stein for offering "a general, all-purpose model which each reader can adapt to fit his own sense of particulars."[38] Such a description applies very well to Ashbery's own poetry, a poetry whose elusive arguments and fractured tales deliver what Bloom rightly calls "a ravishing simplicity that seems largely lacking in any referential quality" (FC, p. 193).

Ashbery's rhetoric of the flux of consciousness and of our lives involves from the start a strategic acceptance of the *loss* of that absolute upon which seers customarily predicate their visions of either multeity or the One. Bloom sees this loss, of course, as a function of the encroaching shadows of visionary history. Remarking on the "difficult serenity" (FC, p. 176) often apparent in the work of Stevens and Ashbery, he suggests that while "perhaps Stevens was addicted to loss," Ashbery "scarcely knows how to proceed except by acknowledging" it.[39] But Ashbery's loss, and the loss of the late Stevens with his poetry "in the predicate that there is nothing else" (CP, p. 527), also might be said to eventuate from defeats other than Bloom's agonistic and oedipal ones. If Stevens's poetry features the scrupulous epistemological hesitance seen by one of Bloom's friendly critical adversaries, Helen Vendler, then we might in turn see in Ashbery's poetry a culmination of such hesitance, as the poet effaces from his vision even the possibility of that essentialized naming of flux that would confer a symbolical mounting into peaks of vision. Stevens's "qualified" assertions (RT, p. 228) lose assertiveness altogether in Ashbery, and become simply qualifications; that is, they become assertions-about-things that, deliberately lacking the force of referential propositionality, exist as propositional "truth-claims" only within the protean world of their own making. To believe in a transcendental signified—even if that belief takes, as it does in Ammons, the skeptically modern form of an avowal (time and again!) that "Overall is beyond me"—is to confer a stability, a coherent progression, on one's arranging of the world through language. Strategically forsaking such a stability, Ashbery builds his entire enterprise upon what Charles Altieri, one of his best critics, calls a "distrust of any dialectical progress," a distrust necessarily involving then, too, a rejection of the "dream of synthesis" at the heart of much Romantic desire.[40]

The question Ashbery was forced to contend with in *The Tennis Court Oath* by his strategy of loss was simply this: What is *left* for poetry, if signification of the Other is eliminated? That the answer of this volume is inadequate—and that Ashbery recognized it to be so—is the key to our understanding of the importance of his work. For, having rent from his poetry the possibility of a referential and essentialized naming, Ashbery in *The Tennis Court Oath* tried to ground the expressions of his art in the only area *seemingly* left it: the flux of his solipsistic consciousness. Poems like "Leaving the Atocha Station" and "Europe" are attempts to circumvent the curse of mediacy entirely by the daringly simple exercise, perhaps derived from Abstract Expressionism, of communing with, or *naming*, only themselves and the vagaries of their randomness as they are created. Thus, "Atocha" determinedly blocks all attempts to fit its particulars within any kind of hierarchy, syntactic or semantic. Thus, "Europe" is not so much written as whimsically collected from snippets of American magazines, odds and ends of children's books.[41]

Poetry, in the characteristic poems of *The Tennis Court Oath*, has given up its very reason for being, for it succeeds finally in erecting a wall between itself and any attempt to understand it, a wall composed of the many objets trouvé of the poet's willfully dispersed and dispersing consciousness. As Paul Carroll, who professes to enjoy

"Atocha," has noticed, Ashbery is not even a successful Dadaist or
Surrealist, because the poems are too *calculated*, they are "too
studied," to capture the distinguishing wit or surprise of a ram-
bunctious dream. Carroll goes on to celebrate the "final freedom" of
our reading of "Atocha" (while insisting somewhat paradoxically
that "Atocha" "isn't a poem which means anything or nothing").[42]
Perhaps we can better use his observation to secure for Ashbery an
escape from the frenzied Many, and back into that world that, since
the disaster of *The Tennis Court Oath*, has been his unflagging object of attention: the world of *our* humanness, of the flux of *our* lives,
our tales together. For the final lesson of Ashbery's artful rambling
in randomness is that it too is compromised by a mediacy of its own;
it too, like all expression, is calculated and strategic, caught within
a prison of its own device. A simple point to make, obviously, yet the
direction of Ashbery's aesthetics forced him *to need* to find it out for
himself—and to find out its corollary wisdom as well. From the fearful but necessary disaster of *The Tennis Court Oath*, Ashbery
learned that all our human knowing and naming is a *telling*, and
that this telling is a telling together whose genesis in the ineluctably
mediated ground of our sharings as language users cannot and
need not ever be denied.[43]

And so we move from the impasse of the elliptical in Ashbery's
work to the liberation of the proverbial. From *Rivers and Mountains*
through *Shadow Train*, this proverbial strain has come to occupy
a position at the center of Ashbery's vision, as the poet, in his
strange and quiet way, has assumed the burdens of the Romantic
universe while at the same time discarding the conventions of
anguished, solitary Romantic posturing to speak to us as one
human among many, to remind us, as "Litany" says:

> How big and forceful some of our ideas can be—
> Not giants or titans, but strong, firm
> Human beings with a good sense of humor
> And a grasp of a certain level of reality that
> Is going to be enough. . . .   (AWK, p. 36)

Thus, we are given a determinedly modest epistemology—an epistemology that is determined to obliterate itself, actually. The point
in this passage is *not* to pin down what "*level of reality*" we "*grasp*"
in any given situation; Ashbery, with his disdain for the easy answers of dialectic, will not slice things up for us, precisely because
whatever is there is "going to be enough." "The Wrong Kind of Insur-
ance," in *Houseboat Days*, might be said to provide the paradigm for
all Ashbery's mature work:

> We too are somehow impossible, formed of so many different
>   things,
> Too many to make sense to anybody.
> We straggle on as quotients, hard-to-combine
> Ingredients, and what continues
> Does so with our participation and consent.   (P. 50)

With cunning honesty, Ashbery's poetics *begins* with loss, with
a rejection of the dream of essence, of dialectic, of synecdoche. "I
wish to keep my differences," Ashbery says in "Litany" (AWK, p. 3),
and, unlike Ammons, who constantly tells us this but continues to
force his "differences" into the tidy hierarchies of his Coleridgean
dialectic, Ashbery remains insistent upon providing what he calls
"a ride in common variety" (p. 107). If the mistake of *The Tennis
Court Oath* was to deliver a journey through a barren and impene-
trable private "variety," the mark of Ashbery's mature mode is to
render his vision open to our "participation and consent" by granting from the start, as a loss that we all share—a "common" loss—
the mediacy of our tales. Ashbery's insistence that we are a conversation—"We are all talkers / It is true," says "Soonest Mended"
(DDS, p. 18)—before we are a knowing, and that our knowing is thus
a telling, should remind us of thinkers as different as Heidegger,
Kenneth Burke, and Richard Rorty, all of whom feature stratagems
to move beyond what Burke calls "scientistic" modes of perception.[44] For Heidegger this involves a radical redefinition of the
Heraclitean Logos as a gathering, not an essence.[45] Ashbery's
ground of verbal being is also a gathering beyond conventional
dualisms, although we may note here a crucial distinction insofar as
Heidegger finally claims ontological status for his Logos as gathering—hence, the Derridean critique[46]—while Ashbery's strategy of
loss dictates that he will not make a truth-claim even for the cosmogony that the crafted flux of his poems seems to presuppose. For
Ashbery, it is important only that, as "Litany" puts it, "*the tales /
Live now, and we live as part of them, / Caring for them and for ourselves, warm at last*" (AWK, p. 37).

Ashbery's strategy of loss gives us the absences of his poetry, the
subdued, often melancholy tone, the empty horizons and empty
afternoons, the broad expanses that are his characteristic images,
the "interstices, between a vacant stare and the ceiling" where "we
live," as "Saying It to Keep It from Happening" instructs us (HD,
p. 29). To forsake the dream of essence means to forsake the hope of
ever naming anything exactly. Ashbery does not deliver peaks of
synecdochal Romantic knowing, where an ecstatic or gnomic nam-

ing of the sublime—whether Bloomian or Coleridgean—is sought. Such an aspiration by design is not even there in Ashbery's work. Similarly, any type of "scientistic" naming is also discredited as an irrelevant and oppressive abstraction from the flux of mind-in-the-world. The poetry of A. R. Ammons, of course, is full of just this kind of knowledge, of detailed and precise observation of the streaks on the postmodern tulip. Ashbery's mode of loss, on the other hand, leaves us with neither this discrete a knowable nature nor this defined a separate knower. Such distinctions have no place within what Ashbery calls the "greater naturalism" of his poetry, a quixotic naturalism based on the mature poet's premise "that we are somehow all aspects of a consciousness giving rise to the poem."[47] The diffidence of the begging of epistemological questions here—"somehow"—should not be overlooked. Ashbery's point is *not* that he "disagrees with" the dualisms that would create a gulf between subject and object in all our knowing and our being. What the strategies of his poetry indicate is that he does not even care to be exercised by such unproductive quandaries—or, rather, that these conundrums of knowing, themselves conventional, will figure in his poetry only insofar as they too are part of the "tales" we live in. "I guess I don't have a very strong sense of my own identity," Ashbery has observed while explaining the "polyphony" of pronouns in his work,[48] and our wonder at the sweeping unpretentiousness of his pronouncement is exceeded only by surprise that the strategies of his poems actually do seek to realize such a modesty beyond the ken of the Romantic mind. Here is a poem I think to be a representative one, from Ashbery's volume of 1979, *As We Know*:

The Wine

It keeps a large supply of personal pronouns
On hand. They awaken to see
Themselves being used as it grows up,
Confused, in a rush of fluidity.

Once men came back here to rot.
Now the salt banners only interrupt the sky—
Black crystals, quartzite. The balm of not
Knowing living filters to the bottom of each eye.

The telephone was involved in it. And bored
Glances, boring questions about the hem no
One wanted to look at, or would admit having seen.
These things came after it was a place to go.

Yet nothing was its essence. The core
Remained as elusive as ever. Until the day you
Fitted the unlikely halves together, and they clicked.
So its wholeness was an order. But it had seemed not to

Be part of the original blueprint, the way
It had appeared in intermittent dreams, stretching
Over several nights, like that. But that was okay,
Providing the noise factor didn't suddenly loom

Too large, as was precisely happening just now.
Where have I seen that face before? And I see
Just what it means to itself, and how it came
Down to me. And so, in like manner, it came to be.   (P. 100)

We need first to note that this poem makes sense in ways that
"Leaving the Atocha Station" does not. While the unity that it presents is obviously not that of the synecdochal Romantic whole or
quest, "The Wine" nonetheless invites a certain kind of "participation." How so? Ashbery could very well take as origin of his mature
art a cryptic remark of the later Wittgenstein: "What has to be accepted, the given, is—so one could say—*forms of life.*"[49] Poems like
"The Wine" are accessible to us because Ashbery bases his explorations of the flux of consciousness on the "forms of life" in which
consciousness comes to us, already mediated. The poet's typically
laconic characterization of his art aptly summarizes the presuppositions governing this curious conjoining: "In the last few years
I have been attempting to keep meaningfulness up to the pace of
randomness. . . . but I really think that meaningfulness can't get
along without randomness and that they somehow have to be
brought together."[50]

Randomness in "The Wine," as always in Ashbery, is realized
through the flux of personal pronouns, often indeterminate,
through the strange shifts in narrative focus, through the bizarre
juxtapositions of semantic counters, of images. This last and very
important point first: we notice that there is not a difference *in kind*
between the semantic field of "Leaving the Atocha Station" and that
of "The Wine." The images still do not create (and thus do not refer
to) a stable and discrete otherness outside the poem; they still
bounce haphazardly off each other. But, whereas "Atocha" had
foregrounded the very disjunctiveness of the semantic field by
thwarting our attempts to place the poem in *any* syntactic frame,
"The Wine," assuming as a form of life the authority of a reasonable
and entirely coherent syntax, *allows us to feel* that we are making

sense of the various scenes, images, and gestures we encounter, and thereby permits us to participate in the "tale" of the poem, although, of course, we may never be entirely certain what the tale is about. The forms of "The Wine," as in most of Ashbery's later poetry, are conventional: six quatrains, a loosely decasyllabic line, a relentlessly ordinary syntax. The quiet, unflamboyant forms the poem comes in serve to convince us, as a matter of calculated effect, that although "we know we can never be anything but parallel / And proximate in our relations" (AWK, p. 117), nonetheless we are justified in granting as a basis for the poet's vision his hope, from "The One Thing That Can Save America," that he may tell us of "the quirky things that happen to me . . . / And you instantly know what I mean" (SP, p. 45).

As Ashbery has learned to exploit the tactical weapons released by his refusal to attempt a naming of the perceptual other, he increasingly has chosen an all-purpose pronoun as a sort of shorthand representation for the "quirky things" and the flux of his tales: "it." An indeterminate "it" is an implied argument against the tyranny of lyric description, against the epistemological arrogance that the quest for conventional exactitude of lyric observation presupposes. Ashbery is always interested in, and has a great facility for, delivering stock descriptions of scenes, but the interest is in the telling as a tale, not as a knowing, and the facility derives from an acute ear for the forms and the formulas of the convention-bound tales of our culture. At the core of the elusive narratives and the disjointed, opaque arguments of Ashbery's mature poetry remains an "it" that, as "Litany" tells us, *emerges as a firm / Enigma, burnished, filled in*" (AWK, p. 15). Since such an "it" deliberately exists without a referent, "it" might be said to occupy that place in Ashbery's vision where randomness and meaningfulness meet. The details in which we see "it" manifest itself in any given poem are all contrivances or rhetorical gambits for saying what is unsayable— unsayable, though, not because transcendent but because immanent and ongoing through multifoliate particulars. The naming of this flux, of this "doing" that, in the words of "As We Know," involves "the whole fabric" (p. 74), must be indefinite, must itself represent a turning away from essence, because Ashbery recognizes that any attempt to say "it," to give expression to the ongoingness of things, necessarily is inadequate—at worst, as the title of one of his canniest poems puts "it," a "Saying It to Keep It from Happening."[51]

And so, in "The Wine," we begin with an "it" that is enigmatic indeed. Ashbery has observed that we should treat his bizarre titles

as ways of "getting into the poem,"[52] so perhaps the "it" moving
through this first stanza with a "rush of fluidity" has a Bacchanalian
cast. But such an orthodox way in will not get us far. We might see
the "it" as a tongue-in-cheek description of Ashbery's own method,
which uncharitable critics often have called "confused"—a too
rushed "fluidity." These speculations are fittingly tentative, for the
second stanza changes the scene of the poem completely: "Once
men came back here to rot." Where is "here"? Customarily, writers
feel obligated to situate "here" in some sort of identifiable mimetic
place. Not so Ashbery. The origin and the place of "here" remain
mysterious, although we do receive an imagistic sketch: surrealistic
"salt banners," a typically empty sky, some unexplained and unex-
plainable rock formations. The humor of the first stanza has taken
a dark turn, into something quite like a lunar waste land. And we
should note that, just as the first sentence of the first stanza set the
scene for "it" with a stock phrase from the economic life of our culture, with its large supplies always on hand, so the second stanza
too is catalyzed by a cliché, this a formula from melodramatic fiction, or perhaps from bad films. "Once" men did this—a "once" that
sets up an expectation, almost a stock response in itself, of a "now"
that will be different.

Ashbery's mature poetry is full of such clichés, such stock
phrases, such readily recognizable patterns of discourse. They too
are forms of life in which consciousness comes to us, to all of us, and
Ashbery's use of them, his probing of them, his purposeful dis-
solving of them one into the other, constitute an integral part of his
poetics, of his attempt to give us that "*living, vibrant turntable*" of
tantalizingly unspecified but somehow common "*events*" that
"Litany" sees as the mark of good art (AWK, p. 36). The scene in
the second stanza is unspecified, not because its details are sloppy,
but because we do not know the context of "here." The scene is
common because it has been elucidated by a stock pattern of response—and the culmination of the pattern is the peculiarly con-
tentless moral observation appended to it: "The balm of not /
Knowing living filters to the bottom of each eye."

Stanza three attempts a clarification, and in the process returns
us to "it." Is this the "it" of the first stanza? The nature of "it" in
Ashbery's poetry should tell us that the question is irrelevant. Since
"it" is the sign of the spot where randomness and meaningfulness
meet, the meaningfulness itself is not referential in intent, but,
rather, is derived from the forms of life amid the flux of the poem. We
do know here that boredom has set in, that it has done so "after it

was a place to go." But we do not know, and do not *need* to know, what the "it" is.

The fourth stanza, with as bold a proposition on the characteristic divagations of Ashbery's art as we will ever see, informs us of the requisite manner of our not knowing. Like many of Ashbery's propositions, this one begins with a coordinating conjunction that implies a logical continuity not discursively merited by the poem. "Yet" is an argumentative gambit; it tells us that a differentiation is about to be established. But what is the previous proposition? Ashbery has likened the movement of his poems to that of an argument "suddenly derailed" and "opaque."[53] Sometimes, as in "Saying It to Keep It from Happening" and "Blue Sonata," the argument is conducted as a sustained exercise in the propositions of a foregrounded "it." Here in "The Wine" the "it" is more elusive, more inviting in its opacity. Ashbery's "yet" seeks to assert, apparently, that the clarifications of the preceding stanza—the telephone's involvement, the boring questions about the "hem"—were unsatisfactory, not because they did not arrive at the "essence" of the matter, but because the "essence" of the matter was not there to be arrived at. "The core / remained as elusive as ever," we are wisely told, and there is a sort of serene power in that summation, although we do not know what the "core" is a core of.

Ashbery's poems since *The Tennis Court Oath* tend to arrive at wisdom of this kind; they tend to settle into domestic aphorism and proverbial knowing as forms of life that are available in a world where "we are somehow all aspects of a consciousness giving rise to the poem." Presenting proverbial wisdom is a way of affirming "as we know"; it is a way, as Kenneth Burke has said, of naming "situations" that are "typical and recurrent" amid a group of people.[54] But, of course, by virtue of their participation within the crafted flux of his poems, Ashbery's proverbs are shorn of their referential substance. The situations that they name are left unspecified, so that, while we are comforted in some way by the gravity of their knowing, we ourselves do not really know what that knowing is about. And so, at this culmination of Ashbery's mature art, we come on the appeal, indeed the solace, of proverbs as epideictic gestures, as central among our many gestures that "have taken us farther into the day / Than tomorrow will understand" (HD, p. 35). As "All Kinds of Caresses" goes on to tell us, the power of such gestures as forms of life, as ways we have lived, is that they come finally to be the given— they come, from our having lived them so often, to "live us."

The rest of "The Wine" crafts gestures upon the proverbial knowing of "wholeness" as "an order," one that is unsatisfactory and yet "okay" at the same time, as long as the conditions that, it seems, do obtain, don't. Ashbery's rehearsal of contradictions would be exasperating if it were not for the calming effect of his reasoned and regular syntax, the appeal of the first and only turning in the poem to an unspecified "you," the very ordinariness of the language— "blueprint," "noise factor," "loom . . . large"—as it moves amid the forms of our culture. "Where have I seen that face before?" is another stock phrase, an expression of bewilderment on the edge of mystery, and it seems that the issue of our knowing returns us to the confusions of "fluidity." But the poem turns again, or, rather, it returns us to the effect of what we know, and by now we know the comfort of the gesture of that knowing: "And so, in like manner, it came to be." That is, in a "manner" like its meaning "to itself . . . it . . . came to be" *it*—and we have now come to see that this "it" continues, as the forms of Ashbery's poems serve to tell us, with our "participation and consent."

Thus, Ashbery's poetics predicated upon loss, upon the only apparent truth that, as "Late Echo" puts it, "there really is nothing left to write about" (AWK, p. 88), succeeds in delivering what the poet, perhaps quixotically, calls "love." "It is necessary," "Late Echo" amends, "to write about the same old things / In the same way" in order for "love to continue and be gradually different." This "love" inheres in our participation together in the tales of our lives, as those tales live and "*we live as part of them / Caring for them and for ourselves, warm at last.*" With the boldness of his sweeping strategic modesty, Ashbery returns us, and returns our poetry, to that ground where we all have our lives, to the situations and the forms of life of our acting together in irreducible difficulty, to the talk on talk that, as Kenneth Burke has affirmed, is the most real and the most realistic knowing that we have.[55]

Ashbery's mature utterance, of course, is somehow too mannered, as many of his critics have charged, too difficult a talking on amid the accepted indeterminacies of time, language, and culture. Certainly there are other ways for contemporary poets to resist the pressures of Romanticism, to refuse to enter the baleful circle of vision and its perplexities. An entire postsymbolist tradition of modern poetry ignored or derided by Bloom—the tradition of Pound, Williams, Olson, Zukofsky, Creeley—has provided a compelling "counter-statement" to Romanticism emphasizing a complex and vivifying interplay of *res* and *verba*, voice, grapholect, history, and culture. Ashbery's special interest lies in the fact that he *does* accept as burden the forms of loss derived from a distinctively Romantic cosmogony, particularly the loss of an essentialized and solitary knowing, but then goes on to release himself from that burden through adherence to a pure principle of discourse—the principle of discourse as a sharing by which we constitute ourselves. What makes this maneuver doubly intriguing is that the rhetorical indeterminacies and wandering, never-quite-synthesized verbal gestures resulting from it, present precisely an *actional* correlative to the world of Bloom's nemesis, Derrida.[56] Bloom, in responding to Derrida, is moved finally to a destructive acceptance of the realm of discourse as either one of two *extremes*, absolute plenitude or absolute dearth of meaning; it matters not which, Bloom says in his essay on Ashbery in *Deconstruction and Criticism*, as long as the dark and uncompromised glory of poetic battle is retained.[57] Ashbery, with his strategic forsaking *even of interest* in any type of essentialized knowing, rejects deconstruction's sterile focus on the problematics of signification at the same time as his turn to a middle realm of shared discourse puts the lie to the presuppositions underlying Bloom's cultivated rhetoric of crisis—the rationale of Romanticism's necessity "in the predicate that there is nothing else."

Bloom's reading of Ashbery, like his reading of Ammons, manages to be both acute and selectively myopic at the same time. Occasionally he shows himself aware of the drama of mediated vision that is crucial to Stevens and Ashbery, and to whatever common ground they do possess:

> For Ashbery, the privileged moments, like their images, are on the dump, and he wants to purify them by clearly placing them there. Say of what you see in the dark, Stevens urges, that it is this or that it is that, but do not use the rotted names. Use the rotted names, Ashbery urges, but cleanse them by seeing that you cannot be apart from them, and are partly redeemed by consciously suffering with them. (FC, p. 190)

Bloom similarly makes a nice distinction between Stevens and Ashbery on the question of transcendence when in an analysis of a late stanza of "Fragment" he observes that Ashbery, "in his moment most akin" to the "sublime self-revelation" of Stevens's "I have not but I am and as I am, I am" (CP, p. 405), does *not* affirm "the Emersonian-Whitmanian Transcendental Self" but, rather, " 'the secret of what goes on' " (FC, p. 200). And yet, having made observations as penetrating as these, Bloom does not go beyond them to assess

their implications for his intensely self-conscious and solipsistic
Romanticism. Just as the circular logic of his map for misreading
has compelled him to ignore the strained, hackneyed, and unintentional conventionality that mars much of Ammons's avidly Romantic verse, so Bloom must ignore in Ashbery's profound and witty
manipulation of the conventions of our tales together the final lesson that such an enterprise has to offer him about the "ends" of his
own Romantic vision. "Yet nothing was its essence," Ashbery says,
which is to say that since "essence," or Ammons's "Overall," is
describable only in the language of things, it is thus, in effect, abol-
ished as "essence," for we know—*and can be content with*—only
what our ineluctably mediated tales tell us. Ashbery's mature art is
characterized, then, by the expansiveness of its voyaging through
a flux of epideictic gestures, a voyaging whose ethical (*not* epistemological) center finally is that

> . . . we are ordinary people
> With not unreasonable desires which we can satisfy
> From time to time without causing cataclysms
> That keep getting louder and more forceful instead of dying
>   away. (AWK, p. 109)

Bloom, whose own ethical center is located in the darkly Romantic principle that "only the agon is of the essence," will neither
recognize nor long abide in a world where "ordinary people" meet
the exigencies of their making "without causing" those cataclysmic
breakings that, for the belated Romantic prophet, constitute the
proper influx of redemptive vision. The "restitution of narcissism,"
which is the beginning and the end of Bloom's critical mission, inevitably entails a refusal to examine the social shapings of language
as they in turn shape the language-bound world of the poet's making. Such a refusal is perhaps too high a price to pay for the indubitable (and coercive) strength that accompanies "unreasonable"
Romantic desires. Harold Bloom's mapping of the poem at the end
of the Romantic mind is itself a highly self-conscious emblem of that
mind in an extremity of its own making. If Bloom's quest to save
A. R. Ammons and John Ashbery from themselves and their time has
any use other than that envisioned by the master mapmaker, it may
be to remind us that self-conscious cunning does not necessarily
redeem solipsistic extremity, even if that extremity is presented as
the "misreading" that the age demands.

Humanism in the Extreme: The Predicament of Romantic Redemption

If the early works of Harold Bloom countered the authoritarian and classical orthodoxies of the waning era of Eliot with a conception of poetry and a version of poetic history that featured the majesty of the autonomous Romantic imagination transcending the dull recalcitrance of nature, language, and society, then the many volumes of his mature phase have expanded upon that earlier visionary Romanticism in order to secure the ground of poetry from the encroachments of even more powerful adversaries who would seek, in Bloom's view, to abolish the authority of poetic vision altogether. In order fully to assess the significance and the appeal of Bloom's critical project since *The Anxiety of Influence*, we must see it in conjunction with those other theories of poetic history and poetic creation that have seemed most pointedly to threaten it. Rather arbitrarily, we might designate as especially salient Bloomian adversaries two critics, Hugh Kenner and Paul de Man, who are completely different in temperament, approach, philosophy, and aims, and in the nature of the critical relation they have to Bloom. Kenner, the author of *The Pound Era, A Homemade World*, and a host of other books elucidating a tenaciously Modernist literary vision, presents a canon of modern literature and a corollary method for reading radically opposed to Bloom's. De Man, a central rhetorician of deconstruction and for many years a colleague of Bloom's at Yale, provides a commentary, at times explicit and at other times implied, upon the logic and the methods of Bloom's own rhetoric of Romantic agon. In the previous chapter we have seen the price that Bloom's version of Romanticism pays for its neglect of the social and conventional side of poetic vision in two important contemporary poets; now, through an examination of his relation to two key contemporaries in criticism, we should be able to judge the full depth of Bloom's enduring commitment to a revision in the awareness of poetry in our time. While Kenner's "philosophy" of poetry and method of reading are foreign enough to Bloom that he seldom deigns to mention them except by way of momentary imprecation, the nihilistic Nietzschean rhetoric of de Man is so unsettlingly close to Bloom's own method for mastery through misreading that over the past decade it has induced in his mapping a profound shadow drama, a subtle lover's quarrel with the tempting demystifications of the deconstructionist regimen that has spurred the development of several of Bloom's most penetrating and controversial ideas. De Man is approached in Bloom's volumes of the late seventies with the "reverence" due an "advanced critical consciousness, the most rigorous and scrupulous in the field today" (WS, p. 393), because he furnishes a formidable critique of Bloom's key assumptions about the nature of "error" in poetic language and in reading. At the same time, however, de Man also serves as an illustration to Bloom of the aridity and the baroque asceticism into which the doctrine of "error" collapses if it is not secured by the final ground of Romantic desire. Bloom's attempt to work out his conflict with de Man and to distance himself from deconstruction forces him to clarify the implications of his own crisis vision of poetics and brings him finally to the culminating subtleties of *Wallace Stevens*, with its featured theory of the visionary crossing, and the ensuing revisionary developments of his subsequent volumes of the late seventies and early eighties.

In an important review of *The Anxiety of Influence* appearing in *Comparative Literature* in 1974 and reprinted in the second edition of *Blindness and Insight* in 1983, de Man made two suggestions that were to be crucial to the development of Bloom's subsequent work. First, he noted that the six revisionary ratios rather sketchily presented by Bloom in the most elliptical of his books could easily be seen to have "paradigmatic rhetorical structures" in the figures and tropes of traditional rhetoric.[1] *A Map of Misreading* in 1975, with its breakdown of the ratios into psychic, imagistic, and tropological components, initiated the quest to chart these structures and thereby to exploit the rich terminological resources of the Aristotelian line of rhetorical criticism. Second, and even more important, de Man, with his usual regard for the rhetoricity of criticism, advanced the claim that Bloom's insight into the systematic swervings of influence suffered from a blindness toward the status of influence itself, which, in de Man's "more linguistic terminology," would have to be seen as "a metaphor that dramatizes a linguistic structure into a diachronic narrative" (p. 276). For de Man, the real subject of *The Anxiety of Influence* is *not* what Bloom himself intends to feature, the mammoth tale of poetic battle in post-Enlightenment poetry; rather, what the volume really concerns is "the difficulty or, rather, the impossibility of reading and, by inference . . . the indeterminacy of literary meaning." "We can forget about the temporal scheme and about the pathos of the oedipal son," de Man suggests (p. 273); "underneath all the drama stands a pretty tight linguistic model that could be described in a very different tone and terminology" (p. 274). The model then extrapolated by de Man from Bloom's map of the six revisionary ratios eliminates the "naturalistic language of desire, possession, and power" of Bloom, representing as it does "a step backward" into "the constraints of natural reference" (p. 271), and replaces the oedipal drama of influence with a deconstruction-ist rhetoric of necessary "patterns of error" that are revealed to be "rooted in language rather than in the self" (p. 272).

De Man's handling of Bloom's subject-centered, intensely psychologistic theory strongly reflects, of course, his own theoretical ties to the continental tradition of poststructuralist thought inspired by Saussurean diacritical linguistics and the Nietzschean revolt against traditional metaphysics. Although the main ideas of deconstruction are by now common currency within the literary establishment, a brief summary nonetheless might be helpful in order to highlight the issues involved in the debate between Bloom and de Man. The deconstructionists seek primarily to subvert what they call the traditional Western "logocentric" belief in the "metaphysics of presence." From Nietzsche, they derive the notion that all human values are ultimately groundless and illusory, all cultural codes arbitrary inventions in a world that one can never really know. From Saussure, they appropriate a model with which to explain the endless play of significations or free-floating signifiers within our language systems when those systems are deprived of the ultimate referent or "transcendental signified" that, in traditional metaphysics, has always given them order and determinate meaning. As presented by Derrida in his important triad of studies, *Of Grammatology*, *Writing and Difference*, and *Speech and Phenomena*, the deconstructionist critique of logocentrism focuses on a dismantling of the Western privileging of speech over writing, a "phonocentrism" that Derrida regards as an especially telling example of the nostalgic desire of Western culture for the unmediated presence or the absolute origins of the signified.[2] Since such moments of pure meaning, of meaning absolutely present to consciousness, can never be had, the Derridean decentering releases us to a world of "free play," of the infinite wandering, or deferment, of signification, for which Derrida invents the elusive punning term, "*differance*."

In literature, the world into which we are liberated is one rid of the tyranny of determinate voice, presence, form, or meaning, a world where the complete range of the significations of the text may be given the full play that criticism characteristically has contrived to deny. J. Hillis Miller delivers a lucid summary of this aspect of the deconstructive enterprise in his unraveling of Wallace Stevens's "The Rock":

> Deconstruction as a mode of interpretation works by a careful and circumspect entering of each textual labyrinth. The critic feels his way from figure to figure, from concept to concept, from mythical motif to mythical motif, in a repetition which is in no sense a parody. It employs, nevertheless, the subversive power present in even the most exact and unironical doubling. The deconstructive critic seeks to find, by this process of retracing, the element in the system studied which is alogical, the thread in the text in question which will unravel it all, or the loose stone which will pull down the whole building. The deconstruction, rather, annihilates the ground on which the building stands by showing that the text has already annihilated that ground, knowingly or unknowingly. Deconstruction is not a dismantling of the structure of a text but a demonstration that it has already dismantled itself.[3]

Deconstruction, at least for most of its American adherents, works not as a destruction but as a *demystified recognition* of what the text has already done to itself, if the critic would only discard the comfortable but finally oppressive fiction of determinate meaning. As de Man explains in *Blindness and Insight*, "That sign and meaning can never coincide, is what is precisely taken for granted in the kind of language we call literary. Literature, unlike everyday language, begins on the far side of this knowledge; it is the only form of language free from the fallacy of unmediated expression."[4] The deconstructive critic's major task, then, is to locate the "*aporias*," or negative moments, where the text, "aware" of the abyss of its own fictionality, in effect cancels itself out, and reveals the final paradoxes of truth and falsehood inherent in the only absolute it can ever know: the supreme fictions of its signifiers' "trace"-like dispersion.

Detractors have charged that the deconstructionist movement as a whole represents little more than a particularly extreme and self-serving stage in a history of Western philosophical skepticism that is almost as long as the history of the "metaphysics of presence" that the movement intends to subvert. Citing Derrida against himself, they argue that it is at best an exercise in futility and at worst a monstrous and antihumanistic terminological game, to seek to deconstruct the language of logocentrism while at the same time acknowledging, as Derrida repeatedly does, that such a language is the necessary and inescapable medium of the critique itself. Yet the movement has gained considerable power in the American academy in the past decade, a power, like Bloom's own, that might be based partly on literary politics and the suasions of intellectual fashion, but that seems to an even greater extent to reside in the very nature of the language-haunted world of literature that it makes possible for us. Without embarking on a Survey Perilous into the heartland of deconstruction and its metaphysical discontents,[5] we can still hope to sketch the predicament of literature and poetics in the past several decades, and the place of Bloom and his deconstructive Yale colleagues within it, by asking ourselves the key question: What do Bloom and his intimate antagonists have *in common*? Or, translated into the terms we have been using in this chapter: What is the nature of Bloom's concern with de Man's challenge?

In his attempt to explain why Bloom is brought to the impasse of the melodramatic tale of the Romantic imagination presented in *The Anxiety of Influence*, de Man acutely observes that the problem arises from the radical conception of the imaginative process advanced by Bloom in his earlier work. Bloom's crucial, if tentative, insight in that work, de Man contends, is "that, all appearances to the contrary, the romantic imagination is *not* to be understood in dialectical interplay with the presumably antithetical category of 'nature' " (p. 269). Rather, as our own discussion in chapters 1 and 3 has shown, Bloom comes increasingly to espouse a theory that sees the Romantic imagination as autonomous, nonreferential, acting according to the sublime guidance of its own "internalized" laws. Precisely because such an imagination exists *by definition* in the realm of the ineffable—exists, that is, in the pure potentiality of what it has ceaselessly ceased to be—any attempt to describe it suffers from the lack of a conceptual language that could be adequate to it. It is at this point, de Man argues, that Bloom makes his key mistake. Faced with the "difficult philosophical predicament" forced upon him by the very acuity of his understanding of the non-

referential nature of the imagination, "Bloom's perhaps unconscious strategy," de Man suggests, "has been to reach out for a new
definition of the imagination by means of near-extravagant over-
statement. Since the imagination is unimaginable, it can only be
stated by hyperbole. Poetry, the product of the hyperbolic imagination, can do anything" (p. 270). In this, the heightening of Romantic
vision granted him by his newly won rhetoric of Romantic triumph,
Bloom becomes for de Man "the subject of his own desire for clarification" (p. 272).

What all this means is that de Man objects to the new Bloom
theory because it takes a wrong turn at a point *far down the line* in its
visionary conception of the imagination. As a deconstructionist,
de Man does not object to Bloom's central insistence on the nonreferential quality of the imagination; it is the very attempt to dismantle the "signified" in Bloom's theory that intrigues him. Rather,
what de Man recognizes here, and thereby forces Bloom to contend
with as well in all his subsequent work of the seventies, is that there
is an abyss beckoning the theorist *whenever* referentiality is aban-
doned as a normative ground for *any* kind of language use. For
de Man, this abyss is the infinite regress of an autonomous textuality as it dances over the deeper void of human insignificance in
a world decreed by Nietzsche to be godless and adrift. The challenge to Bloom, who shares de Man's belief that all the orthodox
gods are dead, who shares his conception of the nonreferential
imagination, and who shares then, too, his Nietzschean certainty
that patterns of "error" determine the reading process, is to legiti-
mize his plea that such error does not plunge us into the nightmare
of Nietzschean perspectivism, but rather still serves, at least in its
moments of deepest defensive majesty, to help us "see ourselves
again as perhaps eternity sees us, more like one another" in
our "egoism and our fallen condition" than "we can bear to believe"
(FC, p. xii).

Bloom's response to the threat posed by de Man takes two primary forms, both involving the development of just such a rhetoric
of misreading as de Man's review recommends. We have already
discussed Bloom's use of the Lurianic tale of limitation-substitu-
tion-restitution as a model for poetic creation. Now we are in a position to see its full significance as a corrective to the desiccations of
the deconstructionist enterprise. For while the first two stages of
poetic creation as envisaged through Luria "can be approximated in
many of the theorists of deconstruction," the third and most important stage, the stage of that visionary representation that *restores*

meaning and thus earns for poetry whatever grandeur it may still attain, cannot be undertaken with the overly limited tools of the deconstructionist project. The deconstructionist reader, "at once blind and transparent with light, self-deconstructed yet fully knowing the pain of his separation both from text and from nature," doubtless, Bloom observes, "will be more than equal to the revisionary labors of contraction and destruction" (MM, p. 5). But, to deconstruct or to demystify in this fashion, to limit reading solely to the limitations and the swervings of signification within the vast labyrinth of our textuality, is only "a limited good" (p. 175) if the reader does not also go about the central task of *re*-centering, which remains the primary burden and the chief responsibility of poetic meaning. The deconstructionist, in declining to scale those heights of restituting hyperbole (and, by extension, synecdoche before and metalepsis after) that de Man finds objectionable in his review of *The Anxiety of Influence*, declines also then to transcend the "destructive weariness" of "Romantic irony" in its "purified form" which de Man's allegories of reading ultimately deliver (DC, p. 16).

To this point Bloom's counterassault exists largely as counterassertion. The problem, as Bloom painfully knows, is in the deeper stratum of "error" itself when considered to be the origin and the end of all utterance. De Man's many allegories of reading over the past decade are all based on his earlier definition and valuation of Romantic allegory as a demystified "rhetoric of temporality," a rhetoric more penetrating than the traditionally conceived rhetoric of symbolic identification insofar as it recognizes "a distance in relation to its own origin, and, renouncing the nostalgia and the desire to coincide," establishes instead a "language in the void of this temporal difference."[6] De Man's response to the obliteration of "identity" before the random diachrony of signification is to accept with grim joy the effacement of truth, self, and presence that he himself has decreed. How can Bloom's own diachronic narrative of the referentless imagination not also, then, acknowledge defeat before the apparent groundlessness of its conceptions of itself? The answer lies in what we have seen to be the crucial turn in Bloom's thinking in his mature phase, the replacement of the master trope, "vision," by the even more cunning and resourceful trope of "influence." This transformation, implicit from the start of Bloom's career in his notion of mythopoeia as the imaginative process whereby vision strives against all threats to become completely itself, is not fully explored and exploited until the mid-seventies, when the challenge of deconstruction forces Bloom to justify the ways of his rhetoric to de Man. *Why* is restoration possible? And how can a theory based on the inevitability of misprision still claim an essential truth for the vision of both criticism and poetry?

Bloom answers these questions with one of his most daring gambits. Against de Man's suggestion that "influence" is but a metaphor that changes a linguistic model for the problematics of signification into a story or a temporal unfolding, Bloom argues in return that metaphor is only one trope among six, and that it is the six *taken together* that "influence" purports to represent. If influence were just a metaphor, Bloom observes, it would "be reduced to semantic tension, to an interplay between literal and figurative meanings" (MM, p. 77). But the story within the "sixfold, composite trope" of influence is *not* a story about semantic tension, about truth or falsehood viewed in mimetic terms; such distinctions, Bloom asserts, are *irrelevant* by de Man's own logic, since language exists by virtue of its initial and engendering referentless autonomy. Bloom's kabbalistic model, on the other hand, "starts" with the "assumption . . . that all distinction between proper and figurative meaning in language has been totally lost since the catastrophe of creation" (WS, p. 394), and then *proceeds from that assumption* to see into the life of what poetic language *really* is about, which is "*the will to utter within a tradition of uttering*" (p. 393). "Still evident even in the most advanced models of post-Structuralist thought," Bloom observes, is a striking confusion of "signification" with "meaning," a mistaken notion that they are somehow the same (PR, p. 240). They are *not* identical, Bloom argues, for the "structures" of poetic meaning consistently and transcendentally "evade the language that would confine them" (MM, p. 77).

And so, through the offices of de Man's counterpointing challenge, we return to the heart of the Bloomian vision already elaborated in chapters 3 and 4. "*There are no tropes,* but only concepts of tropes," Bloom acknowledges in *Wallace Stevens* (p. 393), but his project for misreading nonetheless is saved from the dire fate of Derridean "erasure" or labyrinthine de Manian asceticism by the knowledge that the errors of poetry and of criticism, the lies that are their essential meaning and their only vision, are errors not of signification, of the semantic positives and negatives of our merely referential being, but, rather, lies against that enemy lurking within all of us strong enough to misread and to write, the internalized time or tradition that, even as it establishes the very grounds for meaning, kills. The "poetic equivalent of Freud's concept of defense" (DC, p. 16) is Bloom's answer to the eviscerations of Gallic skepticism; against Derrida's "Scene of Writing" he is able to posit his own more powerful and ennobling "Primal Scene of Instruction" where the "anxiety-inducing transgression" of strong poetry endures "one stage beyond" the mere letter of its deconstruction (FC, p. xii).

And yet there is one more clarification still to be forced on Bloom by the challenge of de Man, a culminating clarification insofar as it involves that crisis point or crossing of vision that Bloom conceives to reside at the center of his drama of defensive creation as a substitutive "breaking" of form *between* the tropes of limitation and representation. In an examination of the rhetoric of Nietzsche initially appearing in *Yale French Studies* in 1975 and reprinted in *Allegories of Reading*, de Man concludes that rhetoric itself may be regarded as the "gap" between its traditional formulation as "persuasion" on the one hand, and as "a system of tropes" on the other:

> Considered as persuasion, rhetoric is performative but when considered as a system of tropes, it deconstructs its own performance. Rhetoric is a *text* in that it allows for two incompatible, mutually self-destructive points of view, and therefore puts an insurmountable obstacle in the way of any reading or understanding. The aporia between performative and constative language is merely a version of the aporia between trope and persuasion that both generates and paralyzes rhetoric and thus gives it the appearance of a history.[7]

With a typically audacious appropriation, Bloom in the final theoretical chapter of *Wallace Stevens* changes de Man's "*aporia* or figuration of doubt" from a "gap" to a "crossing" (p. 392), justifying the change on the expected grounds that "rhetoric considered as persuasion . . . takes us into a realm that also includes the lie" (p. 386). If the rhetoric of poetic argument includes the "lie," the Bloomian logic of visionary desire goes, the tropes of poetry between which the crossings of vision transpire are themselves *not* figures "of knowledge," as de Man's semantics of deconstruction would have them, but figures of "will," of will either "translating itself into a verbal act or figure of *ethos*," or will, by the very force of its transcendent desire, "failing to translate itself and so abiding as a verbal desire or figure of *pathos*" (p. 393). Either way, while the trope might first appear as "a cut or gap made in or into the anteriority of language," such an appearance is illusory since "language" itself must be seen to be an "anteriority" acting "as a figurative substitution for time." Misprision, Bloom deftly summarizes, is "the process by which the meanings of intentionality trope down to the mere significances of language, or conversely the process by which the significations of language can be transformed or troped upward into the meaningful world of our Will-to-Power over time and its henchman, language" (pp. 394–95). Bloom's theory of reading, then, while sharing with the deconstructionists the seemingly nihilistic belief that poems *"don't have* presence, unity, form, or meaning" as criticism traditionally has conceived them (KC, p. 122), nonetheless "triumphs" over mere demystification with its featured principle that what poems *do* deliver is *a desire to continue*, a desire that presupposes a powerful Romantic will prevailing beyond.

The crossing is at the heart of Bloom's final response to the threat of deconstruction because in that catastrophic breaking-of-the-vessels of presence, unity, form, and meaning which propels all strong poetry, there is an equally profound testament to the power of the languageless, relentless "faculty of self-preservation" which gives signification its sole ground. And too, since the crossings occur between *topoi* that are, we will recall, "voices of the dead," the cuts that they make in the language of the poem serve finally to affirm once again the primacy of the inspired prophetic voice over the depredations of deconstructionist "writing" (*"écriture"*). The cunning of Bloom's misprision of de Man's key concept of "gap" or *"aporia"* is representative of the cunning of his entire project to save Romanticism in its time of need. Bloom's strategic genius is to take Romanticism at its putative worst, after the crumbling of the great Romantic truth into the manifold "errors" of a vainglorious and solipsistic imagination, and, in the ringing tones of a "belated" prophecy built upon radically altered assumptions about the nature of poetic meaning, to declare this apparent nadir to be, in fact, the very emblem of Romantic strength and greatness. His tactical triumph in this instance is to present his theory of poetic battle at its seemingly most vulnerable, at a point where the disjunction between the figures of language threatens to proliferate into the endless regress of Derridean *différance*, and to argue that it is exactly here where the unassailable dynamic essence of the Romantic vision is most powerfully revealed.

Of course, in one sense our discussion of the dialogue between Bloom and de Man has simply recapitulated from a different angle some of the most important points of chapters 3 and 4. But the change in angle is important. If the appeal of Bloom's uses for poetry in the Romantic tradition is to be gauged fully, we must consider what alternate ends his theory is fighting most fiercely against. Because it is close to Bloom's revisionary Romanticism in so many crucial ways, the deconstructionist regimen provides a particularly salient focus for comparison. As a prophet after the accomplished fate of our culture's waning, Bloom wants to make the world still possible for the authentic life of strong poetry, even as he is impelled to warn, by the very logic of his theory of Romantic diminishings, that the ravages of time only conspire to make it less so. To save for the errors of poetry a truth that even the most thoroughgoing skepticism of our time could not dismantle, he must make that truth an affair entirely of an agon that transpires beyond language, beyond culture, beyond nature, in a transcendent realm where to be visionary is the grandest blessing and the most majestic curse that the absolute absences of our self-imposed solitude can bestow. "The human writes, the human thinks, and always following after and defending against another human," Bloom asserts against the "humanistic loss" represented by Derrida's elevation of the scene of writing over the oral tradition (MM, p. 60). In that humanity, however savage, willful, and warped by the imperatives of influence, we may still see, Bloom affirms, following a remark of Pater on Coleridge, " 'the true interest of art,' which is to celebrate and lament our intolerably glorious condition of being mortal gods" (FC, p. 41).

II

The analysis of the poetry of A. R. Ammons and John Ashbery in the previous chapter has suggested several ways in which Bloom's theory gravely distorts the import of their work in order to proclaim for these two important contemporary poets an extreme heroism Ammons seems hardly to deserve and Ashbery certainly not to desire. Now, after seeing that such extremity is meant, at the very least, to respond to the different but equally intense extremity of deconstructionist nihilism, we are in a position to assess more fully the nature of Bloom's canonizing as an intended solution for the problems of poetry in our belated time. At this point a comparison to the Poundian poetics of Hugh Kenner becomes helpful, for now the gulf between the two theorists can be revealed to be at bottom a radical divergence in conceptions of the uses of poetry within culture. Kenner's canon, based on the High Modernism derided by Bloom, incorporates not only Pound, Eliot, Joyce, Beckett, and the exemplary ghost of Flaubert, but also William Carlos Williams, Louis Zukofsky, George Oppen, and Charles Olson among poets of more recent reputation. The accompanying method for reading advanced by Kenner tends to treat poetic language on the model of Williams's famous prescription for the poem as a "machine made of words"[8]—or, in Kenner's updated Olsonian metaphors, as a "field of action" made out of various verbal energies.[9] Predictably, Bloom refers to Kenner as an "antiquarian" whose sole achievement consists of having dogmatized the "gossip" grown old of the Pound era into the myth of a chimerical Modernism (MM, p. 28). And indeed, nothing could be further removed from Bloomian misreading or Bloomian literary history than Kenner's "homemade world" of verbal quiddities wedded to what might be called American poetic "know-how" under the general instruction of the cranky American pedagogue, Pound. Bloom's definition of poetry as the extralinguistic, agonistic vision enduring beyond all contact with the Shelleyan dross of mere reality is countered completely by Kenner's contention, from *The Poetry of Ezra Pound* in 1951 through his last major study in poetics, *A Homemade World* in 1975, that poetry is above all the *language* with which culture breathes, the *verbal* forms through which it is shaped and articulates itself. Like Bloom, Kenner affirms the value of poetry over philosophy; like Bloom too, Kenner strongly favors the distinctive world of American poetry making in the twentieth century over the traditional modes of poetic perception still advanced in England. And yet the assumptions behind Kenner's valuations of the American Modernist strain reveal that the distance between his poetics and Bloom's revisionary Romanticism is so great as to be not only aesthetic but ultimately *ethical*.

Poetry's truth is greater than philosophy's, Bloom claims, because poetry's vision, unlike philosophy's, evades the congealed abstractions and codified categories of culture that would confine it. If finally this means that poetry must evade all language in order to be about its own desires to continue, nonetheless that aboutness is sublime in that it bespeaks the grandeur of the solitary will behind it. Kenner, on the other hand, sees poetry as more valuable than philosophy largely because poetry is truer to its own ineluctable *whatness as language*. For Kenner, Williams's famous pronouncement, "no ideas but in things,"[10] does not mean simply that poetry is about the business of presenting images, hard, direct, or otherwise; it means, says Kenner, that poetry *is itself a thing*, that words have thingness as one of their indispensable properties, and that the energies of language are not only connected by, but are *embodied in*, the intricate audiographic, semantic-syntactic web of their relations to each other. Kenner's is thus preeminently a poetics of the spoken and written word—*not* the Word—a poetics of the sensuousness of language cleaving the printed page or the air. "A structure of words, that's the aim," he says in *A Homemade World* about a short poem by George Oppen, "and the 'meaning' is whatever applicability they attract" (p. 186). The taut, sinuous lines of Kenner's own prose—so pronounced a contrast to the sprawling and orotund prophetic encirclings of Bloom's sentences—point to the nature of this attraction. From the Vorticism of the High Modernists to the intricate "word games" of Zukofsky (p. 189), the poetry that Kenner chronicles and praises is distinguished by its abjuring of all those "units of perception detachable from the language" of the poem itself (p. 187), and by its corollary commitment to "new systems of connectedness" (p. xiii) whereby the living, vibrant energies of culture, nature, and language are integrated, released, "made new." Bloom, cherishing above all else the unbounded visionary desire not reducible or confinable to the codifications of language, yet goes on to deliver, with extreme quasi-philosophical rigor, what he says all the great Romantics—Blake, Wordsworth, Freud—have presented: a *map*, a code for a sort of Romantic geometry to be put to a "saving use." Kenner, on the other hand, provides no chart, no elaborately worked out hierarchy of concepts, no extended defense of his own epistemological assumptions. When he observes of the "naive realism" of Williams that "any philosopher would promptly drive a Mack truck" through it (HW, p. 65), he might very well be speaking about the genial air of inductiveness characterizing his own work. Naive realism "sufficed, for Williams," he notes, "to free the poet from anxieties he hadn't the patience for," just as it suffices for Kenner to relieve him from the necessity of critical obeisance to the crises of linguistic belief endemic to our time.[11]

Kenner's impatience with all those questions of vision, imagination, and reference that exercise theorists such as Bloom and de Man is perhaps most apparent in his devaluation of Wallace Stevens before the masters of his Modernist canon, and especially before Williams, that other great modern American poet who chose to stay home. "The American Modernists," Kenner says, are aligned by their "hidden sources of craftsmanship, hidden incentives to rewrite a page" (p. xvii), and by their Dedalian determination "to practice art as though its moral commitments were like technology's" (p. xv). "A fifty-year reshaping of the American language" is what they were all about, Pound through Robert Creeley, a reshaping done under the aegis (all exceptions admitted with alacrity by Kenner, the practicing inductivist) of another famous proclamation of Williams: "It isn't what he [the poet] *says* that counts as a work of art, it's what he makes, with such intensity of perception that it lives with an intrinsic movement of its own to verify its authenticity."[12] The chief problem with the poetry of Wallace Stevens, Kenner contends, the problem that compromises it so profoundly that Stevens's work seems fated to serve posterity only as a marginally interesting illustration of "a phase in the history of poetry" (HW, p. 72), is that it is the work of a poet afflicted precisely with the humanistic burden of having "Something to Say" (p. 57), said something amounting to little more, Kenner goes on sardonically to observe, than "discursive variations on the familiar theme of a first-generation agnostic."

In Kenner's view, Wallace Stevens is a poet hobbled by two misfortunes formidable in their ironic relation: first, he suffers from a typically modern crisis in belief about the ability of language to say anything; and second, he then spends an entire poetic career going about the old-fashioned humanistic business of *saying* how hard (if not impossible) it is to say things. Stevens in his preoccupation with that supreme fiction that, if accepted as a fiction, could still give life, "tended to suppose that he was at grips with a religious or a philosophic crisis," Kenner asserts.

> But it was a writers' crisis purely, a poets' crisis, an episode in the history of nature poetry since Wordsworth. It is entangled in religion and philosophy: of course it is. But it existed, neatly, on the poetic plane: how to make predications concerning snow, or blackbirds. It was on the poetic plane that Stevens coped with it, often magnificently. (Pp. 82 – 83)

The magnificence inheres in Stevens's "chief technical insight," which is that only the techniques of painting could hope to capture the "relationship of the sole man to the mute universe" (p. 77). And yet Kenner is moved quickly to exasperation by this as well. The poetry that results from Stevens's felt philosophical predicament is, he says, reft of "human actions with agents good and bad" (p. 74); lacking in "variety of feeling" (p. 75); "empty of people altogether" (p. 71); and full "merely" with "ways of looking at things" (p. 78). "So many scrupulously arrested gestures," he summarizes, "so laborious an honesty, such a pother of fine shades and nuanced distinctions; yet that forty years' work revolves about nothing more profound than bafflement with a speechless externality which poets can no longer pretend is animate" (p. 81).

Against this sustained exercise in poetic sound and fury about the issue of signifying nothing, Kenner posits the "polar opposite" of Williams's working philosophy of language, featuring the "assumption that words share thinghood with things, and that language is a social fact needing no explanations" (p. 81). Such an assumption, unlike Stevens's endless puzzling over "how words relate to reality," accomplishes, says Kenner, what a poetic epistemology should accomplish; with quiet efficiency, it allows the poet to write his poems, to forge his red wheelbarrow as a patterned verbal energy or a "thing" made, while at the same time assuming that such thinghood is shared with the correlative real object one might espy, red and dependable, on any given farm.

It is obvious how remote Kenner's analysis of Stevens is from Bloom's, both in particulars and in general assumptions about poetic meaning. As we have seen, Bloom passionately repudiates any reading of Stevens as a painterly poet or a mere crafter of relational "dilapidations." More important, Bloom's entire operation on Stevens is designed, like all his rescue attempts, to save the poet from the Ulro into which he would fall if his work were to be regarded as merely a trafficking in the problematics of signification, a worrying over the difficult task of having "Something to Say." The very substance of Kenner's charge against Stevens—itself a dyslogistic variant of the sort of reading given Stevens by Vendler—will not even be admitted by Bloom, since according to his conception of Romanticism no Romantic poet ever really writes about the externality of nature anyway, not even to take such a subject as a predicament in predication. "Wallace Stevens was the Last Romantic," Kenner intones, "the last poet of a long era that believed in 'poetry,' something special to be intuited before the words had been found, something of which one's intuition guided the precious words" (p. 185). Bloom, of course, from his radically different perspective, tells us much the same thing (adding several poets beyond Stevens to prove that the situation is not completely hopeless). But while Bloom sees the waning of Romanticism hyperbolically as nothing less than the death knell for an entire culture, Kenner is quite content to bring in the new poems *beyond* the end of the Romantic mind, for the new, he would affirm, is where *we all live our lives*, poets, critics, computer scientists, and garbage collectors alike." 'Is there any *poetry* here?' the Romantic reviewer would ask, looking up from the book; do I detect those harmonies that transcend the crass and the quotidian, that ignore the Ford car and the asphalt and the computer?" (p. 185). Thus Kenner lampoons the likes of

Bloom, piercing what he sees as the foggy air of gothic nostalgias
with the light of his witty prescription for the new that "*The poem is
the Gestalt of what it can assimilate.*" The analogue for poetry that he
then advances marks his quirky contemporaneity in the same way
that the oedipal battles and heroic defeats of the map of misreading
mark Bloom's willful nostalgia for an earlier age of Romantic
grandeur. A poem, Kenner repeats, with his eye on a world far removed from Grasmere or Cumberland, shady bowers or vales sublime, is

> the Gestalt of what it can assimilate, like New York City; and a
> visitor to New York City at any time is apt to feel the place is in
> process of being improvised. Structures run up, abandoned, left
> behind in a night; graffiti, sound and light shows, iridescences;
> neon; footnotes to history; registrations of the current, persis-
> tences in the memory, in tacit defiance of paperback transcience;
> so the domain of the 1970's Muse. (P. 185)

My own point is not to poke fun at Bloom's eloquent and impassioned "persistences in the memory" of the Romantic mind. Rather,
the intriguing aspect of the conflict between Kenner and Bloom lies
in the depth of their divergence on crucial questions of what I have
been calling "poetic ethics," after Bloom's Emersonian pragmatics
of the "uses" of poetry. Kenner's credo, perhaps best seen as a
secularization of the High Modernist religion of art advocated by
Joyce (a Shelleyan in his youth) and Pound (early an accomplished
imitator of certain of the late Romantic poets), would hold that
poetry is important only insofar as it *does* "make it new," only
insofar as the poet forces himself to live on the cutting edge of the
life and the language of the culture around him. "When a man
makes a poem, makes it, mind you, he takes words as he finds them
interrelated about him and composes them—without distortion
which would mar their exact significances—into an intense expression of his perceptions and ardors . . .":[13] another pronouncement
of Williams's that could stand as Kenner's own, and what it implies
for Kenner's method of reading poetry is that the words on the page
matter *more than anything else*, more than the abstractions of philosophy, more too than the imperatives of Romantic vision and redemption, because not only are those words the life of the poet, his
authentic homemade *logos*, they are also, since the poet necessarily
lives in culture and expresses his perceptions through the language
that he finds around him, verbal embodiments of the cultural
energy that has helped to give them shape. Bloom, on the other

hand, with ethics predicated on the solipsistic *logos* of a Romantic will deliberately placed beyond the encroachments of all mere sharing, either social or linguistic, would maintain that the proper function, and the only hope, for poetic art is continually to remake the old, to forge again through the fires of vision and its battles a breaking of shape equal to the primal desires of the great prophets of the past.

Bloom's broodings on the fate of reading and misreading in our time always have been heavy with apocalyptic foreboding over the very survival of poetry in a culture that will not heed its true prophets. Even in the mature period marked by the darker "internalized" complications of the anxiety of influence as a master principle for his work, Bloom continues to retain his original Blakean faith in the all-important role of the imagination in human life and an equally intense Blakean conviction that society by the very nature of the constraints it imposes as a *fallen* social body can never accept the vision delivered by its embattled poet-prophets. Los, "the imaginative principle in man" (BA, pp. 385 − 86), may be bloodied by savagery and parricide in the final incarnation of Bloom's theory, but his function still is to redeem us, to make us gods once again after our fall into the fractured ordinariness of our common humanity. Like Emerson, the cunningly chosen avatar of the map of misreading's program for an American "*re-centering*" against the decenterings of deconstruction (MM, p. 176), Bloom will never cease affirming that "that is always best which gives me to myself" (CW, 1:82), even if such a self is driven, by the forces featured by Bloom, to the grisly oedipal battles evermore about to be of influence. Like Bartleby, the perversely heroic prisoner of his own self-imposed solitude amid the sterile Gestalt of a not very fictional New York City of Emerson's time, Bloom "would prefer not to" if asked to quit his self-communings for the life of those at large within the exile of modern civilization. Extremity in itself becomes yet another defense in the formidable Bloomian arsenal, an extremity and, stylistically, a hyperbole, designed to transmute the curse of time into the heroism of desperate resistance before all that in our culture and within ourselves that, remorselessly and inevitably, schemes to defeat us.

III

What does Harold Bloom give us, then? What is there in his self-styled critical prophecy that seems to be central to the way we read poetry in our time, central not only for the praise it has garnered and the influence it has amassed, but for the heated and keenly personal condemnation with which it also has been met? Defining Bloom by the nature of his opponents, we have located his poetics as a response, on the one hand, to the absolute obliteration of the ontic self argued by Derrida and de Man, both of whom tend to regard the self-conscious, self-glorifying "I" of the Romantic era as an elaborate and now obsolete historical fiction. On the other hand, if Bloom is precisely a self-conscious, self-glorying resister to the brave and monstrous world of autonomous inhuman textuality promulgated by the legions of Derrida, he is also an unwilling participant in the world of our ordinary, culture-ridden lives as our poets might live them now under the benison of Kenner. Where *do* we live our lives, then, according to the revisionary Romanticism of Harold Bloom? Time and again, throughout all stages of his career, he tells us: we are happy only when we are most our selves, when, temporarily free from the miserable dualisms to which we have been condemned by both our society and our mortality, we are most within "that solitary and inward glory we can none of us share with others" (FC, p. 109).

It seems a suggestive, though not necessarily a damning, coincidence that the decade in which Bloom's theory of the anxiety of influence rose to prominence recently has been labeled, through the writings of Christopher Lasch, Tom Wolfe, and a host of others, the "me decade" or an "age of narcissism," a time when glorification of the self became a defining American passion, especially among the leisured classes and the cultured elite.[14] Whatever the final authority of commentators such as Lasch and Wolfe (Lasch in particular has been used as a starting point for prognostications of cultural malaise by everyone from Jimmy Carter to Gerald Graff), they do provide an accurate enough thumbnail sketch of a decade in which, among a good many other things, preoccupation with the inner meanings of the innermost self became a leading American growth industry.[15] The deconstructionist effacement of the constitutive self, like most culminations of philosophical skepticism, has little enough to do with the way anyone, from the most intellectually haunted ideologue to the gas station attendant down the street, actually lives his or her life (a point Samuel Johnson, with typically hard-headed rationality, made of an earlier skepticism in an earlier time). In contrast, Bloom's theory, pronouncing itself in Stevensian fashion as a theory of poetry that is also a theory of life, is *meant* to take us—those of us who still read poetry, at any rate, a lonely enough crowd to be sure—to the wellsprings of our solitary being by furnishing a map that will guide us through the dim and daemonic realms of our hidden and untranslatable desires. As Kenneth Connelly, in a fascinating and fatidic review of *Yeats* appearing in the *Yale Review* in 1971, has observed:

> Bloom's Romanticism seems an exalted, tremendously erudite, and consistently noble form of Consciousness III; it postulates the duty of every man and every poem to strive for the triumph of man, not under God or in the hope of heaven but here and now. The notion of the divine is secularized and placed with mathematical equality in each human breast, and salvation is to be realized not after death but in historical progress. It is a brilliant, learned, impassioned version of "Wishing Will Make It So."[16]

It is precisely, of course, Bloom's overwhelming erudition, his loftiness of temperament, and his passionate intelligence in service of a complex, historically grounded conception of the Romantic psyche, that distinguish him from the many recent gurus and popularizers of consciousness, poetic and otherwise, whom he quite properly scorns. For what is especially interesting about Bloom and the "restitution of narcissism" espoused by him as a primary poetic principle, is that he takes us and our poets inside the map of misreading *not* to adjust or, in his all-purpose term for the neurasthenic quick-fixes of contemporary psychology, to "idealize," the tangle of poetic influence relations he sees governing all reading, but, rather, to *intensify* existing conflicts by making us even more aware of the savagery and the sublime self-ishness that, he warns, are our only defense against the shadows of our own belatedness. Connelly, writing as he was at the crucial juncture in Bloom's career between the early theory of vision and vision's culmination in influence and the wars of poetic desire, of course could not see that the motto for Bloom's project in the years ahead would become something like "Wishing Won't Make It So, but in the Wishing and Its Losses There Is the Saving Strength of Sublime Defeat." But this is only to say that the unique interest of Bloom's Romantic myth lies in the resourceful way in which it contrives seemingly to make the worst of an already bad situation for poetry, for reading, and for the self, only at the last moment, and in fittingly melodramatic fashion, to salvage the victory of triumph-in-defeat out of all that would seem most to condemn it.

"Rivalry, misinterpretation, repression, and even plain theft and savage misprision" (FC, p. xii): Bloom stands as the chronicler and the prophet of a host of apparent vices upon which, he says, "literature itself is founded," a roster of deadly agonistic sins formulated by the founding fathers of revisionism, Nietzsche and Freud, whose darkest insights Bloom himself revises to make yet more alarming. Bloom's entire project, like the ratio of *apophrades* which not only concludes but, in effect, summarizes his map for post-Enlightenment poetry, is marked by a "conscious rhetoricity" (MM, p. 102) as it attempts to subvert the usual categories of humanism in order to save the dark heart of Romantic vision beneath. What Bloom quite consciously gives us as a theory of poetry and of life is a mythographic chart for Psychological Man forced first to live within the abyss of the constitutive inner self, and condemned then to the most excruciating manner of solipsistic grandeur by the realization that this is his inescapable plight. That there are other, and happier, charts possible, even for *daemon*-ridden modern humanity, is irrelevant to the true Bloomian believer, for such charts—Freud's own, for instance, which features the hope of "adjustment," or Kenneth Burke's, which emphasizes the consubstantial sharings of symbol-using humanity—do not admit the cultivated crises and crossings of imaginative desire that alone, in Bloom's universe, confer redeeming value upon our alienation and our despair.

In presenting the elaborate map of his mature phase that purports to tell the true tale of the poetic psyche, Bloom, a Blakean as always, is following through on the wisdom gleaned from his early studies of Blake's intricate mythography, a wisdom perhaps encapsulized in the observation from *Blake's Apocalypse* that "a psychology . . . is necessarily a cosmology" (p. 325). When Los proclaims early in *Jerusalem* that "I must create a System, or be enslav'd by another Mans" (1.10.20), he is providing not only the "guiding principle of Blake's poetry" (BA, p. 376), but also the ruling precept for all Bloom's own systematizing in the years following, a systematizing that comes to feature just the sort of radical polysemism as a principle for reading that Blake pioneered in the Romantic mode. Yet Bloom's myth must depart from Blake's at a rare and crucial moment, for Blake, too, in his primal strength, overidealized the psychology and the cosmology of the redemptive Romantic imagination. "I will not Reason & Compare: my business is to Create," Los boldly announces in the line succeeding his proclamation of visionary emancipation, but Bloom is impelled, by the privileged position of his despair almost two centuries later, to go about the business of comparison, of weighing and judging the outcome of all the visionary strife in the years since Blake. "Comparison" is now not only the central duty of the canonizer but also, then, the characteristic *topos* of the Romantic sublime (WS, p. 399), and the assumption about poetry making upon which it rests is that Blake was *wrong* when he called the imagination the "Real Man." Or, rather, he was not so much wrong as he was engaged in the happy fallacy of wishing it were so. "Perhaps there is" a "Real Man" of the imagination, Bloom observes several times in his later work, "but he cannot write poems, at least not yet" (MM, p. 198; FC, pp. 140—41). The inevitable correction follows: "poetry is written by the natural man who is one with the body" (MM, p. 198), and, among other things, this means that the anxiety of influence determining all strong poetry is itself "the fear of death," which for the poet-as-poet is translated into the fear "that *there is not enough for him*, whether of imaginative space or in the priority of time" (MM, p. 198).

The "central strife" of the Blakean cosmology as presented by Bloom in his early work, the strife over "the fate of Orc, the natural Man, the human energy warred over by the contraries of Los and the opposing Spectres of Urizen and Urthona: art against the doctrines and the circumstances that restrict" (VC, p. 33), is "internalized" in Bloom's later Freudian theorizing by the recognition that it is what transpires *within* the psyche of man that presents the greatest restriction, and thus the gravest danger, to imaginative life. And since the "recalcitrance" within, represented by the master trope of influence, is a *necessary* precondition, or ground of meaning, for whatever vision a poet achieves, it only follows that the modern poet is cursed most profoundly by *having to be himself*, by having to be what he is, the miserable and afflicted pawn of his own belated godhood. Since influence is terminal, an inescapable *end* as well as a beginning, there is no "cure of the ground" for its afflictions; there is only a tone, a style fit for triumph-in-despair. "The secret of Romanticism, from Blake and Wordsworth down to the age of Yeats and Stevens, increasingly looks like a therapy in which consciousness heals itself by a complex act of invention." So Bloom observes in *The Ringers in the Tower* (p. 337), and it is one of the most trenchant insights he has ever provided, not only into Romanticism as he conceives it, but, necessarily then, too, into Romanticism as he cunningly and powerfully exemplifies it in his own complex act of invention, his theory of Romantic man in extremis.

Of course, if Bloom's campaign to save Romanticism follows the old military adage that the best "defense" (in Bloom's case, Freudian) is a good "offense" against tradition and its encroachments, his rescue operation also has opened itself to the charge of having fulfilled its intentions in a way that would be anathema to any competent military strategist. "He had to destroy Romanticism in order to save it," might be the motto volunteered for Bloom's project by an entire army of unpersuaded critics, scholars, and readers of poetry, and the delicious absurdity of the formula, so

grim and so comical in the true manner of our time, would seem to
have a resonance not wholly inappropriate to Bloom's own conscious designs toward Romantic redemption. What is destroyed by
Bloom's conception of the Romantic mind? Above and beyond all
else, *innocence* perhaps is—innocence defined as the hope for
vision and for an imaginative life that would liberate us from our
squalor and our apparently ineluctable alienation, innocence defined as the joy of reading when reading is affirmed to be an authentic sharing with the life of the vision of another. To highlight the full
extremity of Bloom's working out of the consequences of his conception of the Romantic psyche, we need only compare him to his
former teacher and mentor, M. H. Abrams, a magnanimous critical
father whose scene of instruction Bloom has schemed relentlessly
to subvert. From *The Mirror and the Lamp* through his culminating
magisterial study of the Judeo-Christian millennial patternings of
Romantic thought, *Natural Supernaturalism*, Abrams, like Bloom,
has concentrated almost exclusively on delineating the contours of
Romantic vision and imagination as they are both represented in,
and expressed by, the great works of the Romantic mind. Like
Bloom, too, he has premised his entire undertaking upon an awareness of the dumbfounding gulf that stands between imaginative
man and the fulfillment of his hopes and desires, so infinite and
majestic. And yet Abrams, unlike Bloom, has steadily maintained
a position within the mainstream of our inherited humanism and
modern critical culture with his eloquent insistence that the lamp
of the Romantic mind is not, and can never be, darkened by the
dilemmas brought on by its own uncompromising aspiration.
Against Bloom, who first adopts Blake and Shelley, and later Freud
and Nietzsche, as his instructors for the scene of Romanticism revised, Abrams has steadfastly pledged an allegiance throughout his
career to the poet he conceives to be the grand moderator and the
greatest figure of the visionary company, Wordsworth, especially
the Wordsworth who announces, in the "Prospectus" to his intended masterpiece, *The Recluse*, that he will sing

> Of Truth, of Grandeur, Beauty, Love, and Hope,
> And Melancholy Fear subdued by Faith;
> Of blessèd consolations in distress;
> Of moral strength, and intellectual Power;
> Of joy in widest commonalty spread.... (PW, p. 590, 1.14−18)

With an exegetical structure based on Wordsworth's "Prospectus," *Natural Supernaturalism* is based as well on these high
Wordsworthian hopes for the continuing relevance of the liberating

Romantic imagination, even in an age whose faithlessness and whose myriad linguistic frustrations seem destined to subvert past glories. All of Abrams's hopes for literature and for Romanticism are in the passage in *Natural Supernaturalism* where he posits the enduring "Romantic positives" against a time that he sees as contriving either to subsume or to destroy them:

> In our own age a number of the most talented authors have turned against the traditional values of the civilized order, to voice the negatives of what Lionel Trilling has called an "adversary culture." Some envision the end of our world as an apocalyptic bang, others as a plaintive whimper; in the latter version, an anti-hero plays out the moves of the end-game of civilization in a non-work which, in some instances, approaches the abolition of meaningfulness in language itself. The Romantic writers neither sought to demolish their life in this world in a desperate search for something new nor lashed out in despair against the inherited culture. The burden of what they had to say was that contemporary man can redeem himself and his world, and that his only way to this end is to reclaim and to bring to realization the great positives of the Western past. When, therefore, they assumed the visionary persona, they spoke as members of what Wordsworth called the "One great Society . . . / The noble living and the noble Dead," whose mission was to assure the continuance of civilization by reinterpreting to their drastically altered condition the enduring humane values, making whatever changes were required in the theological systems by which these values had earlier been sanctioned. Chief among these values were life, love, liberty, hope, and joy. These are the high Romantic words, the interrelated norms which always turn up when the poets get down to the first principles of life and of art, which they proclaim without unease and with no sense that these commonplaces may have outworn their relevance.[17]

It is not surprising that, given his acceptance of the spirit of the Romantic enterprise, Abrams does not worry unduly about the possible treachery of the letter; for him, as he has explained in response to an attack by J. Hillis Miller,[18] all writers, even the most exuberant Romantic prophets chafing at the bounds of language, may be assumed not only to have a definable and determinate authorial status, but to have written their works "in order to be understood."[19] In his important review of *Natural Supernaturalism*, Miller objects that Abrams begs crucial questions raised by the Romantic

texts themselves on the final adequacy of any common norms for
interpretation within tradition, and also "pays notably little attention throughout to the question of signs or of language." The consequence of this lack of reflection on the problematics of language and
of meaning in Romantic expressiveness, Miller contends, is that
"Abrams perhaps takes his writers a little too much at face value,
summarizes them a little too flatly, fails to search them for ambiguities or contradictions in their thought, does not 'explicate' in the
sense of unfold, unravel, or unweave."[20] Since this would very likely
be the objection that Bloom, as a theorist of a related type of misreading and wandering textuality, would offer against the methodology of *Natural Supernaturalism*, Abrams's reply to Miller is intriguing. He defends his relatively straightforward reading of
Wordsworth, Coleridge, Schelling, Schiller, and the other great
heroes of his Romantic corpus by arguing that since these writers
did write "in order to be understood," certain "interpretive assumptions" may be employed in reading them. To escape the prison of
solipsism and to assure the goal of vital communication, the Romantic poets, Abrams suggests,

> had to obey the communal norms of their language so as to turn
> them to their own innovative uses. The sequences of sentences
> these authors wrote were designed to have a core of determinate
> meanings; and though the sentences allow a certain degree of
> interpretive freedom, and though they evoke vibrations of sig-
> nificance which differ according to the distinctive temperament
> and experience of each reader, the central core of what they
> undertook to communicate can usually be understood by a
> competent reader who knows how to apply the norms of the lan-
> guage and literary form employed by the writer. The reader has
> various ways to test whether his understanding is an "objective"
> one; but the chief way is to make his interpretation public, and so
> permit it to be confirmed or falsified by the interpretations of
> other competent readers who subscribe to the same assump-
> tions about the possibility of determinable communication.[21]

In this lucid expression of the orthodox creed that reading remains possible for our time, Abrams can be seen to be responding to
the powerful heterodoxies of both Bloom and de Man, and to the
obliteration of "communal norms" of language as a basis for interpretation and reading that Bloom's Romanticism and de Man's
deconstruction represent. Indeed, in an essay appearing in *Partisan
Review* in 1979, "How to Do Things with Texts," Abrams explicitly

groups Bloom with Derrida (and Stanley Fish) as exemplary figures in what he calls the brazen new world of "Newreading," a world in which reading at first seems to be liberated by its movement beyond traditional interpretive standards, but in which it is finally freed, Abrams argues, only to perform the endlessly subtle gamesmanship and the slow self-reflexive suicide of the subverter who needs the order that he passionately attacks. "Newreading" is suicidal, Abrams asserts, because it knowingly "destroys the possibility that a reader can interpret correctly either the expression of his theory or the textual interpretations to which it is applied." It is merely gamesmanship, after all, because the Newreader himself knows "that he is playing a double game, introducing his own interpretive strategy when reading someone else's text, but tacitly relying on communal norms when undertaking to communicate the methods and results of his interpretations to his own readers."[22]

Bloom's assault on innocence, of course, cuts much deeper than just an attack on the methodology of reading. If Derrida is, in the words of Abrams's witty thrust, "an absolutist without absolutes" (p. 569), Bloom, on the other hand, is unabashedly an absolutist who endeavors to save, at the languageless cynosure of his map, an essence of defeated but inviolable Romantic will. Deconstruction as an exercise in extremity claims that all linguistic signification is ultimately empty, an endless wandering in language without a home. Bloom, making his rapprochement with Derrida and de Man in *Deconstruction and Criticism*, argues that either the theory of language as "dearth of meaning" *or* the opposite theory of language as "plenitude," as a "Kabbalistic magical absolute," is acceptable to him. "All I ask," he concludes, "is that the theory of language be extreme and uncompromising enough" (DC, p. 4). Thus, Bloom's theory strategically and ruthlessly eliminates the entire middle ground of language in which we usually think ourselves to live, the ground of language as a communal activity, as a medium that defines us in our reducible but nonetheless essential sharings. The necessary corollary of this cut, as Abrams observes (p. 586), is that Bloom's map eliminates from the scene of literature "the great diversity of motives for writing poetry, and in the products of that writing, the abundance of subject-matters, characters, genres, and styles, and the range of the passions expressed and represented, from brutality and terror and anguish, indeed, to gaiety, joy, and sometimes sheer fun." In attempting to force us to the dubious Romantic redemption of an ever more agonized awareness of our fallen innocence and our consequent life within the agonistic ex-

tremes of the map of misreading, "what Bloom's tragic vision of the
literary scene systematically omits," Abrams contends, "is almost
everything that has hitherto been recognized to constitute the
realm of literature."

Bloom's audacious subversion of the traditional possibilities of
humanism, of "adjustment" or hope or the "joy" that Abrams identifies in *Natural Supernaturalism* as the liberating Romantic "norm
of life,"[23] amounts in its larger designs to nothing less than a giant
fable of alienation, a conceptual Dark Tower of the Romantic Imagination before which all the great questings of vision in the Romantic
tradition are seen to end. It is no accident that one of Bloom's favorite poems is Browning's haunted version of quest romance, "Childe
Roland to the Dark Tower Came."[24] The nightmarish landscape
through which Roland journeys, so rich with grotesquerie and unnatural distortion, is a resonant correlative for the grim subjective
life that the poet, perhaps against his conscious will, divulges. The
quester himself, identified typically and tellingly by Bloom as "the
modern poet-as-hero" (MM, p. 122), seems uncannily like a figure
from the wells of modern nightmare, driven from within by he
knows not what to an end he knows not where, to be possessed
finally by the terror that becomes defiance before the malign and
singular presence of a tower that, despite its apparent otherness,
seems to mirror the quester's own darkest and most treacherous
desires. All Bloom's own obsessive readings of Romanticism are
about just such a "triumph of life" as threatens Roland at the end of
his journey; all his readings of Romanticism recognize that the
malignity that we confront is primarily an alienation, profound and
irreducible, that devours us from within. Finally, all Bloom's revisions of Romanticism wrest from the quester's predicament the
only victory to be calculated in a moment of such imminent peril,
the triumph of noble defiance before the self-induced, self-fought
specter of self-destruction. All our vision, Bloom cries, slughorn set
to lips, surveying the dark and distorted landscape of his Romantic
history, is a savage phantasm, a lie not just in its telling but in the
very ground of its existence as imagination, and this necessary self-
same identity of vision and error is the only glory that we should
want, or that we shall ever have, from the remorseful and relentless
questings of the Romantic imagination.

CONCLUSION

The critical project of Harold Bloom, taken as a whole, has many
merits that even his detractors would not deny. Bloom's fourteen
major volumes feature countless seminal readings of important
Romantic and modern poetic texts, all the readings invested with
a passionate erudition entirely appropriate to an exegete of the
grand Romantic tradition, none of them completely compromised
by our disagreement with the hubristic designs of the map for misreading. Bloom has introduced an unarguably sophisticated mode
of psychopoetics and psychohistory into the generally moribund
realm of the traditional scholarly study of literary influence, thereby
compelling a trenchant reexamination of those *idées reçues* concerning influence, self, and the role of psychobiography which for
so many years have stultified critics interested in the dynamics of
literary tradition.[1] Yet to suggest that Bloom's enterprise is most
notable for his accomplishments in the mode of "practical criticism" (AI, p. 13) that he has always claimed to value is to ignore the
larger significance of his work. Perhaps above all, what Bloom has
given us, with his self-styled critical prophecy for a belated age, is an
idea of criticism whose deliberate extremes and contrived rhetoric
of crisis do not so much address as *reflect* the very real crisis in
vision troubling not only the profession of literary criticism but also
the entire tradition of humanistic culture in the last half of the
twentieth century.

Humanism in its larger sense as an inherited body of beliefs
about our essential nobility within the wealth of our culture and its
artistic creations has foundered badly in our time before the apocalyptic realities of our other creations—genocide, mass starvation,
the threat of nuclear annihilation, and the catastrophes awaiting us
in our progressive destruction of the earth's fragile environment.

The divisions between literature and science, value and fact, the culture of liberalism and the cult of applied science, seem no closer to fruitful mediation now than they did almost two centuries ago in the first formulations of the first Romantics. Our best fiction writers explore a "literature of exhaustion"[2] as they undertake a task no more sublime than what Bloom, speaking of Pynchon in particular, quite rightly calls an immense and brilliantly wrought "voluntary parody" of literature itself (MM, p. 38), an exhaustive recycling of the materials of past Western culture performed with the debilitating awareness that none of it—none of what the writers themselves now are doing, none of what was written or thought in the great book of the past—really matters or ever really can halt the headlong "progress" of humankind toward, at best, an unplanned obsolescence, or, at worst, a final nuclear meeting with a gravity's rainbow of falling bombs.

The general crisis in humanism—a crisis that, for all its newfound sense of urgency, is itself as new as *The Prelude* or "Dover Beach"—has been intensified within the realm of literary criticism and the profession of teaching during the past twenty years by bitter intramural squabbles over the proper role of criticism within culture, and by the growing perception among many scholars, critics, and teachers of the humanities, whatever their critical positions, that the society at large has become indifferent, if not actively hostile, to *any* claims for the continuing importance of humanistic culture, no matter how those claims might be presented. At a time of steadily declining interest in the humanities and of a perceived "crisis in literacy," which together seem to guarantee that our English departments on the university level, if they have any relevance at all, will have it only insofar as they package themselves as glorified "trade schools" in the "communication arts," a widespread feeling has arisen that, while literature itself may not be played out on the stage of Western culture, the tradition of explicating and interpreting it by professors of college English nonetheless *might* be through, a victim both of its own past richness and of its current lack of coherence or confidence in its many disparate undertakings.

How do we make the humanities important again? The question is not easily answered at a time when the profession of academic criticism lacks common standards for reading, evaluating, and making use of literary texts—when, in fact, major elements of academic culture have embraced philosophies (or antiphilosophies) such as deconstruction on the one hand and Marxism on the other, which call radically into doubt the assumptions, methods, and goals of liberal humanism itself. For a deconstructionist, of course, the case for liberal humanism is no stronger than the case for any other logocentric endeavor; concealed within humanism's rhetoric of voice, presence, truth, beauty, and determinate textual authority are the inevitable abysses that finally undermine the status of humanism as a redemptive project. For a Marxist such as Terry Eagleton, liberal humanism has "dwindled to the impotent conscience of bourgeois society, gentle, sensitive and ineffectual"; the response of the liberal humanist to the current cultural situation is weak because, in making grossly overstated claims for the "transformative power" of literature, it fails to consider that power in relation to the social, economic, and political contexts within which it necessarily finds its place, and thus condemns literature (and criticism) to continued isolation and irrelevance.[3]

Whatever the enduring merits of Marxism as an analytical methodology, there can be no doubt that social, economic, political, and professional factors are deeply relevant to the crisis in the academy today, with most of them working to ensure that literary critics exist, as Edward Said has put it, in conditions of "institutionalized marginality."[4] Intense and restrictive codes of professionalism, the impetus (not confined to literary studies) toward extreme specialization, the demands of the tenure system for production regardless of merit, the material pressures of budget cuts and drops in enrollment in literature courses, the appalling rate of unemployment for a whole generation of younger scholars: all these factors would contribute mightily toward a crisis in the profession, even if literary scholars had been able to arrive at a united front concerning the precise nature of the importance of the humanistic experience of literature to society as a whole.[5] Paradoxically, the very circumstances that have produced fragmentation, disunity, and disillusionment have also resulted in the most remarkable proliferation of scholarly and theoretical works in the history of literary criticism, to the point that Thomas Carlyle's prophecy of 1831 seems uncannily and unhappily fulfilled in the Library of Babel today: "By and by it will be found that all Literature has become one boundless self-devouring Review; and, as in London routs, we have to do nothing, but only to see others do nothing. —Thus does Literature also, like a sick thing, superabundantly 'listen to itself.' "[6]

Are we sick beyond cure? Can literary critics, caught within a time at odds with itself, set that time right, when they seem to have forfeited, both by their practice and by the disease of their intensely self-reflexive beliefs, the moral authority to offer orthodox modes of humanistic salvation? Questions such as these hover uneasily about, or behind, the discourse of many literary critics today, and they are questions that Bloom's enterprise, often without wholly intending to, bears revealingly upon. For, in one sense, Bloom, with his relentlessly single-minded focus on the strivings of the context-less visionary imagination, very seldom explicitly concerns himself with the time in which he lives, except to lament that he is forced to live in it at all. Similarly, in his theorizing on the dynamics of tradition in poetry, he never sees the poetic imagination as responding to a *historical* moment, only to intrapsychic forces of influence whose temporality is solely a function of the continuing compulsions of the isolate Romantic imagination. As Elizabeth Bruss has remarked in her formidable discussion of Bloom in *Beautiful Theories*, Bloom's is a "theory of literature that is literary to the core." Aesthetic considerations govern the design and structure of his map, and if the aesthetic sometimes conflicts with the historic—if, say, Shakespeare seems not to fit tidily into the story of poetic influence—Bloom is not unduly troubled, since the "only consistency" he "truly cares for is atmospheric and passional."[7]

Bloom's aestheticism and the limitations in his use of history have discomfited many other scholars besides Bruss. Said notes that Bloom's story of poetic influence "conceals . . . a radically mythologized conception of the individual determinants of culture, and a total disregard for culture's anonymous and institutional supports"; by way of example, he cites Bloom's lack of reference in his treatment of the English Romantics to the "materially productive agencies" of the time: the journals, reviews, and "competing discourses," as well as larger collective supports such as the university, the press, the class system, and Foucault's "archive-discourse-statement (*enoncé*)."[8] Frank Lentricchia, speaking from a related Foucaultian perspective in his polemical overview of recent literary theory, *After the New Criticism*, also accuses Bloom of brandishing an ultimately empty and self-defeating aestheticist historicism. Behind Bloom's history of poetry Lentricchia discovers "a need to construct an inclusive and formally self-sufficient totality which would eternalize and isolate literary discourse."[9] While Lentricchia sees the possibility of modifying Bloom's position to open it up to a vision of discourse in history as a more capacious network of force relations,[10] another critic of Bloom's totalizing and aesthetic tale of poetic history, Paul Bové, finds nothing at all salvageable in the project. Discussing recent critical theory and modern American poetics from a Heideggerian framework in *Destructive Poetics*, Bové summarizes Bloom's work as an attempt to develop "a series of metaphors to stabilize 'tradition' as a defense against time"—an attempt doomed to fail because of the sterility of its dualistic and ultimately atemporal model for poetic creation. Bloom's "need for a center, for ontological security, cannot conceive the living in a productive but unaccommodated relationship with the past," Bové asserts; a reified and monolithic tradition is Bloom's only "bulwark" against the chaos and fragmentation that, ironically enough, his own persistent dualism has decreed.[11]

And yet, despite his ahistoricism, despite his lack of interest in any crises other than the cultivated crossings of the strife-ridden Romantic soul, Bloom does finally deliver an answer of sorts to the manifold troubles of academic humanism in our time. He seeks to make literary criticism important again by unburdening it of much of the excess baggage of its traditional humanism, its gentility, its idealism, its sense of literary tradition as an "ideal order," and by replacing all these musty accoutrements with his own highly melodramatic mapping of crisis-ridden Romantic desire. He attempts to ameliorate the distress associated with the common perception that works of "high art," especially poetry, are increasingly less read in an age of electronic illiteracy, by reminding us that all tradition is necessarily elitist, and by arguing as well that, in the greater bloody parricide of literary history as he envisions it, the Titans of true poetic vision *will* win out in the end (an end that may be nearer than we think for literature, he portentously warns) to assume their deserved preeminence. Above all, he endeavors to tell us, through the exemplary visionary instance of his own audacity in framing such an intensely charged tale of the "vast visionary tragedy" of Romantic desire (AI, p. 10), that nobility and majesty, heroism and greatness, are *still* ours, if only we can marshal the strength and, yes, he affirms darkly, the desperation, necessary to imagine them as our belated being's heart and home. Bloom's answer for our ills is, in other words, a "therapy"—a therapy for Romanticism and thus a palliative, if not a cure, for the maladies afflicting the humanistic culture in which Romanticism continues to earn its salience. All that is required to be both solaced and heartened by the mythographic fable of Bloomian Romanticism is a willing suspension of our disbelief in the premises and assumptions that make Bloom's story possible. Once this is accomplished, once we accept the world of the isolate yet embattled Romantic visionary as the only world possible for modern poetry, our malaise is transformed into desperation and thereby ennobled, our directionlessness becomes defeat and is thereby made tragic.

Of course, we may rightly question whether Bloom affords us sufficient grounds for accepting his willfully extreme positions. If contemporary theory is, in the words of Bruss, the "faith of the faithless" (BT, p. 485), does Bloom's version of revisionary Romanticism succeed in surmounting our doubts about its designs upon us? Bruss herself does not think that it does; Bloom's aesthetic, so "inflexible and all-engulfing," cannot "possibly invent a way out of old aesthetic impasses," she argues, but instead seems to "mire us further in the polarities—of literature vs. life, heart vs. head, imagination vs. reason, beauty vs. truth—" (p. 362) from which the experimental texts of critical theory, in her view, ought to seek deliverance. Certainly there is a sense in which Bloom's project can be characterized by its very need *never* to show the "weakness" of theoretical flexibility, never to allow encroachment by theoretical universes less agonistically charged than its own. Beginning with a definition of visionary Romanticism so intensely circumscribed that, as Lentricchia wittily observes, "it is difficult to say what, outside of the testimony of the devil himself, would sanction" it (ANC, p. 329), Bloom proceeds inexorably to the desired end of his quest, which is nothing less than the recognition that vision itself, as a supreme fiction of the embattled Romantic imagination, can save us only if we engage ourselves fully in the seductive vainglories of its lies about time. Thus, Bloom finally delivers both myth and fiction, myth as a totalizing structure or tale allowing poetry its own self-contained universe apart from all the threats of external reality, fiction as the inevitable grounds for examining and enacting our myths in a faithless time.[12] Romanticism defined in this fashion can no longer give us what one of Bloom's critical fathers, Northrop Frye, heralded in *An Anatomy of Criticism*: the "work of imagination" as "the vision of a decisive act of spiritual freedom, the vision of the recreation of man" (p. 94). Rather, it renders, under the torn, bloody flag of influence, only *the illusion of such freedom*, and the poignant suspicion—to use Lentricchia's observation about Wallace Stevens's species of ironic secular humanism—that fictions, which we might like to see as "heroic evasions," may just as easily be understood to be "pitifully unheroic lies" (ANC, p. 33).

Viewed from another angle, as a prescription for a critical method, Harold Bloom's program for Romantic revision seems above all a response to the many lingering explication-oriented conceptions of practical criticism still commanding support in the academy today, including the mainstream tradition of explication and paraphrase of Romantic texts represented by M. H. Abrams. Bloom's profound and polemical enlargement of the bounds of the critical enterprise attempts to blur, if not obliterate, the distinctions that have usually operated between literature and criticism, primary and secondary texts. "All criticism is prose poetry," Bloom proclaims in his "Manifesto for Antithetical Criticism" (AI, p. 95) as a necessary corollary to his continuing contention that all poetry is "poetic argument." Both positions dissent rigorously from that residual New Criticism that would condemn interpretation to the dungeon of explication and poetry to the prison of "pseudostatement"; both positions testify to the power of Bloom's belief in the imagination as the single defining element in *all* interpretive discourse. While Bloom shares with deconstruction, then, an emphasis on the ineluctable primacy of interpretive activity and, concomitantly, an awareness of the labyrinths of intertextuality that implicate any given utterance, he departs once again from the deconstructionist regimen insofar as he transforms the activities of interpretive textuality into gestures grounded by the dark enduring *logos* of the Romantic will. As such, the mixed poetics and rhetoric of his own work represent an especially extreme instance of the sort of creative criticism that his colleague at Yale, Geoffrey Hartman, has eloquently called for and much more hesitantly embodied.[13] If Hartman's crisis mentality in a book such as *Criticism in the Wilderness* produces a rhetoric so self-conscious in its "creative" textuality as to be paralyzed into virtual nonpropositionality, Bloom's sense of crisis takes him to the opposite pole of prophetic stridency, as he hurls dark truths into the faithless void like visionary lightning bolts.[14]

Ultimately, Bloom as a critic is most tellingly placed within the company he has selected for himself. Emerson, Kenneth Burke, Ruskin, Pater, Wilde, and Yeats are obvious influences on Bloom's mode of meditative discourse, but even closer to his temperament and to his practice, perhaps, are the outlaws of Gnostic and kabbalistic tradition whose appropriation by Bloom we examined in chapter 3. Here we need only note that Bloom is drawn to the Kabbalah and to Gnosticism not only because of their shared status as bodies of creative misinterpretation about the origins of creation, but also because both systems of interpretation provide Bloom a model for his conflation of the languages of poetry and criticism. Both Kabbalah and Gnosticism, that is, are primarily nondiscursive forms of interpretation that find their meaning not so much within the structures of ratiocinative argument as within the figures and symbols of the imaginative universe—the universe that finally, in Bloom's own misreading, is seen to rule over the deathly world of literal meaning.[15]

Bloom's canonizing tale of revisionist literary history belongs, in another sense, to the tradition of Midrashic commentary on the Old Testament, a type of commentary that Angus Fletcher usefully defines as "turned to the revelation of a continuing hidden truth assumed to inhere in the unity and therefore to locate the center, of a canonic tradition."[16] We have already noted how Bloom capitalizes on his relationship to the prophetic works of the Old Testament by referring to himself as a "kakangelist," and by continually invoking the rhythms and the tonalities of prophecy in order to present as vibrantly as possible the tragic grandeur of the central Romantic canon. Less obviously, he uses Midrash as a model, and as an implicit justification, for his own strenuous canonizing practice, a practice that involves not only eliminating everything in the history of literature over the previous two centuries that does not conform to the requirements of visionary Romanticism, but even within the Romantic tradition itself, excising much that other critics have deemed important—Coleridge's theorizing, German Romanticism, Romantic art and music, Romantic prose fiction—but that does not admit of the predominantly lyric "centrality" that is the only real object of Bloom's critical vision. The prophet and the canonizer are finally of a piece in the critical project of Harold Bloom, a project whose goal, as Hartman has observed in appropriately biblical language, is to use "*the voice of the critic* to keep the tower of literature from becoming a tower of Babel."[17]

Beyond biblical exegesis, Bloom in his mature incarnation as mapmaker of misreading continues to rely more heavily on Blake— another revisionary reader in the scriptural tradition—than on any other single figure to buttress his critical prophecy. As Cynthia Ozick has ably summarized, Bloom's many theorizing volumes in his incarnation as prophet of influence contrive to give us not criticism as we usually know it but "a long theophanous prose poem, a rationalized version of Blake's heroic Prophetic Books."[18] Bloom intends to stand, she says, "as a vast and subtle system-maker, an interrupter of expectations, a subverter of predictability—the writer, via misprision, of a new Scripture based on discontinuity of tradition." Perhaps it is this underlying Blakean symmetry in all Bloom's books that allows his project for criticism to come completely into focus. Too self-conscious to possess Blake's primal and direct imaginative power, too belated to be able really to deliver the life of authentic visionary prophecy as the master does in *The Four Zoas* and *Jerusalem*, Bloom nonetheless answers the confusions of our time with a scripture whose "saving use" is itself derived from a revisionary reading of Blake's most revisionary prophetic poem, *Milton*. The fearful ratios of the visionary imagination at war will be the sole subject of this new scripture; the blocking of all the blocking agents of art will be its prime visionary desire. Harold Bloom's defense of the Romantic vision endangered from within as well as without, emerges as a brilliantly resourceful mythographic expression of its own need to justify itself. That the scripture delivered by Bloom offers bold new possibilities for the art of criticism is hardly to be doubted. That it escapes the treacherous tautologies of its complex, self-imposed "therapy" is a tale, fittingly enough, that only time will tell.

NOTES

Preface

1 At the time of the writing of this preface, a new volume by Bloom, *The Poetics of Influence: New and Selected Criticism*, has been announced as forthcoming.

2 Martin is quoting Bloom on Yeats to characterize Bloom. See the introduction to *The Yale Critics: Deconstruction in America*, ed. Jonathan Arac, Wlad Godzich, and Wallace Martin, Theory and History of Literature, vol. 6 (Minneapolis: University of Minnesota Press, 1983), p. xxviii.

Introduction

1 The following are Bloom's books that I cite throughout this volume and the shortened form by which I will refer to them in textual references:

Agon   *Agon: Towards a Theory of Revisionism* (New York: Oxford University Press, 1982).

AI   *The Anxiety of Influence: A Theory of Poetry* (New York: Oxford University Press, 1973).

BA   *Blake's Apocalypse: A Study in Poetic Argument* (1963; reprint, Ithaca: Cornell University Press, 1970).

BV   *The Breaking of the Vessels* (Chicago: University of Chicago Press, 1982).

FC   *Figures of Capable Imagination* (New York: Seabury Press, 1976).

KC   *Kabbalah and Criticism* (New York: Seabury Press, 1975).

MM   *A Map of Misreading* (New York: Oxford University Press, 1975).

PR   *Poetry and Repression: Revisionism from Blake to Stevens* (New Haven: Yale University Press, 1976).

RT   *The Ringers in the Tower: Studies in Romantic Tradition* (Chicago: University of Chicago Press, 1971).

SM   *Shelley's Mythmaking* (1959; reprint, Ithaca: Cornell University Press, 1969).

VC   *The Visionary Company: A Reading of English Romantic Poetry*, rev. ed. (Ithaca: Cornell University Press, 1971).

WS   *Wallace Stevens: The Poems of Our Climate* (Ithaca: Cornell University Press, 1977).

Yeats   *Yeats* (New York: Oxford University Press, 1970).

DC   *Deconstruction and Criticism*, ed. Harold Bloom (New York: Seabury Press, 1979).

I will use the 1971 revised edition of *The Visionary Company* throughout this study because it is more widely available and because it has important additional materials. In 1971 Bloom added a preface, an introductory essay on the backgrounds of English Romantic poetry, and an epilogue on the "persistence" of Romanticism, but his other changes are not significant, and the text itself remains virtually the same as the original 1961 edition. All my quotations from *The Visionary Company* have been checked against the earlier edition whenever it appeared that a discrepancy might be significant to a consideration of the development of Bloom's thought.

2 See Wasserman's review, "Shelley for the Present," in *Yale Review* 48 (1959): 609 – 12. The safer, saner study to which Wasserman is comparing *Shelley's Mythmaking* here is Milton Wilson's *Shelley's Later Poetry: A Study of His Prophetic Imagination* (New York: Columbia University Press, 1959).

3 The relevant publishing information of all the sources cited in this and the next paragraph follows the order in which the sources are mentioned:

Kenneth Burke, "Father and Son," review of *A Map of Misreading*, *New Republic*, 12 Apr. 1975, pp. 23 – 24.

Edward Said, "The Poet as Oedipus," review of *A Map of Misreading*, *New York Times Book Review*, 13 Apr. 1975, pp. 23 – 25.

J. Hillis Miller, "J. Hillis Miller on Literary Criticism," *New Republic*, 29 Nov. 1975, pp. 30 – 33.

Helen Vendler, "Defensive Harmonies," review of *Poetry and Repression*, *Times Literary Supplement*, 25 June 1976, pp. 775 – 76.

Paul de Man, review of *The Anxiety of Influence*, *Comparative Literature* 26 (1974): 269 – 75. The essay is reprinted in de Man's *Blindness and Insight: Essays in the Rhetoric of Contemporary Criticism*, 2d ed., Theory and History of Literature, vol. 7 (Minneapolis: University of Minnesota Press, 1983), pp. 267 – 76.

Frank Kermode, "Notes toward a Supreme Poetry," review of *Wallace Stevens*, *New York Times Book Review*, 12 June 1977, pp. 9, 44.

Charles Altieri, review of *Figures of Capable Imagination* and other books, *Criticism* 19 (1977): 350 – 61.

Christopher Ricks, "A Theory of Poetry, and Poetry," review of *Poetry and Repression*, *New York Times Book Review*, 14 March 1976, p. 6.

Howard Nemerov, "Figures of Thought," review of *The Anxiety of Influence* and other books, *Sewanee Review* 83 (1975): 161 – 71. The essay is reprinted in Nemerov's *Figures of Thought: Speculations on the Meaning of Poetry and Other Essays* (Boston: David Godine, 1978), pp. 18 – 29.

David H. Hirsch, "Deep Metaphors and Shallow Structures," review of *Kabbalah and Criticism, Poetry and Repression, Figures of Capable Imagination*, and other books, *Sewanee Review* 85 (1977): 153 – 66.

Robert Towers, "The Ways and Means of Literary Critics," review of *Kabbalah and Criticism* and other books, *New York Times Book Review*, 21 Dec. 1975, pp. 15 – 16.

Joseph Riddel, "Juda Becomes New Haven," review of *Wallace Stevens, Diacritics* 10, no. 2 (1980): 17 – 34.

M. H. Abrams, "How to Do Things with Texts," *Partisan Review* 46 (1979): 566 – 88.

Sandra M. Gilbert and Susan Gubar, *The Madwoman in the Attic: The Woman Writer and the Nineteenth-Century Literary Imagination* (New Haven: Yale University Press, 1979).

4 The Frye and Abrams influences will be discussed extensively in chapter 1. For Pottle, see "The Case of Shelley," in *English Romantic Poets: Modern Essays in Criticism*, ed. M. H. Abrams, 2d ed. (New York: Oxford University Press, 1975), pp. 366 – 83.

5 R. P. Blackmur, "W. B. Yeats: Between Myth and Philosophy," in *Language as Gesture: Essays in Poetry* (New York: Harcourt, Brace and Co., 1952), pp. 122 – 23.

6 John Hollander, "Let a Thousand Blooms . . . ," review of *Yeats, Poetry* 117 (1970): 43 – 45.

7 This is an often repeated Bloomian point. See especially the discussion of "the dialectics of poetic tradition" in chapter 2 of *A Map of Misreading*, pp. 27 – 40.

8 See ibid., p. 89. Bloom is responding here to Geoffrey Hartman's review of *The Anxiety of Influence*, "War in Heaven," which appeared originally in *Diacritics* 3, no. 1 (1973): 26 – 32, and is reprinted in Hartman's *The Fate of Reading and Other Essays* (Chicago: University of Chicago Press, 1975), pp. 41 – 56. Hartman compares Bloom unfavorably to Freud. Both writers, he says, rely on "the analogical method," but Bloom's style is too "precariously assimilative," with the result that he "cannot always make the rich and echoing thoughts his own" (*Fate*, p. 51). Hartman's review is generally laudatory, of course.

9 Hartman, *The Fate of Reading*, p. 46.

10 "Harold Bloom on Poetry," *New Republic*, 29 Nov. 1975, p. 24.

1. The Visionary Company in Its Own Time

1 Northrop Frye, *Fearful Symmetry: A Study of William Blake* (Princeton: Princeton University Press, 1947), and *Anatomy of Criticism* (Princeton: Princeton University Press, 1957). All subsequent quotations from *Anatomy of Criticism* will be documented in parentheses in the text.

2 See the introduction to *Shelley's Mythmaking*, pp. 1 – 10. In his preface to the 1969 Cornell edition, Bloom tells us that the first draft of *Shelley's Mythmaking* was written in 1955, thus antedating Frye's *Anatomy of Criticism* by two years. The influence of *Anatomy* begins to be felt in *The Visionary Company*, while *Fearful Symmetry* is a strong presence even in Bloom's first volume.

3 For Frye's dismantling of the Blakean critical context, see chapter 1 of *Fearful Symmetry*, pp. 3 – 29. Frye's discussion of Blake's earlier English and Hebraic connections is conducted throughout the study.

4 See *The Visionary Company*, p. vii.

5 See *Milton*, in *The Complete Poetry and Prose of William Blake*, ed. David Erdman, with commentary by Harold Bloom, rev. ed. (Berkeley: Univer-

sity of California Press, 1982), 1.29.3. All subsequent quotations from this edition of Blake will be documented in parentheses in the text.

6 See *The Prelude* (1850 edition), in *Wordsworth: Poetical Works*, ed. Thomas Hutchinson, rev. Ernest de Selincourt (New York: Oxford University Press, 1969), 6.608. All subsequent quotations from this edition of Wordsworth will be documented in parentheses in the text as PW.

7 For Lewis's objections, see "Poetry and Exegesis," review of *The Visionary Company, Encounter* 20, no. 6 (1963): 74 – 76. Lewis faults Bloom not only for his imposition of Blakean categories on the other English Romantic poets, but also for his use of a barbarous and fuzzy critical language. Wellek comments on Bloom in "Romanticism Re-examined," in his *Concepts of Criticism*, ed. Stephen G. Nichols (New Haven: Yale University Press, 1963), p. 218. Noting with disapproval that Bloom "sees only the prophetic, the visionary of the company," Wellek concludes that "we shall not, I think, make much progress with the problem of romanticism if we seek its prototype in such an exceptional and lonely figure as Blake, who seems to me rather a survival from another century, however much he may also anticipate the issues of our own time."

8 M. H. Abrams, *The Mirror and the Lamp: Romantic Theory and the Critical Tradition* (New York: Oxford University Press, 1953), p. viii.

9 For Frye on Blake's reaction to Wordsworth, see *Fearful Symmetry*, pp. 39, 324.

10 For Keats's reference to the "deceiving elf" of the imagination, see "Ode to a Nightingale," in *The Poems of John Keats*, ed. Jack Stillinger (Cambridge: Harvard University Press, Belknap Press, 1978), p. 372, ll. 73 – 74. Keats also speaks of imagination as "Lost in a sort of purgatory blind," in "Epistle to John Hamilton Reynolds" (listed in the Belknap edition under the first line of the poem, "Dear Reynolds, as last night I lay in bed"; see pp. 241 – 44). For trenchant readings of Keats as a skeptic about visionary experience, see Stillinger's "The Hoodwinking of Madeline: Skepticism in 'The Eve of St. Agnes,' " *Studies in Philology* 58 (1961): 533 – 55, and "Imagination and Reality in the Odes," which serves as the introduction to *Twentieth Century Interpretations of Keats's Odes: A Collection of Critical Essays*, ed. Jack Stillinger (Englewood Cliffs, N. J.: Prentice-Hall, 1968), pp. 1 – 16. Both essays are reprinted in Stillinger's *"The Hoodwinking of Madeline" and Other Essays on Keats's Poems* (Urbana: University of Illinois Press, 1971), pp. 67 – 93 and 99 – 119, respectively.

11 "The Internalization of Quest Romance" first appeared in *Yale Review* 58 (1969): 526 – 36. It was then reprinted in expanded form in *Romanticism and Consciousness: Essays in Criticism*, ed. Harold Bloom (New York: W. W. Norton and Co., 1970), pp. 3 – 24. Finally, it was included in *The Ringers in the Tower* (1971), pp. 13 – 35. All quotations from the essay will be documented in the text with reference to the latter volume. I have called the essay an effort of 1968, despite the fact that it was not published until 1969, because Bloom himself assigns the date of 1968 to it at the end of the printing in *Ringers* (p. 35).

12 Hartman, "Structuralism: The Anglo-American Adventure," in *Beyond Formalism* (New Haven: Yale University Press, 1970), p. 14.

13 For precisely this objection, see James Benziger's review of *The Visionary Company* in *Criticism* 5 (1963): 185 – 88.

14 See *Anatomy of Criticism*, pp. 203 – 6. Frye defines "epiphany" as "the symbolic presentation of the point at which the undisplaced apocalyptic world and the cyclical world of nature come into alignment" (p. 203).

15 See "Epipsychidion," in *Shelley's Poetry and Prose: Authoritative Texts, Criticism*, ed. Donald H. Reiman and Sharon B. Powers, Norton Critical Edition (New York: W. W. Norton and Co., 1977), ll. 573 – 91. All subsequent quotations from this edition of Shelley will be documented in parentheses in the text as SPP.

16 This quotation is taken from the epilogue added to the 1971 edition of *The Visionary Company*.

17 In "Auden: Christianity and Art," Bloom announces his preference for Auden over Eliot as the lesser of two evils: "Auden is wittier, gentler, much less dogmatic, and does not feel compelled to demonstrate the authenticity of his Christian humanism by a judicious anti-Semitism." Auden also "has more wisdom and more humor than Eliot, and his talent is nowhere near so sparse . . ." (RT, p. 209).

18 Robert O. Preyer, "Voyagers of the Imagination," review of *The Visionary Company*, *Yale Review* 51 (1961): 316 – 19.

19 For this particular angle on Emerson, see especially chapter 9 of *A Map of Misreading*, pp. 160 – 76.

20 For Pottle's overview of the dynamics of the Shelleyan critical reception, see "The Case of Shelley," in Abrams, *English Romantic Poets*, pp. 366 – 72.

21 For this most famous of attacks on Shelley, see F. R. Leavis, "Shelley," in *Revaluation: Tradition and Development in English Poetry* (New York: George W. Stewart, 1947), pp. 203 – 40. Leavis observes that Shelley's poetry "depends for its success" on inducing "a kind of attention that doesn't bring the critical intelligence into play . . ." (p. 207). He accuses Shelley of having a "weak grasp upon the actual" (p. 206), and concludes that even in Shelley's best work, "it is impossible to go on reading him at any length with pleasure; the elusive imagery, the high-pitched emotions, the tone and movement, the ardours, ecstasies and despairs, are too much the same all through. The effect is of vanity and emptiness . . . as well as monotony" (p. 211). Leavis's discussion is reprinted in Abrams, *English Romantic Poets*, pp. 345 – 66.

22 See "The Unpastured Sea: An Introduction to Shelley," in *The Ringers in the Tower*, pp. 87 – 116. This essay, originally written to introduce *The Selected Poetry and Prose of Shelley* (New York: New American Library, 1966), pp. ix – xlv, and also appearing in *Romanticism and Consciousness*, pp. 374 – 401, is the clearest and most straightforward treatment by Bloom of a poet as important to him as any.

2. Yeats and the Spectre of Modernism

1 Preyer, "Voyagers of the Imagination," p. 316.

2 Benziger, review of *The Visionary Company*, p. 186.

3 W. B. Yeats, *A Vision*, rev. ed. (New York: Macmillan Co., Collier Books, 1966), p. 142. In this study I will use the final version of *A Vision*, incorporating all the author's changes. All subsequent quotations from

this work will be documented in parentheses in the text as AV.

4 See especially "The Tower," in *The Collected Poems of W. B. Yeats* (New York: Macmillan Co., 1976), p. 195:

> Did all old men and women, rich and poor,
> Who trod upon these rocks or passed this door,
> Whether in public or in secret rage
> As I do now against old age?

All subsequent quotations from this volume will be documented in parentheses in the text.

5 "Intellectual Beauty has not only the happy dead to do her will, but ministering spirits who correspond to the Devas of the East, and the Elemental Spirits of mediaeval Europe, and the Sidhe of ancient Ireland, and whose too constant presence, and perhaps Shelley's ignorance of their more traditional forms, give some of his poetry an air of rootless fantasy" (W. B. Yeats, "The Philosophy of Shelley's Poetry," in Yeats, *Essays and Introductions* [New York: Macmillan Co., Collier Books, 1973], p. 74).

6 Ibid.

7 See *Shelley: Poetical Works*, ed. Thomas Hutchinson, rev. G. M. Matthews (New York: Oxford University Press, 1970), p. 823.

8 Whitaker, *Swan and Shadow: Yeats's Dialogue with History* (Chapel Hill: University of North Carolina Press, 1964), p. 309. Whitaker is perhaps Bloom's most formidable adversary in Yeatsian criticism. He provides not only a consistently penetrating analysis of the Blake-Yeats relationship, but also delivers—to use Bloom's own description—a "strong" argument for "the relevance of certain esoteric traditions" in Yeats's work (*Yeats*, p. vii). Whitaker's thesis on the Yeatsian attitude toward history is less uncompromising, not as single-minded, as Bloom's. Whitaker suggests that "history was for Yeats a mysterious interlocutor, sometimes a bright reflection of the poet's self, sometimes a shadowy force opposed to that self"; he finds in Yeats's doctrine of history a passage beyond "facile subjectivism" to complex and authentic wisdom (p. 4).

9 See *Yeats*, p. 73. Also see the discussion of Bloom's use of Blake's Beulah in my first chapter.

10 See *The Works of William Blake, Poetic, Symbolic, and Critical*, ed. Edwin J. Ellis and W. B. Yeats (London: Bernard Quaritch, 1893), 1:290, 288.

11 See Ezekiel, 28:14 – 16. The cherub, like most of the figures that preoccupy Bloom, is discussed extensively in Frye's *Fearful Symmetry*.

12. See Eliot, "*Ulysses*, Order and Myth," in the *Dial* 75 (1923): 480 – 83. The essay is reprinted in *Selected Prose of T. S. Eliot*, ed. Frank Kermode (London: Faber and Faber, 1975), pp. 175 – 78. Eliot sees in myth the possibility for art to manipulate "a continuous parallel between contemporaneity and antiquity. . . ." Such a device, Eliot notes, "is simply a way of controlling, of ordering, of giving a shape and a significance to the immense panorama of futility and anarchy which is contemporary history." Eliot cites Yeats as a pioneer in this type of Modernist mythmaking:

> It is a method already adumbrated by Mr. Yeats, and of the need for which I believe Mr. Yeats to have been the first contemporary to be

conscious. It is a method for which the horoscope is auspicious. Psychology (such as it is, and whether our reaction to it be comic or serious), ethnology, and *The Golden Bough* have concurred to make possible what was impossible even a few years ago. Instead of narrative method, we may now use the mythical method. It is, I seriously believe, a step toward making the modern world possible for art. . . ." (*Selected Prose*, pp. 177 – 78)

13 Both options for dealing with *A Vision* are employed by Northrop Frye in "The Rising of the Moon," perhaps the most penetrating exegesis of the philosophy and symbology of *A Vision* yet offered. Frye first locates Yeats's cosmology within the framework of other great symbolic orders in the Western poetical tradition, including those of Dante and Blake, and then goes on to note the strong affinities of Yeats's cyclical historicism with Spengler's. For Frye, Yeats's elaborate cycles of history and the individual exhibit not only a deficient sense of evil but an inadequate conception of the fundamental identity in great art between subject and object, creative imagination and created image. Frye concludes that most of Yeats's best poems do not require the apparatus of *A Vision* in order to be understood. The reductive cyclical orderings of *A Vision* are irrelevant, he says, to the profound union of sensuous image and timeless artifice found in poems such as "Byzantium" and "Sailing to Byzantium." Frye's essay first appeared in *An Honoured Guest: New Essays on W. B. Yeats*, ed. Denis Donoghue and J. R. Mulryne (London: Edward Arnold, 1965), pp. 8 – 33, then was reprinted in Frye's own *Spiritus Mundi: Essays on Literature, Myth, and Society* (Bloomington: Indiana University Press, 1976), pp. 245 – 74.

14 Ellis and Yeats, *Works of William Blake*, 1:238.

15 See Yeats's discussion of this most crucial of phases in *A Vision*, pp. 135 – 37. Bloom argues that the "contrast between Phases 1 and 15 is Yeats's only genuine dialectical distinction in the whole of *A Vision*; the other distinctions are merely cyclic" (*Yeats*, p. 237). Nonetheless, for Bloom the dialectic remains empty because phase 15, the very center of Yeats's vision and his values, "is opaque both as image and as concept" (p. 241)—"really fit stuff for Yeats's spooks to have instructed him in" (p. 240).

16 Yvor Winters, *The Poetry of W. B. Yeats* (Denver: Alan Swallow, 1960), p. 10.

3. Vision's Revision

1 See *Yeats*, p. 218, and *The Anxiety of Influence*, p. 35.

2 Ellis and Yeats, *Works of William Blake*, 1:288.

3 I will not discuss Bloom's often touted relation to Bate in this study. While Bloom does acknowledge that Bate's *The Burden of the Past and the English Poet* (Cambridge: Harvard University Press, Belknap Press, 1970) is an important contribution to the study of poetic influence, he also correctly sees that his own attempt at writing a literary history on the model of Freud's family romance shares little or nothing with the methods and the working philosophy of Bate's more conventional historiography (see *The Anxiety of Influence*, p. 8). Bate's thesis that the modern poet is haunted by the excessive richness of the poery of the past

takes its place within the tradition of humanistic scholarship known as the "history of ideas." Bloom's vision of all post-Enlightenment poetry as a savage grappling for imaginative space between poetic sons and fathers is designed to subvert some of the key ideas of that tradition, especially the assumption of an essential continuity and "objectivity" in literary history.

4 See especially Nemerov's scathing review, "Figures of Thought," in *Figures of Thought*, pp. 18 – 29.

5 Denis Donoghue, "Stevens at the Crossing," review of *Wallace Stevens, New York Review of Books*, 15 Sept. 1977, p. 39.

6 In "Blake's *Jerusalem:* The Bard of Sensibility and the Form of Prophecy," an essay appearing in *The Ringers in the Tower*, Bloom concludes that the form of Blake's epic is "twisted askew by too abrupt a swerve or *clinamen* away from" the precursor, in this case the prophecies of Ezekiel. Thus, though his formidable conceptual powers enable him "heroically" to formulate and confront the dread subject of anxiety of influence in *Milton*, even Blake is not fully exempt from the disfigurings of the "baneful aspect of Poetic Influence" before a biblical Titan such as Ezekiel (pp. 75 – 76). Bloom's rereading in *Poetry and Repression* of his earlier "canonical" treatment of Blake's "London" and "The Tyger" ultimately provides the picture of a poet who, by Bloom's admission, is "not so much a visionary as a shrewd revisionist, obsessed with his own defensive gestures" (*Agon*, p. 50).

7 Abrams, *The Mirror and the Lamp*, p. 251.

8 See *Paradise Lost*, in *The Complete Poetry of John Milton*, ed. John T. Shawcross, rev. ed., Anchor Seventeenth-Century Series (Garden City, N. Y.: Doubleday and Co., Anchor Books, 1971), 4.110. All subsequent quotations from this volume will be documented in parentheses in the text.

9 *The Letters of John Keats*, ed. Edward Hyder Rollins (Cambridge: Harvard University Press, 1958), 2:212. This letter was written by Keats to George and Georgiana Keats in late September 1819.

10 The entire chart is presented by Bloom in *A Map of Misreading*, p. 84, and in *Poetry and Repression*, as a frontispiece. In my discussion of the ratios in this chapter, I will be emphasizing the psychic and rhetorical components simply because these aspects of the Bloomian map are more important to his thought than the imagistic and topical components. The topics, a late addition to the map in *Wallace Stevens*, will be discussed briefly in my fourth chapter.

11 Emerson, of course, is also an important contributor to Bloom's revisionism, and often serves as a point of reference in Bloomian discussions of Gnosticism, Nietzsche, and Freud. I do not treat Emerson in this chapter because the Emersonian "religion" of American Orphism described by Bloom is a central subject of my discussion in the next chapter.

12 Isaac Luria's thought survives only in the writings of his disciples, whose accounts of his theories often conflict. The most powerful of these accounts is *Ez Hayyim*, by Hayyim Vital Calabreze. Bloom's use of the Kabbalah of Luria, as well as of de Leon and of Luria's master, Moses Cordovero, relies heavily on the scholarship of Scholem. See especially Scholem's most famous studies: *Major Trends in Jewish Mysticism*, rev. ed. (New York: Schocken Books, 1946); *Jewish Gnosticism, Merkabah*

Mysticism, and Talmudic Tradition, 2d ed. (New York: Jewish Theological
Seminary of America, 1965); *On the Kabbalah and Its Symbolism,* trans.
Ralph Manheim (New York: Schocken Books, 1969); and *Kabbalah* (New
York: Quadrangle/New York Times Book Co., 1974).

For a key to Bloom's perspective on the significance of Scholem's work,
see his review of *Gershom Scholem: Kabbalah and Counter-History,* by
David Biale (Cambridge: Harvard University Press, 1979), in *New Republic,* 23 June 1979, pp. 36–37. "In our post-Holocaust time, the unknown
God of Scholem, contracted and withdrawn from our cosmos, seems
more available than the normative God of Akiba and Maimonides,"
Bloom observes (p. 37). "Without wholly intending to take up such a
stance, Scholem has become a kind of prophet of a still-emerging Jewish
spirituality that has little or no relation to the normative rabbinical tradition. His writings, however insistently historical, begin to provide the
basis for another Jewish Gnosis, perhaps the inevitable religion of Jewish
intellectuals for whom the doctrine of Akiba is dead" (p. 36).

13 The standard English edition of de Leon is *The Zohar,* trans. Harry
Sperling, Maurice Simon, and Paul P. Levertoff, with an introduction by
J. Abelson, 5 vols. (New York: Soncino Press, 1970). Abelson's introduction to vol. 1 provides a capsule summary of the long controversy in
Hebrew scholarship over the writing of *The Zohar,* with Abelson himself
concluding that the work could not possibly "have emanated from the
brain of one man" ((pp. x–xi).

Bloom is especially concerned with the rhetorical implications of the
Sefirot. In *Kabbalah and Criticism,* he notes that Scholem gives "a very
suggestive list of Kabbalistic synonyms for the *Sefirot:* sayings, names,
lights, powers, crowns, qualities, stages, garments, mirrors, shoots,
sources, primal days, aspects, inner faces, and limbs of God" (p. 26). The
list is suggestive for Bloom since rhetorically these attributes "range over
the entire realm of the classical trope," a realm that Bloom will go on
more fully to assimilate into his own map in the theoretical chapter that
concludes *Wallace Stevens.* For Scholem's most pointed discussion of
the imagistic attributes of the *Sefirot,* see *Kabbalah,* pp. 96–116.

14 Hans Jonas, *The Gnostic Religion: The Message of the Alien God and the
Beginnings of Christianity,* 2d ed. (Boston: Beacon Press, 1963), p. 42.

15 My summary here is taken from Jonas's account of Valentinian Gnosticism in *Gnostic Religion,* p. 174–97.

16 Ibid., p. 327.

17 Ibid., p. 338.

18 For a clearly written speculation on the sociopolitical aspects of the
Gnostic revolt against the early Church, see Elaine Pagels, *The Gnostic
Gospels* (New York: Random House, 1979).

19 Jonas, *Gnostic Religion,* p. 34.

20 I am quoting the translation that Bloom uses in *Agon,* p. 90, not the
slightly different rendering in Jonas, *Gnostic Religion,* pp. 45, 334.

21 I am quoting the version of the passage that Bloom presents in *Poetry
and Repression,* p. 205. For a different translation, see Jonas, *Gnostic Religion,* p. 190.

22 Jonas, *Gnostic Religion,* p. 109. For the entire account of Simon Magus
from which my remarks here are taken, see pp. 103–11.

23 In particular, Bloom finds Nietzsche's opposition of the "ascetic" ideal

to the "antithetical" will to be crucial to Yeats's conception of the "primary" and the "antithetical". See Bloom's discussion in *Poetry and Repression*, pp. 207 and 221. For the pertinent Nietzschean passages, see the third essay of *On the Genealogy of Morals*, in *Basic Writings of Nietzsche*, trans. Walter Kaufmann (New York: Modern Library, 1968), especially sects. 23 – 28, pp. 581 – 99. Kaufmann, it should be noted, translates the German adjective, "*gegnerisch*," as "opposing," not "antithetical" (p. 582). Of course, what Bloom has in mind is the radical suggestion toward which Nietzsche's polemic against the "ascetic" ideal is advancing: that it is in art, not science, where "precisely the *lie* is sanctified and the *will to deception* has a good conscience . . ." (p. 589).

24 See the second essay of *On the Genealogy of Morals*, in *Basic Writings of Nietzsche*, sect. 19. In the text of this chapter I have quoted the slightly different translation that Bloom uses. See *The Anxiety of Influence*, p. 118.

25 See *Thus Spake Zarathustra*, trans. Thomas Common (New York: Carlton House, 1900), pt. 2, sect. 42. In the text of this chapter I have quoted the slightly different translation that Bloom uses. See *Agon*, pp. 120 – 21.

26 See "A Special Type of Choice of Object Made by Men," in *The Standard Edition of the Complete Psychological Works of Sigmund Freud*, ed. James Strachey, in collaboration with Anna Freud, assisted by Alix Strachey and Alan Tyson, 24 vols. (London: Hogarth Press, 1953 – 74), 11:173. In the text of this chapter I have quoted the slightly different translation that Bloom uses. See *The Anxiety of Influence*, pp. 63 – 64.

27 For Freud's most cogent discussion of the parallels between tradition and the impulses of the unconscious, see *Moses and Monotheism*, chap. 3, pt. 1, in *Works*, 23:92 – 102, 132 – 37. In the text of this chapter I have quoted the translation of Freud that Bloom uses—here from the American edition of *Moses and Monotheism* (New York: Alfred A. Knopf, 1949). In *Works*, "tradition" is translated less elegantly as "something in a people's life which is past, lost to view, superseded and which we venture to compare with what is repressed in the mental life of an individual" (p. 132). For Bloom's discussion, see *The Anxiety of Influence*, p. 109, and *Kabbalah and Criticism*, pp. 97 – 98.

28 See "A Special Type of Choice of Object Made by Men," in Freud, *Works*, 11:173.

29 For the classic discussion of the primal killing of the father as an engendering cultural deed, see *Totem and Taboo*, pt. 4, in *Works*, 13:140 – 61.

30 Thomas Mann, "Freud and the Future," in *Essays of Three Decades*, trans. H. T. Lowe-Porter (New York: Alfred A. Knopf, 1968), p. 427.

31 Geoffrey Hartman, ed., *Psychoanalysis and the Question of the Text: Selected Papers from the English Institute, 1976 – 77* (Baltimore: Johns Hopkins University Press, 1978), p. vii.

32 Lionel Trilling, "Freud and Literature," in *The Liberal Imagination: Essays on Literature and Society* (New York: Viking Press, 1950), p. 53.

33 See Anna Freud, *The Ego and the Mechanisms of Defence*, rev. ed., trans. Cecil Baines (London: Hogarth Press, 1968). Chapter 4 is especially relevant, with its listing and brief description of the ten mechanisms.

34 See Burke's "Four Master Tropes," in *A Grammar of Motives* (Berkeley: University of California Press, 1969), pp. 503 – 17. Bloom follows Burke in associating metaphor with "perspective," irony with "dialectic," metonymy with "reduction," and synecdoche with "representation" (p. 503).

35 See Abrams, "Structure and Style in the Greater Romantic Lyric," in *From Sensibility to Romanticism: Essays Presented to Frederick A. Pottle*, ed. Frederick W. Hilles and Harold Bloom (New York: Oxford University Press, 1965), pp. 527 – 60; reprinted in Bloom, *Romanticism and Consciousness*, pp. 201 – 29.

36 Philip Reiff, *Freud: The Mind of the Moralist*, 3d ed. (Chicago: University of Chicago Press, 1979), p. 38.

37 For Freud's discussion of reaction-formation and sublimation, their differences and their similarities, see *Three Essays on the Theory of Sexuality*, pt. 2, in *Works*, 7:178. For Freud on how repression can itself employ reaction-formation, see "Repression," in *Works*, 14:157. For a pointed later discussion of the roles of repression and reaction-formation as distinct defenses, see *Inhibitions, Symptoms, and Anxiety*, in *Works*, 20:101 – 18.

38 Bloom, in fact, now labels Frye disparagingly "the Arnold of our day" in *The Anxiety of Influence* (p. 31) and "the Proclus or Iamblichus of our day" in *A Map of Misreading* (p. 30).

39 Freud, "The 'Uncanny,' " *Works*, 17:240 – 41. In the text of this chapter I have quoted the slightly different translation that Bloom uses. See *Poetry and Repression*, pp. 208 – 9.

40 Freud, *Beyond the Pleasure Principle*, *Works*, 18:36. All the pivotal chapter 5 of *Beyond the Pleasure Principle* should be consulted.

41 Freud, "The 'Uncanny,' " *Works*, 17:241. In the text of this chapter I have quoted the slightly different translation that Bloom uses. See *Poetry and Repression*, p. 210.

42 Bloom's treatment of Yeats's conception of the *daimonic* is discussed in my second chapter. For Bloom, the final sections of "Anima Hominis" in *Per Amica Silentia Lunae*, Yeats's brief reverie of 1917, present a far more profound vision of the relation of the *daimon* to poetry than anything Yeats went on to offer in the overelaborations of *A Vision*. Bloom sees great significance in the Yeatsian lines opening section 10 of "Anima Hominis": "It is not permitted to a man who takes up pen or chisel, to seek originality, for passion is his only business. . . ." Bloom's reading of Yeats's symbolism in the ensuing sections of "Anima Hominis" as a *clinamen* away from Blake is one of the most ingenious discussions in all his work; see *Yeats*, pp. 182 – 84. For the relevant sections of *Per Amica Silentia Lunae*, see W. B. Yeats, *Mythologies* (New York: Macmillan Co., Collier Books, 1969), pp. 339 – 42.

43 Bloom in *Poetry and Repression* acknowledges Pater's use of "*ascesis*" as a source for his own conception of this most counterproductive of Romantic ratios: "Pater was attempting to refine the Romantic legacy of Coleridge, with its preference for mind/nature metaphors over all other figurations. To Pater belongs the distinction of noting that the secularized epiphany, the 'privileged' or good moment of Romantic tradition, was the ultimate and precarious form of this inside/outside metaphor" (p. 19). Pater's importance for Bloom's reading of Yeats and the passage from Romanticism to Modernism is briefly discussed in chapter 2.

44 See, in particular, "On Narcissism: An Introduction," in *Works*, 14:67 – 102, for its distinction between "ego-libido" and "object-libido." This essay, since it crucially anticipates in many ways the themes of Freud's mature ego psychology in *The Ego and the Id* and *Inhibitions*,

Symptoms, and Anxiety, is especially important to Bloom, who urges us "never to forget" that the concept of narcissism "was the actual engine of change in Freud's theory" (*Agon*, p. 127). For a cogent and less partisan account of the role of narcissism in Freud's developing theory, see Richard Wollheim, *Sigmund Freud* (New York: Cambridge University Press, 1981), pp. 124–30.

45 For Bloom's treatment of the concept of narcissism in Freud, see the comments on Freud and on Laplanche's reading of Freud in *Agon*, p. 128. For a key Freudian observation on primary narcissism, see chapter 2 of *An Outline of Psycho-Analysis:*

> It is hard to say anything of the behavior of the libido in the id and in the super-ego. All that we know about it relates to the ego, in which at first the whole available quota of libido is stored up. We call this state absolute, primary *narcissism.* It lasts till the ego begins to cathect the ideas of objects with libido, to transform narcissistic libido into object-libido. Throughout the whole of life the ego remains the great reservoir from which libidinal cathexes are sent out to objects and into which they are also once more withdrawn, just as an amoeba behaves with its pseudopodia. (*Works*, 23:150–51)

46 Freud, *Inhibitions, Symptoms, and Anxiety,* in *Works,* 20:108–9.

47 For the Freudian view of the death drive to which Bloom is alluding, see chapters 6 and 7 of *Beyond the Pleasure Principle,* in *Works,* 18:44–64. In chapter 6 Freud makes his famous observation that "the dominating tendency of mental life, and perhaps of nervous life in general, is the effort to reduce, to keep constant or to remove internal tension due to stimuli"; borrowing from Barbara Low, he calls this the "Nirvana principle," and finds this tendency, which is expressed "in the pleasure principle," to constitute "one of our strongest reasons for believing in the existence of death instincts" (pp. 55–56). In chapter 7 Freud identifies the urge to repose more explicitly as "the most universal endeavor of all living substance—namely to return to the quiescence of the inorganic world" (p. 62).

48 This is the final import of both of the essays on Freud in *Agon*. See especially the summarizing comments on pp. 137–40, which are useful also for their aligning of Freudian origins specifically with the Gnostic tale of creation. For Bloom's argument that "contamination is not a trope but the necessary condition of all troping (or all defending)," see *The Breaking of the Vessels,* pp. 65–67.

A cogent critique of Bloom's appropriation of the Freudian theory of the death instinct is provided by Elizabeth Bruss in *Beautiful Theories: The Spectacle of Discourse in Contemporary Criticism* (Baltimore: Johns Hopkins University Press, 1982). In Freud, Bruss argues, death takes its salience as an "ideal equilibrium or homeostasis," with the paradox being that psychic exertion is "directed toward the end of exertion, a life force bent on bringing itself back to death." Freud's truly despairing account becomes in Bloom's hands the predictable melodrama of a poetic "struggle for survival," whose exertions "retain a dim if baffled grandeur, which the Freudian version of the death drive—less martial in every way —would make impossible, even risible" (p. 325). Bloom "uses the death

instinct as a compositional resource to arouse and to excite—in ways
that seem the precise reverse of Freud's intentions," Bruss concludes
(p. 342); she sees Bloom's conflation of instinct and defense to reveal an
inconsistency in his thought, not the richness of paradox (though, it
must be noted, Bruss is not treating Bloom's fuller and more subtle examination of these matters in *Agon* and *The Breaking of the Vessels*).

49 The goal of the transference situation, as Freud himself puts it in chapter
3 of *Beyond the Pleasure Principle,* is "to force as much as possible into
the channel of memory and to allow as little as possible to emerge as
repetition" (*Works,* 18:19). That repetition-compulsions nonetheless
retain so much power is a basis, of course, for the Freudian speculations
later in *Beyond the Pleasure Principle,* as well as for Bloom's rehearsal
of the untidy paradoxes of "contamination" in his own account of the
forces of memory and repetition in poetic creation.

50 See Angus Fletcher, *Allegory: The Theory of a Symbolic Mode* (Ithaca:
Cornell University Press, 1964), p. 241 n. 33. For Quintilian's discussion of
metalepsis, see vol. 3 of the Loeb Classical Library edition of *The Instituto
Oratoria,* trans. H. E. Butler (New York: G. P. Putnam's Sons, 1921),
8.6.37 − 39.

Bloom's indebtedness to Fletcher's *Allegory* extends far beyond this
one borrowing. In particular, chapter 1 of Fletcher's study, "The Daemonic Agent," which finds in the quest of such an agent in allegory "a
maximum of will and wish-fulfillment with a maximum of restraint"
(p. 69), is salient to Bloom's whole enterprise. For Bloom's enthusiastic
critical response to *Allegory,* see his review, "Myth, Vision, Allegory," in
Yale Review 54 (1964): 143 − 49. Here is an especially telling nugget of
praise from that review: "No book on literary theory since Frye's *Anatomy
of Criticism* has excited me as much as this continually inventive and
exuberant attempt to bring a flexible order into an outrageously chaotic
area" (p. 147).

4. Influence and the Map of American Poetic History

1 See Roy Harvey Pearce, *The Continuity of American Poetry* (Princeton:
Princeton University Press, 1961). In particular, Pearce's chapters on the
American Renaissance (pp. 137 − 91) and on Wallace Stevens (pp. 376 −
419) are concerned with many of the questions of priority and contextlessness in the Adamic tradition of American poetry that will later be
treated by Bloom via the theory of the anxiety of influence.

2 R. W. B. Lewis, *The American Adam: Innocence, Tragedy, and Tradition in
the Nineteenth Century* (Chicago: University of Chicago Press, 1955), p. 5.

3 Richard Poirier, *A World Elsewhere: The Place of Style in American Literature* (New York: Oxford University Press, 1966), pp. ix, 69.

4 The distinction between mythic and Adamic poets is at the heart of
Pearce's book. For his assessment of the achievements and the failures
of both traditions as makers of a more human imaginative world, see
Continuity, pp. 420 − 34.

5 See "Circles," in *The Collected Works of Ralph Waldo Emerson,* ed.
Alfred R. Ferguson et al. (Cambridge: Harvard University Press, Belknap
Press, 1971 −), vol. 2, ed. Joseph Slater, Alfred R. Ferguson, and Jean

Ferguson Carr (1979), p. 182. All subsequent quotations from this edition of Emerson will be documented in parentheses in the text as CW.

6 See "The Poet," in *The Complete Works of Ralph Waldo Emerson*, Autograph Centenary Edition, 12 vols. (Cambridge, Mass.: Riverside Press, 1903 – 04), 3:26. All subsequent quotations from this edition of Emerson will be documented in parentheses in the text as EW.

7 Yvor Winters, "Jones Very and R. W. Emerson: Aspects of New England Mysticism," in *In Defense of Reason*, 3d ed. (Denver: Alan Swallow, 1947), p. 279.

8 Bloom's brief discussion in *Figures of Capable Imagination* (pp. 69 – 71) of the Orphic religious rituals in ancient Greece seems to be mediated by Jane Harrison's seminal scholarship in the field, just as his knowledge of the Kabbalah often derives from a close reading of Gershom Scholem. For Harrison's most extensive analysis of the origins, eschatology, and cosmogony of the Orphic cults, see *Prolegomena to the Study of Greek Religion*, 3d ed. (New York: Meridian Books, 1955), pp. 454 – 658. As usual, comparing Bloom with his sources reveals little more than the remarkable consistency of his deliberate "misreadings."

For a completely different approach to the Emersonian Orphic tradition, see R. A. Yoder, *Emerson and the Orphic Poet in America* (Berkeley: University of California Press, 1978). Yoder provides a much closer—and less polemical—reading of Emerson's expression of the Orphic strain. He also devotes a chapter to the Emersonian tradition in modern poetry, covering both Stevens and A. R. Ammons (see pp. 173 – 205).

9 See *The Journals and Miscellaneous Notebooks of Ralph Waldo Emerson*, ed. William H. Gilman et al. (Cambridge: Harvard University Press, Belknap Press, 1960 –), vol. 5, ed. Merton M. Sealts, Jr. (1965), pp. 253 – 54.

10 Emerson, *Journals*, vol. 8, ed. William H. Gilman and J. E. Parsons (1970), p. 228.

11 See *Walt Whitman: Complete Poetry and Collected Prose*, ed. Justin Kaplan (New York: Library of America, 1982), pp. 394 – 95. All subsequent quotations from this volume will be documented in parentheses in the text as WW.

12 Randall Jarrell, "Reflections on Wallace Stevens," in *Poetry and the Age* (New York: Alfred A. Knopf, 1953), pp. 141, 139.

13 For the Pearce discussion from which I quote in this paragraph, see *Continuity*, pp. 423 – 24.

14 For the most impressive treatment of Stevens as an essentially comic poet, see Daniel Fuchs, *The Comic Spirit of Wallace Stevens* (Durham, N. C.: Duke University Press, 1963).

15 See Helen Vendler, *On Extended Wings: Wallace Stevens' Longer Poems* (Cambridge: Harvard University Press, 1969). Noting that Stevens's themes, "abstractly considered . . . are familiar, not to say, banal, ones," Vendler locates his crucial difference from the Romantics in the "new form" and "elaborately mannered movement of thought" in which these themes are expressed (p. 13). Needless to say, Bloom sees nothing banal in Stevens's Romantic themes.

16 See *The Collected Poems of Wallace Stevens* (New York: Alfred A. Knopf, 1954), p. 477. All subsequent quotations from this volume will be documented in parentheses in the text.

17 For Miller's phenomenological reading of Stevens, see chapter 6 of *Poets of Reality: Six Twentieth-Century Writers* (Cambridge: Harvard University Press, Belknap Press, 1965), pp. 217 − 84. For his deconstructionist analysis of Stevens's "The Rock," see "Stevens' Rock and Criticism as Cure," *Georgia Review* 30 (1976): 5 − 31, 330 − 48.

18 For this definition, see *The Rhetoric of Aristotle*, trans. Lane Cooper (New York: Appleton-Century-Crofts, 1960), 1.2. For a full discussion of the types of character as they pertain to oratory, see 2.12 − 17.

19 Bloom acknowledges his indebtedness to Geoffrey Hartman's notion of the "after-image" in Wordsworth's poetry. "The after-image could be defined as a re-cognition that leads to recognition," Hartman observes in *Wordsworth's Poetry, 1787 − 1814* (New Haven: Yale University Press, 1964), p. 270. With the help of Freud and Luria, Bloom easily assimilates Hartman's theory into his own paradigms of misprision.

20 Bloom cites two sources for his notion of the "crossing." In his essay, "The Breaking of Form," in *Deconstruction and Criticism* (pp. 25 − 27), he announces his indebtedness to Angus Fletcher, especially to Fletcher's essay " 'Positive Negation': Threshold, Sequence and Personification in Coleridge," in *New Perspectives on Coleridge and Wordsworth: Selected Papers from the English Institute*, ed. Geoffrey Hartman (New York: Columbia University Press, 1972), pp. 133 − 64. Fletcher reads Coleridge's avowed love of "method" as a desperate defense against the greater anxieties of the "diachronic" imagination, an imagination that he sees at the heart of Coleridge's greatest work. According to Fletcher, the diachronic imagination works through "thresholds," where "both sight and sound create a sense of time" that is finally "enigmatic." The threshold itself is aligned with "the prophetic speech that marks its liminal apprehension" (p. 137); thus poetry in a Coleridgean effort such as "Ne Plus Ultra" emerges into a vision whose perception of a higher order is only enhanced by the enigmatic nature of its temporal impetus. Fletcher summarizes the concept of threshold in *The Prophetic Moment: An Essay on Spenser* (Chicago: University of Chicago Press, 1971): "Thresholds are openings or doorways between two spaces or places. Moments are doorways between two spaces of time. These metaphors diagram the emergence of vision. At the theoretical meeting place between the temple and the labyrinth there bursts forth a higher order, which the great syncretist of ancient allegory, Philo Judaeus, would call '*the Immanent Logos*' " (pp. 45 − 46). In *Agon* (p. 24), Bloom reveals that a passage in Emerson's "Self-Reliance" gave him the idea of the "crossing": "Life only avails, not the having lived. Power ceases in the instant of repose; it resides in the moment of transition from a past to a new state, in the shooting of the gulf, in the darting to an aim" (CW, 2:40).

21 Bloom's quarrel here is with Paul de Man. Although Bloom announces his own debt to de Man's audacious redefinition of "poetic thinking *as* the process of rhetorical *substitution* rather than as a thinking by particular trope" (WS, p. 392), he cannot accept the other's overly ascetic conception of *logos* as the negative moments that collect in language reft of origin, essence, and end—a conception that, Bloom cautions, "isolates too purifyingly the trope from the *topos* or commonplace that generates it" (p. 393). For Bloom, as a belated Romantic humanist, the tropes

and errors of language presuppose an essential and engendering visionary will; for de Man, as a deconstructionist, the tropes and errors of language *are* language in its endless deferring of itself. The essay by de Man to which Bloom often refers in the final chapter of *Wallace Stevens* is "Action and Identity in Nietzsche," *Yale French Studies*, no. 52 (1975), pp. 16 – 30; reprinted in de Man's *Allegories of Reading* (New Haven: Yale University Press, 1979), pp. 119 – 31. Bloom's reconceiving of de Man's "*aporia*" or "figuration of doubt" as a "crossing" or "crisis-point" is entirely representative of the differing epistemological and linguistic choices made by these two prominent literary theorists. My sixth chapter will examine in some depth the lessons of the powerful de Man-Bloom dialogue.

22 Bloom's reading of Emersonian "surprise" as "the *pathos* of Power, the sudden manifestation of the vital will" (WS, p. 5), is based on Emerson's use of the word in several essays, most notably in "Experience," "History," and the late effort "Poetry and Imagination." "Surprise" is one of the seven "lords of life" in "Experience" (EW, 3:43). In "History," Emerson praises the second part of Goethe's *Faust* for its "wild freedom" of design and "the unceasing succession of brisk shocks of surprise," which awaken "the reader's invention and fancy" (CW, 2:19). In "Poetry and Imagination," the poet's use of the tropes of nature for their "ulterior" significance is seen to produce "a shock of agreeable surprise" (EW, 8:15). From these instances and a few others of Emersonian praise of "surprise," Bloom eventually draws the formidable conclusion that "surprise" is at the heart not only of Emerson's own work but of the entire American poetic tradition. "For *surprise* is the American poetic stance, in the peculiar sense of surprise as the poet's Will-to-Power over anteriority and over the interpretation of his own poem" (WS, p. 6).

23 See *Letters of Wallace Stevens*, ed. Holly Stevens (New York: Alfred A. Knopf, 1966), p. 464.

24 See Miller, *Poets of Reality*, pp. 277 – 79, for a discussion of the nothingness of being that is presented in "The Snow Man."

25 Wallace Stevens, *Opus Posthumous: Poems, Plays, Prose*, ed. Samuel French Morse (New York: Alfred A. Knopf, 1957), p. 118.

26 Miller, *Poets of Reality*, p. 277.

27 Kermode, "Notes toward a Supreme Poetry," p. 9.

28 Pettingell, "A Text That Is an Answer," *Poetry* 131 (1977): 169.

29 See Riddel, "Bloom—A Commentary—Stevens," *Wallace Stevens Journal* 1 (1977): 111 – 19, and "Juda Becomes New Haven."

30 Riddel, "Bloom—A Commentary—Stevens," pp. 115, 119, 117.

5. The Poems at the End of the Romantic Mind

1 See "A New Look at Lit Crit," *Newsweek*, 22 June 1981, pp. 80 – 83. Most of the article is devoted to the deconstructionist side of the Yale School, with Jacques Derrida getting the lion's share of attention. Bloom is called, not entirely accurately, "a brilliant critic of American literature who eschews linguistic argot."

2 For documentation of many of these charges against Bloom, see the introduction.

3 Bloom's use of Nietzschean insights on the nature of reading and interpretation is best seen as part of his dialogue with de Man, which will be
discussed in chapter 6. In general, Nietzsche for Bloom is a "prophet of
the antithetical" (AI, p. 8) and a great philosopher of revisionism,
although Nietzsche, like Emerson and Blake, apparently suffered little
from the anxiety of influence himself. For a more rigorous examination of
the Bloom-Nietzsche relation than I have offered here or in chapter 3, see
Daniel O'Hara, "The Genius of Irony: Nietzsche in Bloom," in Arac,
Godzich, and Martin, *The Yale Critics*, pp. 109 – 32.

4 See "Terministic Screens," in Burke's *Language as Symbolic Action:
Essays on Life, Literature, and Method* (Berkeley: University of California
Press, 1966), pp. 44 – 62. In this important essay, Burke analyzes the
mechanisms whereby any terminology that we use will condition the
knowledge gained through using it: "Even if any given terminology is
a *reflection* of reality, by its very nature as a terminology it must be a
selection of reality; and to this extent it must function also as a *deflection*
of reality" (p. 45). Of course, a similar point has been made often in the
philosophy of science and mathematics in this century, as well as in the
hermeneutics of reading; Burke's particular relevance to Bloom is that
he presents a philosophy of *rhetoric*, and one, furthermore, that Bloom
has found to be of "use."

5 Ammons's books cited in this chapter are:

CP   *Collected Poems, 1951 – 1971* (New York: W. W. Norton and Co.,
         1972).

Snow   *The Snow Poems* (New York: W. W. Norton and Co., 1977).

Sphere *Sphere: The Form of a Motion* (New York: W. W. Norton and Co.,
         1974).

Tape   *Tape for the Turn of the Year* (Ithaca: Cornell University Press,
         1965).

6 The observation by Stevens to which Bloom alludes is: "It is not every day
that the world arranges itself in a poem." See "Adagia," in Stevens, *Opus
Posthumous*, p. 165. Ashbery's "completion" of Stevens is "antithetical"
apparently in that, according to Bloom, Ashbery would delete the "not"
from Stevens's pronouncement.

7 Ashbery's books cited in this chapter are:

AWK *As We Know* (New York: Viking Press, 1979).

DDS *The Double Dream of Spring* (New York: The Ecco Press, 1976).

HD   *Houseboat Days* (New York: Viking Press, 1977).

SP   *Self-Portrait in a Convex Mirror* (New York: Viking Press, 1975).

TCO *The Tennis Court Oath* (Middletown, Conn.: Wesleyan University
        Press, 1962).

    Although I do not quote directly from them, other Ashbery books that
are discussed in this chapter are: *Rivers and Mountains* (New York: The
Ecco Press, 1977); *Shadow Train* (New York: Viking Press, 1981); *Some
Trees*, Yale Series of Younger Poets, 52 (New Haven: Yale University Press,
1956); and *Three Poems* (New York: Viking Press, 1972).

8 My phrasing intentionally echoes the title of Ammons's "Extremes and
Moderations" (CP, p. 328).

9 Hartman, "Romanticism and Anti-Self-Consciousness," in *Beyond Formalism*, p. 309.

214

10 See Richard Howard's essay, "A. R. Ammons: 'The Spent Seer Consigns Order to the Vehicle of Change,' " in *Alone with America: Essays on the Art of Poetry in the United States since 1950*, enlarged ed. (New York: Atheneum, 1980), pp. 1–24. It should be noted that the appreciation of Ammons published in the first edition of Howard's book in 1969 antedates Bloom's earliest essay on Ammons by a year.

11 *Diacritics* 3, no. 4 (1973) features essays on Ammons by Bloom, Josephine Jacobsen, David Kalstone, Jerome Mazzaro, Josephine Miles, Linda Orr, and Patricia A. Parker, as well as an interview with Ammons by David Grossvogel.

12 Hyatt H. Waggoner, "The Poetry of A. R. Ammons: Some Notes and Reflections," *Salmagundi*, nos. 22–23 (1973), p. 293.

13 Alicia Ostriker, "Drought and Flood," review of *Sphere, Partisan Review* 47 (1980): 153–61. For Denis Donoghue's reading of Ammons, see "Ammons and the Lesser Celandine," *Parnassus* 3, no. 2 (1975): 19–26.

14 A. R. Ammons, "A Poem Is a Walk," *Epoch* 18, no. 1 (1968): 114. For Coleridge's definition of the imagination, see *The Collected Works of Samuel Taylor Coleridge*, ed. Kathleen Coburn et al., 16 vols. (Princeton: Princeton University Press, 1969–), vol. 7, pt. 2, ed. James Engell and W. Jackson Bate (1983), p. 16.

15 *Collected Letters of Samuel Taylor Coleridge*, ed. Earl Leslie Griggs, 6 vols. (Oxford: Clarendon Press, 1956–71), 2:810.

16 See especially part 1 of Derrida, *Of Grammatology*, trans. Gayatri Chakravorty Spivak (Baltimore: Johns Hopkins University Press, 1977), pp. 3–93. Also see the still apt summary of Derrida's project, "Structure, Sign, and Play in the Discourse of the Human Sciences," printed in *The Languages of Criticism and the Sciences of Man: The Structuralist Controversy*, ed. Richard Macksey and Eugenio Donato (Baltimore: Johns Hopkins University Press, 1970), pp. 247–72, and reprinted in slightly different form in Derrida's *Writing and Difference*, trans. Alan Bass (Chicago: University of Chicago Press, 1978), pp. 278–93.

For the central Coleridgean definition of the imagination in relation to the "infinite I AM," see chapter 13 of the *Biographia Literaria*, in *Collected Works of Samuel Taylor Coleridge*, vol. 7, pt. 1, p. 304.

17 See "Coleridge," in *The Works of Walter Pater* (London: Macmillan and Co., 1901), 5:68–69. Pater observes that it was this restless "scheming," this "effort of sickly thought" that "saddened" Coleridge's "mind, and limited the operation of his unique poetic gift."

18 *Specimens of the Table Talk of Samuel Taylor Coleridge* (Edinburgh: John Grant, 1905), p. 61. The date for this entry is 1 May 1830.

19 It is "the business of the philosopher," Coleridge says, "to desynonymize words originally equivalent, therein following and impelling the natural progress of language in civilized societies." See *The Philosophical Lectures of Samuel Taylor Coleridge*, ed. Kathleen Coburn (New York: Philosophical Library, 1949), p. 152.

20 *Collected Letters of Samuel Taylor Coleridge*, 1:626.

21 This "miraculism" is behind much of Krieger's rigorous reworking of Coleridgean poetics. See especially his *Theory of Criticism: A Tradition and Its System* (Baltimore: Johns Hopkins University Press, 1976), which strikes me as a culmination of his work. See also "Mediation, Language,

and Vision in the Reading of Literature," in *Interpretation: Theory and Practice*, ed. Charles S. Singleton (Baltimore: Johns Hopkins University Press, 1969), pp. 211 – 42. The essay is reprinted in Krieger's *Poetic Presence and Illusion: Essays in Critical History and Theory* (Baltimore: Johns Hopkins University Press, 1979), pp. 270 – 302.

22 David Grossvogel, "Interview / A. R. Ammons," *Diacritics* 3, no. 4 (1973): 52.

23 In his discussion of Ammons's "The Wide Land," Bloom typically sees the wind as an "emblem of the composite precursor," Emerson and Whitman (FC, p. 213). More interesting, in his treatment of "Hibernaculum," Bloom defines the wind in all of Ammons's work as "a metonymy for the lean word, and then for the empty word" (p. 224)—a figure that *undoes* the traditional Romantic identification of the wind with fullness of spirit.

24 See *The Ringers in the Tower*, pp. 261 – 62.

25 See Abrams, "Structure and Style in the Greater Romantic Lyric."

26 Ammons is especially fond of Whitman imitations. An example of brave footloose Walt: "oh I will be addled and easy and move / over this prairie in the wind's keep, / . . . I will glide and say little / (what would you have me say? I know nothing; / still, I cannot help singing) . . ." (Ammons, CP, p. 83). An example of compassionate all-embracing Walt: ". . . I know them: I love them: I am theirs . . ." (*Sphere*, p. 18). An example of Walt as democratic philosopher: ". . . a united, capable poem, a united, capable mind, a united capable / nation, and a united nations! capable, flexible, yielding, / accommodating, seeking the good of all in the good of each . . ." (*Sphere*, p. 79). And so on.

27 *Collected Works of Samuel Taylor Coleridge*, vol. 4, pt. 1 (1969), ed. Barbara E. Rooke, p. 441.

28 Cynthia Haythe, "An Interview with A. R. Ammons," *Contemporary Literature* 21 (1980): 188. It is interesting to consider Ammons's almost licentious use of the colon as a stylistic device in light of his addiction to hierarchy and his corollary fear of undissected flux. As Alan Holder and Linda Orr have noted, Ammons's colons sustain movement, they sustain the "motion" of the poem. But, it must be added, colons at the same time provide Ammons's verse with a kind of visual and grammatical geometry that is perhaps best seen as the typographical analogue to the self-conscious symbolic schemes of the poet. Colons furnish little prisons for a poet fearful of the motion his poems threaten to engender. It is no accident that the colon tends to be most liberally employed in Ammons's longer poems, for it is in these poems that the dangers of unbridled motion are particularly acute. See Holder's *A. R. Ammons* (Boston: Twayne, 1978), pp. 106, 161. Linda Orr's essay, "The Cosmic Backyard of A. R. Ammons," in *Diacritics* 3, no. 4 (1973): 3 – 12, is valuable on Ammons's stylistic devices.

29 For an important treatment of deconstruction along this line, see Charles Altieri, "Wittgenstein on Consciousness and Language: A Challenge to Derridean Literary Theory," *Modern Language Notes* 91 (1976): 1397 – 423. Also see Gerald Graff, *Literature Against Itself: Literary Ideas in Modern Society* (Chicago: University of Chicago Press, 1979), for cogent attacks on the presuppositions of much contemporary literary theory.

30 This distinction strikes me as central to the work of Kenneth Burke. See especially *A Rhetoric of Motives* (Berkeley: University of California Press, 1969), pp. 145 – 49, 174 – 80. Burke's emphasis on the primacy of form is countered by recent Marxist thinkers such as Fredric Jameson and Terry Eagleton. See Jameson's *Marxism and Form* (Princeton: Princeton University Press, 1971).

31 Even an effort such as "Extremes and Moderations," one of Ammons's more interesting long poems, is compromised by Ammons's characteristic inability to conceive of the ethical dimension of societal relations in any terms other than the dialectical ones he uses to describe and categorize natural phenomena.

32 Miller, *Poets of Reality*, p. 1. All subsequent quotations from this volume will be documented in parentheses in the text.

33 See Ammons, "Note of Intent," *Chelsea Review*, nos. 20 – 21 (May 1967), pp. 3 – 4.

34 See Auden's foreword to *Some Trees*, pp. 11 – 16. The foreword has not been reprinted in subsequent editions of *Some Trees* in 1970 and 1978.

35 The phrase is Ernst Cassirer's, from *Language and Myth*, trans. Susanne K. Langer (New York: Dover, 1953), p. 7.

36 Bloom notes that "Ashbery necessarily began in a poetic world emptied of magical images and acts" (FC, p. 170); he also observes, while discussing *Three Poems*, that Ashbery "backs away from" the "sudden glory" of the " 'privileged moment' " at the center of Romantic tradition (pp. 205 – 6). But, of course, since "we can surmise" that this backing off is done "for defensive reasons, involving both the anxiety of influence and more primordial Oedipal anxieties" (p. 206), the lineaments of Ashbery's visionary quest are still somehow intact.

37 Perloff, " 'Mysteries of Construction': The Dream Songs of John Ashbery," in *The Poetics of Indeterminacy: Rimbaud to Cage* (Princeton: Princeton University Press, 1981), p. 266. Ashbery's comment on subjects in his poetry is quoted by Perloff in her " 'Transparent Selves': The Poetry of John Ashbery and Frank O'Hara," *The Yearbook of English Studies*, Modern Humanities Research Association, 8 (1978): 178.

38 Ashbery, "The Impossible," *Poetry* 90 (1957): 251.

39 Bloom, "Viewpoint," *Times Literary Supplement*, 30 May 1980, p. 611.

40 Altieri, "Motives in Metaphor: John Ashbery and the Modernist Long Poem," *Genre* 11 (1978): 671.

41 For information on the composition of "Europe," see Perloff, *The Poetics of Indeterminacy*, pp. 268 – 69.

42 Paul Carroll, "If Only He Had Left from the Finland Station," in *The Poem in Its Skin* (Chicago: Follett, 1968), pp. 12, 22, 20.

43 My phrasing alludes to Kenneth Burke's "definition of man" as "the symbol-using animal." See "Definition of Man," in *Language as Symbolic Action*, pp. 3 – 24. Like Burke, Ashbery defines man in a "dramatistic" fashion that deliberately begs epistemological questions in order to explore more fully the suasions of our being-within-culture. Unlike Burke, whose later work has come to be preoccupied with those consummations of dialectical symbolicity that deliver what he calls the "god-terms" of literature and culture, Ashbery does not finally seek a controlling perspective amid the plethora of symbolic forms through which people live.

44 Burke's entire career is built upon this "dramatistic" battle with "scientistic" or knowledge-oriented modes of perception; no specific work need be cited. For Rorty in *Philosophy and the Mirror of Nature* (Princeton: Princeton University Press, 1979), the task of "edifying" philosophy—as opposed to analytical philosophy and traditional modes of essentialist epistemological inquiry—is "to keep the conversation going rather than to find objective truth" (p. 377). Wisdom is thus defined as "the practical wisdom necessary to participate in a conversation" (p. 372).

45 See Martin Heidegger, *An Introduction to Metaphysics*, trans. Ralph Manheim (New Haven: Yale University Press, 1977), pp. 124−35. Although I am obviously not employing a fully developed Heideggerian terminology, the points I am making in this chapter about Ashbery and Bloom are similar to the arguments marshaled against Bloom in explicitly Heideggerian terms by Paul Bové in *Destructive Poetics: Heidegger and Modern American Poetry* (New York: Columbia University Press, 1980). See especially chapters 1 and 2, pp. 1−92.

46 For a particularly pointed critique of Heideggerian "Being," and for Derrida's replacement of that ontic term with his own deconstructing "trace," see "Differance," in *Speech and Phenomena and Other Essays on Husserl's Theory of Signs*, trans. David B. Allison (Evanston, Ill.: Northwestern University Press, 1973), pp. 129−60.

47 Janet Bloom and Robert Losada, "Craft Interview with John Ashbery," *New York Quarterly*, no. 9 (1972), p. 24. The interview is reprinted in *The Craft of Poetry: Interviews from the New York Quarterly*, ed. William Packard (Garden City, N.Y.: Doubleday and Co., 1974), p. 123, and it is this reprinting I will cite hereafter.

48 Bloom and Losada, "Craft Interview," pp. 123−24.

49 Ludwig Wittgenstein, *Philosophical Investigations*, trans. G. E. M. Anscombe, 3d ed. (New York: Macmillan Co., 1968), p. 226.

50 Bloom and Losada, "Craft Interview," p. 121.

51 For a more detailed discussion of Ashbery's use of pronouns and other of his rhetorical stratagems, see David Fite, "On the Virtues of Modesty: John Ashbery's Tactics against Transcendence," *Modern Language Quarterly* 42 (1981): 65−84.

52 Bloom and Losada, "Craft Interview," p. 111.

53 Louis A. Osti, "The Craft of John Ashbery: An Interview," *Confrontation*, no. 9 (1974), p. 87.

54 Kenneth Burke, "Literature as Equipment for Living," in *The Philosophy of Literary Form: Studies in Symbolic Action*, 3d ed. (Berkeley: University of California Press, 1973), p. 297.

55 Burke himself strategically skirts epistemological traps in *A Grammar of Motives* by calling his Pentadistic terms and ratios "necessary 'forms of talk about experience' "—*not* " 'forms of experience' " themselves (p. 317). In *A Rhetoric of Motives*, rhetoric is seen to be "*rooted in an essential function of language itself, a function that is wholly realistic, and is continually born anew; the use of language as a means of inducing cooperation in beings that by nature respond to symbols*" (p. 43).

56 Altieri is penetrating on the relation between Ashbery and Derrida in "Motives in Metaphor: John Ashbery and the Modernist Long Poem." While observing that "for Ashbery the mind stands towards its own

knowing in the same condition of infinite regressiveness" as is presented in Derrida, Altieri goes on to make the crucial distinction that "for Ashbery the problematics of relation are not primarily of sign to signified but of act to other acts as the mind tries to identify secure resting places" (p. 662).

57 See "The Breaking of Form," in *Deconstruction and Criticism*, pp. 4 – 5.

6. Humanism in the Extreme

1 Paul de Man, *Blindness and Insight*, p. 275. All subsequent quotations from this review of *The Anxiety of Influence* will be documented in parentheses in the text.

2 The Derridean critique of the "metaphysics of presence" is the basis of all his work. For pointed dissections of "phonocentrism," see chapter 6 of *Speech and Phenomena*, pp. 70 – 87, and pt. 1 of *Of Grammatology*, pp. 3 – 93.

3 J. Hillis Miller, "Stevens' Rock and Criticism as Cure," p. 341.

4 De Man, "Criticism and Crisis," in *Blindness and Insight*, p. 17.

5 There is an abundance of criticism on the Derridean movement, both expository and argumentative. For especially provocative attacks on Derrida's ends, means, and philosophical assumptions, see M. H. Abrams, "The Deconstructive Angel," *Critical Inquiry* 3 (1977): 425 – 38, and "How to Do Things with Texts," *Partisan Review* 46 (1979): 566 – 88 (the latter also treats Bloom and Stanley Fish); Charles Altieri, "Wittgenstein on Consciousness and Language: A Challenge to Derridean Literary Theory," and *Act and Quality: A Theory of Literary Meaning and Humanistic Understanding* (Amherst: University of Massachusetts Press, 1981); Denis Donoghue, "Deconstructing Deconstruction," review of *Deconstruction and Criticism* and *Allegories of Reading, New York Review of Books*, 12 June 1980, pp. 37 – 41; Gerald Graff, "Deconstruction as Dogma, or, 'Come Back to the Raft Ag'in, Strether Honey,' " review of *Deconstruction and Criticism, Georgia Review* 34 (1980): 404 – 21, and *Literature Against Itself*, pp. 61 – 62, 81 – 82, 145 – 46, and 192 – 93. Recent book-length studies of deconstruction include Jonathan Culler, *On Deconstruction: Theory and Criticism after Structuralism* (Ithaca: Cornell University Press, 1982); Vincent Leitch, *Deconstructive Criticism: An Advanced Introduction* (New York: Columbia University Press, 1983); Christopher Norris, *Deconstruction, Theory and Practice* (New York: Methuen, 1982); and Michael Ryan, *Marxism and Deconstruction: A Critical Articulation* (Baltimore: Johns Hopkins University Press, 1982).

Obviously, my own very brief summary of deconstruction is not meant to do justice to the subtle differentiations advanced by the most gifted theorists of deconstruction, nor to the pointed disagreements they have among themselves.

6 Paul de Man, "The Rhetoric of Temporality," in *Blindness and Insight*, p. 207. This essay first appeared in Singleton, *Interpretation: Theory and Practice*, pp. 173 – 209.

7 De Man, *Allegories of Reading*, p. 131.

8 See the author's introduction to *The Wedge* (Cummington, Mass.: Cummington Press, 1944), p. 8; reprinted in *Selected Essays of William Carlos Williams* (New York: Random House, 1954), p. 256.

9 For Kenner's discussion—and endorsement—of the poetics of the post-Poundian poets Zukofsky, Oppen, and Olson, see chapter 6 of *A Home-made World: The American Modernist Writers* (New York: Alfred A. Knopf, 1975), pp. 158 – 93. All subsequent quotations from this work will be documented in parentheses in the text.

10 William Carlos Williams, *Paterson* (New York: New Directions, 1963), p. 6. Also see chapter 58 of *The Autobiography of William Carlos Williams* (London: MacGibbon and Kee, 1968), p. 390.

11 The "naive realism" of Kenner is quite consciously a strategy, of course. For the basis of Kenner's working philosophy of induction, we might turn to R. Buckminster Fuller, whose theorizing on the properties of systems has provided Kenner not only with ideas but with an idiosyncratic critical vocabulary—"patterned integrity," "vector," and so on. Kenner's *Bucky: A Guided Tour of Buckminster Fuller* (New York: William Morrow and Co., 1973) is an invaluable guide to both the philosophy and geometry of Fuller and the logic underlying Kenner's own method of literary criticism. Like Fuller, Kenner takes as first principle not the Cartesian "I think, therefore I am," but, as Kenner puts it, "I experience, whatever I am" (p. 161).

For a deft analysis of some of the contradictions and gaps in Kenner's own rhetoric, see Denis Donoghue's discussion of Kenner in *Ferocious Alphabets* (Boston: Little, Brown and Co., 1981), pp. 63 – 71. An important question not treated by Donoghue is the relation between Kenner's poetics and his politics.

12 *Selected Essays of William Carlos Williams*, p. 257.

13 Ibid.

14 See Lasch's *The Culture of Narcissism: American Life in an Age of Diminishing Expectations* (New York: W. W. Norton and Co., 1978). Wolfe, of course, coined the famous phrase in his "The Me Decade and the Third Great Awakening," in *Mauve Gloves & Madmen, Clutter & Vine* (New York: Farrar, Straus and Giroux, 1976), pp. 126 – 67.

15 See Graff's *Literature Against Itself*, chapters 1 and 3, pp. 1 – 29, 63 – 101. Graff's basic argument is that the "power of powerlessness" (p. 90) displayed by contemporary radical or adversary culture itself represents yet another capitulation to the decadent consumerism of late capitalist culture.

16 Kenneth Connelly, review of *Yeats*, *Yale Review* 60 (1971): 398.

17 M. H. Abrams, *Natural Supernaturalism: Tradition and Revolution in Romantic Literature* (New York: W. W. Norton and Co., 1971), pp. 430 – 31.

18 J. Hillis Miller, "Tradition and Difference," review of *Natural Supernaturalism*, *Diacritics* 2, no. 4 (1972): 6 – 13. While professing admiration for Abrams's learned and eloquent contribution to "the grand tradition of modern humanistic scholarship" (p. 6), Miller nonetheless challenges the very assumptions upon which he sees *Natural Supernaturalism* as founded, and he offers a brief deconstructive reading of Romantic language and tradition to take their place.

19 See M. H. Abrams, "Rationality and Imagination in Cultural History: A Reply to Wayne Booth," *Critical Inquiry* 2 (1976): 447 – 64. The essay is reprinted in Wayne Booth, *Critical Understanding: The Powers and Limits of Pluralism* (Chicago: University of Chicago Press, 1979), pp. 175 – 94. See "Rationality and Imagination in Cultural History," *Criti-*

cal Understanding, pp. 186 – 88, for Abrams's most pointed discussion of Miller's objections.

20 Miller, "Tradition and Difference," pp. 8, 11.

21 Abrams, "Rationality and Imagination in Cultural History," *Critical Understanding*, p. 187.

22 Abrams, "How to Do Things with Texts," pp. 568, 587. All subsequent quotations from this article will be documented in parentheses in the text.

23 Abrams, *Natural Supernaturalism*, p. 431.

24 Bloom's two major readings of "Childe Roland" mark the movement in his thought from the transitional phase of the late sixties featuring the "internalization of quest romance" to the phase in which all quests are revealed to be part of the oedipal drama of poetic influence. For the earlier reading, see "Browning's 'Childe Roland': All Things Deformed and Broken," in *The Ringers in the Tower*, pp. 157 – 67; for the later reading, designed by Bloom as a showcase for his new map, see *A Map of Misreading*, pp. 106 – 22.

Conclusion

1 An especially interesting commentary on Bloom's intensely patriarchal conception of literary history is offered by Sandra Gilbert and Susan Gubar in *The Madwoman in the Attic*, pp. 46 – 53. Acknowledging that Bloom's model might seem "offensively sexist to some feminist critics" (p. 47), they nonetheless maintain that it is precisely Bloom's courage in recognizing and formulating a psychology of the essentially male structures and dynamics of our Western literary experience that makes him important to theorists in the new field of literary psychohistory.

2 The phrase is from John Barth's famous essay, "The Literature of Exhaustion," *Atlantic*, Aug. 1967, pp. 29 – 34.

3 Terry Eagleton, *Literary Theory: An Introduction* (Minneapolis: University of Minnesota Press, 1983), pp. 199, 207.

4 Edward Said, "Interview," *Diacritics* 6, no. 3 (1976): 38.

5 For probing reflections on the role of the humanist scholar in contemporary society, see Edward Said, *The World, the Text, and the Critic* (Cambridge: Harvard University Press, 1983), especially his "Introduction: Secular Criticism" (pp. 1 – 30) and "Reflections on American 'Left' Literary Criticism" (pp. 158 – 77). No doubt the most sweeping recent critique of the crisis in the humanities is Gerald Graff's *Literature Against Itself*. Graff's antidote for the malaise in humanism and for the nihilism of much modern art and literary criticism is, unfortunately, a call for a return to old shibboleths such as "mimesis," "realism," and the "liberal arts" that he leaves relatively unexamined. For a much more theoretically resourceful defense of the meanings of humanism, see Charles Altieri, *Act and Quality*.

6 See "Characteristics," in *Carlyle's Complete Works*, Sterling Edition (Boston: Estes and Lauriat, 1885), 14:366.

7 Bruss, *Beautiful Theories*, pp. 345, 320. All subsequent quotations from this volume will be documented in parentheses in the text.

8 Said, "Interview," p. 34.

9 Frank Lentricchia, *After the New Criticism* (Chicago: University of Chicago Press, 1980), p. 344. All subsequent quotations from this volume will be documented in parentheses in the text.

10 See the afterword to *After the New Criticism*, pp. 349 – 51.

11 Bové, *Destructive Poetics*, pp. 29, 21, 53.

12 My use of the terms "myth" and "fiction" here is derived from Lentricchia's discussion of Northrop Frye and Wallace Stevens in chapters 1 and 2 of *After the New Criticism*, especially pp. 16 – 35.

13 See Geoffrey Hartman, *Criticism in the Wilderness: The Study of Literature Today* (New Haven: Yale University Press, 1980), especially the introduction (pp. 1 – 15) and the concluding essay, "A Short History of Practical Criticism" (pp. 284 – 301).

14 See Gerald Graff's review of Hartman's *Criticism in the Wilderness*, *New Republic*, 1 Nov. 1980, pp. 34 – 37, for this view of Hartman's style. Also see Michael Sprinkler's perceptive comments on Hartman's style in "Aesthetic Criticism: Geoffrey Hartman," in Arac, Godzich, Martin, *The Yale Critics*, p. 45.

15 It seems appropriate at this point to take note of Bloom's own foray into fiction, *The Flight to Lucifer: A Gnostic Fantasy* (New York: Farrar, Straus, Giroux, 1979). The subtitle is especially apt; as Bloom himself has observed in *Agon*, in a discussion of *A Voyage to Arcturus*, David Lindsay's fantasia, Bloom's *Flight to Lucifer* undertakes the difficult task of assimilating Lindsay's characters and narrative movement to "the actual, historical cosmology, theology and mythology of second-century Gnosticism" (p. 222). Brief paraphrase cannot do justice to the complicated, fantastic world of *Lucifer*, with its clotted diction, its elaborate machinations of plot, and its many bewildering characters and symbols drawn from a wide range of Gnostic, Romantic, and Freudian cultural reference. Rather, let the volume's author deliver the verdict on his own catastrophic creation: "Though a violent narrative, freely plagiarized by misprision of endless fantasy-sources from Spenser to Kafka, *The Flight to Lucifer* has too much trouble getting off the ground, not because it knows too well what it is about, but because it is rather too interested in the ground, which is to say, too interested in the pleasure/pain principle" (*Agon*, p. 222). This in turn says (it seems to one unpersuaded reader) that the volume features precisely that flaw that Bloom fails to note in the poetry of A. R. Ammons: it is excruciatingly self-conscious, archly and awkwardly aware of "what it is about" as a "fiction" whose imaginative life is drawn almost solely from its author's encounters with the many texts of his chosen tradition.

16 Angus Fletcher, "The Central Commentary: Notes for a Review," review of *The Ringers in the Tower*, *Diacritics* 1, no. 1 (1971): 17.

17 Hartman, "The Sacred Jungle 3: Frye, Burke, and Some Conclusions," in *Criticism in the Wilderness*, p. 106. Hartman's comment suggests that Bloom, despite his radical reading methods, is in some respects a rather conservative defender of the literary canon. Such has been the charge made against Bloom by Bruss in *Beautiful Theories* (p. 475). Such also is the diagnosis of the entire Yale School of critics made by Jonathan Arac in his afterword to *The Yale Critics*. Arac contends that Bloom, Hartman, Miller, and de Man are all more profitably regarded as "wily conserva-

tives" than as "iconoclasts" (p. 179). Edward Said makes a similar point about the "safeguarding" of the canon by the Yale critics in "Traveling Theory," in *The World, the Text, and the Critic*, p. 229.

18 Cynthia Ozick, "Judaism & Harold Bloom," *Commentary* 67, no. 1 (1979): 46. Ozick delivers a fierce indictment of Bloom's false prophecy, arguing that Bloom is "engaged in the erection of what can fairly be called an artistic anti-Judaism" (p. 46), and seeing in his self-conscious prophecies about literary history the activity of "idol-making" (p. 47).

INDEX